WRITING THE INFORMATION SUPERHIGHWAY

William Condon
Washington State University

Wayne Butler
University of Michigan

Allyn and Bacon
Boston • London • Toronto • Sydney • Tokyo • Singapore

Vice President, Humanities: Joseph Opiela
Editorial Assistant: Kate Tolini
Marketing Manager: Lisa Kimball
Production Administrator: Susan Brown
Editorial-Production Service: Matrix Productions Inc.
Cover Designer: Suzanne Harbison
Composition Buyer: Linda Cox
Manufacturing Buyer: Suzanne Lareau

Library of Congress Cataloging-in-Publication Data

Condon, William.
    Writing the information superhighway / William Condon, Wayne Butler.
        p.   cm.
    Includes index.
    ISBN 0-205-19575-X
    1. English language—Rhetoric—Data processing—Problems, exercises, etc.   2. Academic writing—Data processing—Problems, exercises, etc.   3. Internet (Computer network) in education.
    4. Information superhighway in education.   I. Butler, Wayne.
    II. Title.
    PE1413.C575   1997
    808'.042'0285—dc20

                                        96-43596
                                        CIP

Printed in the United States of America

10 9 8 7 6 5 4 3 2 1   01 00 99 98 97

CONTENTS

iii

PREFACE

Every day computer technology becomes a larger part of our lives. As computers have progressed from massive vacuum tube–burning mainframe machines to silicon chip–driven laptop and notebook-sized personal micros, these devices have moved from the military world and research facility into the home and school. Computer culture, once the domain of scientists and engineers, has permeated mainstream culture to such an extent that much of what we do during the course of our daily activities—from banking to shopping, from using the microwave oven to communicating with others—is facilitated, in outward and in more and more transparent ways, by computer technology. In 1997 it is nearly impossible to read a newspaper or magazine or watch TV news and not read or hear a story about technology. In fact, many of you may now be using computers to get the news and advertising you used to get through newspapers and magazines.

Even if what we hear and read is not directly related to technology, the language of technology has made its way into our collective consciousness. The infopike. The Internet. Cyberspace. Hypertext. Interactive TV. CD-ROM. Virtual communities. The World Wide Web—or, to those in the know, simply "the Web." No clear consensus yet exists on what overall terms will be used to describe the conglomeration of technologies that are transforming the ways people gather information, communicate, and create knowledge, the ways groups of human beings interact and form the social groups that lie at the center of what it means to be human. For the time being, anyway, we will use the most popular term—the information superhighway.

When thinking of the information superhighway, most in the academic community think first of the Internet, the amorphous, nonhierarchical and distributed "network of networks" with no owner or central controlling agencies. *Information superhighway,* as a descriptive term, is more encompassing. The information superhighway also embraces cable television, which in the near future promises to offer not only broadcasting but also interactivity and not only will include programming for entertainment and news but will permit on-line shopping, video conferencing, and on-demand videos. The information superhighway includes the various commercial information systems such as America Online, Prodigy, and CompuServe. And, the open-ended term *information superhighway* also allows us to name those technologies and information services not yet developed.

In one sense, the information superhighway can be considered a technological phenomenon. At its technological core it is personal, mini-, and mainframe computers linked together through cabling into local networks that are in turn linked together by more cabling into wide area networks. Special software allows one computer on one network on one side of the world to communicate with another computer on another network on the other side of the world.

More important, however, is what these networks of networks allow human beings to do. The information superhighway lets individuals communicate with individuals and groups and allows groups to communicate with groups via computer-mediated communication (CMC) such as E-mail, newsgroups, electronic bulletin boards, and chat programs. CMC allows people separated by vast distances and time to distribute, gather, and share information, data, and software through databases, Gopher sites, FTP servers, and World Wide Web sites. This information, and the people who create it, share it, and use it, are really the substance of the information superhighway. If the hardware, cabling, and software are the skeleton and vascular systems of the information superhighway, then the information is the heart of it and the people who produce and share the information are the brains and soul of it.

Although the technological wizardry that ties all the computers together is a wonder, perhaps eventually rising to the ranks of one of the Great Wonders of the World, the information superhighway is only as good as the *information* that speeds along the wires. The superhighway is a distributed system where there is no central font of information, and where anyone may send an E-mail message, create a World Wide Web homepage, or make data and information available on his or her personal computer to the rest of the network; so the quality of the information superhighway will only be as good as what people put on it.

That is where this book comes in. We have chosen the title *Writing the Information Superhighway* for a number of reasons. Of course, we are playing off a pun that grows out of the highway metaphor, which for better or worse dominates the ways our culture has come to describe the phenomenon. But taking the pun a bit further also reveals our feeling toward the roles those who will contribute to and use the content will play. "Riding" implies passivity, like riding on a bus that someone else drives on a route someone else selects. "Writing," on the other hand, is an act of creation. Writers are active, not passive. Writers must invent ideas, gather materials, synthesize, analyze, and otherwise sort out those ideas, and then communicate them to others. Writing, and the critical thinking activities that effective writing requires, is the process by which information is transformed into knowledge.

TRANSFORMATIONS IN EDUCATIONAL SETTINGS

Until the introduction of the personal microcomputer into the classroom, one could predict with a high level of certainty what people might see if they peeked into almost any writing classroom anywhere in the United States. Inside a traditional school building, those classrooms might have forward-facing desks bolted to the floor, or movable integrated chairs with writing surfaces, or movable tables or desks with chairs. If the furniture was movable, the pieces might be arranged into rows, into clusters, into a full or semicircle. In some writing classrooms, teachers might be standing at the front of the room lecturing, giving demonstrations on a chalkboard or overhead projector, or leading a discussion. In more workshop-oriented writing classrooms, students and their desks might have been clustered in tight circles to facilitate small-group discussion. Although throughout the years there have been examples that fall outside this range of options, for the most part the material conditions of educational settings consisted of one or more variations of these scenarios.

In a growing number of schools, colleges, and universities, however, the places where writing is taught, learned, and accomplished are undergoing radical transformations. Some writing classrooms may have as few as one or two computers in the back of the traditional classroom. These might be stand-alone computers used primarily for word processing, or they might be connected to the outside world via a modem. In other places, one or two or even a number of rooms might have been transformed into public-use computer labs where teachers can make appointments to bring students from the traditional classroom for one or several meetings a week. These labs might include a couple of printers and a dozen to two dozen or so stand-alone personal computers, but by this point they have probably been linked together on a local area network at least, and perhaps into a wide area network with full Internet access. Other institutions have opened general computing sites that are not dedicated to or available for instructional purposes but can be used by students to word-process papers, read and send E-mail, use the Internet, and conduct on-line research. At the far end of the technology-rich writing environment in education are those relatively few sites around the country that have computer-based classrooms used primarily by the English department or writing program. These are not places merely for word-processing papers but rather places where actual writing instruction occurs and where at least half and maybe all the class meetings for each section of each course are held.

Traditional writing textbooks could assume many common denominators among those who might use the books. The teacher was the experienced writer and writing teacher with years of study and experience with language and with helping students grow as writers. Students would enter rather traditional classrooms that looked much like the classrooms of their previous educational experiences with a wide range of writing abilities, but they would come in with relatively equal abilities with such technologies of writing as pencils, pens, typewriters, and paper.

This book, too, strives to help teachers help students become better writers, but the potential audience is more diverse. The teacher may be either a novice or advanced computer user who is taking the first or second steps to teach writing with computers and for the first time may be stepping into the educational setting without full confidence born of previous experience or deep knowledge. In fact, some or even many of the students might have more technological knowledge, ability, and confidence than the teacher. For both the teacher and the student, this relationship will most likely be new—and intimidating. Furthermore, we cannot know, like composition textbook writers before us, what the learning place will look like, that is, what technology will be available to the teachers or students.

So, in this world of changing, diverse learning environments, new roles emerge for all the entities that come together in a learning environment, including teachers, students, and educational materials. And with these new roles come new burdens of responsibility. But, if even a portion of what futurists like the Tofflers predict comes true in the twenty-first century, if, that is, knowledge—the gathering of data and information, the processing and synthesizing of that information into knowledge, and the communicating of that knowledge to others—will become the dominant resource of the twenty-first century, we, teachers and students alike, will be obliged to accommodate these changes and share the burden of shouldering these responsibilities. Taking on such responsibilities, however challenging it may sound, is nothing new for education. In fact, the central role of education has always been to prepare young people for the civic and economic duties they will inherit.

TRANSFORMATIONS IN TECHNOLOGY

Another challenge of writing on the information superhighway is the constant and rapid rate of change in technology itself. The introduction of the personal computer occurred only fifteen years or so ago. And in that short time, we have gone from stand-alone machines with limited functionality—cumbersome word processors and drill-and-practice software that amounted to mere electronic workbooks—to the Internet with its various forms of computer-mediated communication such as electronic bulletin boards, electronic mail, MUDs and MOOs, and the hypermedia of the World Wide Web. Whereas early computer users grappled with the special and idiosyncratic logic, languages, and commands of mainframe computers and then personal computers that mimicked those mainframes, those using computers for the first time today will be accommodated by the more "user-friendly" graphic interfaces of the Macintosh and Windows operating systems. When one compares today's technology to that of a mere fifteen years ago, one might be tempted to think, "Ah, how far we've come." Indeed, the computer world is a more friendly place than it once was, but it is still a complex one. Thinking in terms of the automobile, we are driving on pneumatic tires in an enclosed passenger space, with an engine that will start and run with some reliability. We are sitting on padded seats in a vehicle that furnishes us with some amenities—a heater, fuel gauges, a speedometer, shock absorbers. And we can buy this automobile at a reasonable price. In other words, we're driving a Model T—with a long way to go before we operate anything like the sleek, reliable, accommodating vehicles we drive today. Those computers are still a long way down the road.

Still today, those who endeavor to get on the information superhighway must first deal with all the incompatibilities that exist among competing hardware and software products. Ever since IBM-compatibles and Macintoshes forged different paths in personal computing, users have been faced with a dilemma, an either/or decision. Macintosh software would not work with IBM-compatibles and vice versa. So, either users were wedded to one or the other or they became sort of "bilingual." The advent of Windows 95 is closing the gap between the two platforms, and contemporary software packages are doing a better job of making files created for one platform compatible with the other, but as far as personal computing goes, we still live in a somewhat bifurcated world. To further complicate matters, a great range of possibilities exist for connecting to the Internet, sending and receiving E-mail, copying files from one computer to another, creating Gopher and World Wide Web sites, and browsing those sites.

Finally, yet another variable can lead to great frustration among those who would use computer technology: obsolescence. Just as soon as we are dazzled with how far computer technology has come over the last two decades, we become baffled by how much more quickly it changes in the next two years. Computer manufacturers introduce new hardware with faster processors, more random access memory (RAM), and more hard disk space. Such upgrades are welcomed, but shortly after each new hardware upgrade, software developers crank up their programs with more features that quickly use up the potential of the faster processors and increased RAM and hard disk space. This "progress" makes the computer model you owned just before to the latest and greatest upgrade unable to use the latest and greatest software, thus making your machine, which may only be a couple of years old, stuck in a time warp. So, that Macintosh LC with four megabytes of RAM and a forty-megabyte hard disk and that snappy 2,400-baud modem you bought just a few years ago will let you send and receive E-mail, but it won't let you access the World Wide Web using the most recent version of Netscape.

Unfortunately, computer hardware and software are not the only things that become obsolete quickly. So does your own knowledge. If you first dabbled in computers and word processing during the mid 1980s and cut your word processing teeth on Applewriter II or Word Perfect 1.0 for DOS, for example, you would not recognize today's versions of the same programs. You would have to learn a whole new set of commands to perform the same functions. You would not, however, be starting from scratch because the word-processing and computer literacy concepts you learned would serve as the basis for the new operating procedures. If you learned the concepts of entering and formatting text, of moving text around with copy and paste techniques, of saving and printing files, all you would need to learn is how to use different keystrokes or menu-based commands, or now icon-based commands, to complete the same concept-based tasks.

In fact, this emphasis on concepts rather than skills underlies the purpose and structure of this book. As textbook writers, we cannot anticipate or control the technological realities in which every writing teacher and student might live. There is no way any book written for a large, general audience could address in a detailed, specific way the pedagogical differences and needs of different learning sites because what one can do in the fully networked, Internet-accessible computer classroom dedicated specifically to the teaching of writing is vastly different from what one can do in the institution where classes are conducted in traditional classrooms and students have access to the technology only outside of class in public, general computing sites. Likewise, we cannot address the particular skills of word processing or E-mail in terms of specific applications such as Microsoft Word for Windows or the Macintosh version of Eudora, a popular E-mail program. What we can and will do, however, is focus on the conceptual underpinnings of word processing, computer-mediated communication, and information retrieval and offer activities designed to help teachers and writers work collaboratively to learn the technological topographies and application skills particular to their specific learning sites.

WRITING EDUCATION IN THE INFORMATION AGE

For perhaps the first time in educational history, teachers need not be the main authority for all knowledge to be attained in a class. Indeed, the teacher will still be a more experienced writer and will bring to the mix her experience as a teacher, but if she has considered using this book, she may or may not have the breadth and depth of knowledge about the technology that even some of her students will bring (each of us authors has been in such a situation, and we continue to be amazed at the level of expertise that some students bring to our classes). And students, many of whom are already more fully integrated members of contemporary electronic culture, will still need the teacher's help to develop advanced literacy skills. But, in comparison with previous educational settings, anyway, the distribution of responsibility for learning literacy will be less lopsided. The information superhighway metaphor implies that all those who use it are on some sort of journey. In the case of college writers, that journey is a quest for improved academic literacies. But because this journey will take us through sometimes uncharted territories, students will at times rely on teachers as seasoned trail guides. However, the territory can change so quickly and completely (witness the rapidity with which the World Wide Web transformed from side road to interstate highway) that no guide, however experienced, can really know the way. Teachers cannot send writers off into the wild unknown and say simply, "Go forth and survive." Instead, teachers and students must forge new relationships and work together as expedition teams to which each member of the team contributes unique knowledge, whether that knowledge involves techniques of reading critically, writing well, using a particular piece of software to find electronic information, or uncovering a well-spring of on-line resources.

Writing the Information Superhighway, then, is not merely a composition textbook written for students, a pedagogical "how-to" book for teachers, or a technology manual for learning the Internet. This is the case in part because a plethora of books for each of those audiences and purposes already exists. Students and teachers can already choose from hundreds of composition textbooks and style manuals, but those grow out of more traditional modes of writing, conceptions of learning how to write, and relationships between teachers and learners. Although such books offer *detailed information on writing and language* concepts such as the writing process, modes of discourse, structures of argumentation, and so forth, few address the needs, techniques, and skills of writing on-line. Plenty of books already exist for teaching teachers how to integrate technology into their teaching, but these serve more as resource guides for teachers and not for students. Take a casual stroll through the "new media" section of almost any bookstore, and you will find scores of books about the Internet, but those typically focus on the technological aspects of the information superhighway with little information about how to read and write on it effectively.

This book, then, strives to bridge the traditional gaps between what teachers do and what students do and what writers do and what net surfers do. Ultimately, we have designed *Writing the Information Superhighway* as a guidebook to help learning communities that consist of students and teachers working together to use new technologies to learn not only traditional academic literacy but also the new literacies engendered by the new technologies.

ABOUT THE STRUCTURE OF THIS BOOK

As you prepare to embark on this journey along the information superhighway, it will be useful for you to understand the map we've laid out for you. Part I, "Producing and Accessing Digital Texts," includes five chapters that focus on the kinds of activities writers pursue using computers. Chapter 1, "Manipulating Text," emphasizes the principles of creating digital texts using word processing. Chapter 2, "Communicating on the Internet: One on One," focuses on one-on-one communication via electronic mail. Chapter 3, "Communicating on the Internet: Accessing Virtual Communities," includes a definition and purpose for each of the ways of accessing and participating in a variety of electronic communities, a description of common applications, and practice activities that will help students learn how to find appropriate lists, groups, and MOOs for English-related communications. Chapter 4, "Gathering Information on the Internet: Reaching Out and Bringing Back Resources," describes the "information" portion of the information superhighway and advises writers about gathering information in the form of facts, texts, graphics and other pictorial resources. Chapter 5, "Constructing Texts On-Line," explains how the advent of the World Wide Web has created a virtual workspace where writers not only can give others access to their documents but also collaborate, with as large a group of other writers as they wish, in constructing documents. Moreover, hypertext markup language (HTML) provides a means of linking these individual documents together so that the individual document changes, in effect, because of its juxtaposition with other documents. This chapter discusses the world of on-line texts that writers can explore and participate in, using, again, constantly evolving tools.

Whereas Part I sets the context by introducing members of the electronic learning community to the technologies and the "rules of the road," so to speak, Part II, "Writing Projects for the Information Age," leads learning community members through a number of writing projects that ask writers to use what they've learned in Part I and apply those techniques and principles in inventing, composing, sharing, and revising the kinds of texts typical of academic writing. Chapter 6 focuses on issues of assessment. We start there based on our belief that writing communities must reach a consensus on standards. Once such standards are in place, then the rest of the writing completed during the semester is done within a shared context. Chapters 7, 8, 9, and 10 include projects that lead writers through assignments that require them to write narratives, use writing to learn, and report, analyze, and argue. During these activities, writers will learn how to use the information and resources available on the information superhighway to help them write more traditional academic texts, how to write about the Internet itself, and how to write texts specifically for the information superhighway. Chapter 11 addresses writing in the disciplines. Although this section does not set out to teach writers everything they need to know about writing in different disciplines, it does address the differences among writing in various disciplines and what resources exist on the Internet to help writers learn more about the disciplines they seek to join, how to join the various virtual communities their disciplines have created, and how to conduct disciplinary research using the Internet. Part II wraps up with three projects in Chapter 12, "Writing for the World Wide Web." These projects lead students through analyses of Web Sites, introduces them to converting their linear electronic texts into hypertextual World Wide Web documents using HTML, and then finally leads them through the process of constructing Webfolios, World Wide Web versions of hypertextual writing portfolios.

The Appendices include "A Directory of On-Line Resources for Writers" that presents addresses of newsgroups, listserv discussion lists, appropriate reference books, and helpful FTP, Gopher, and World Wide Web sites. Finally, you will find a "Glossary of Key Terms" that includes definitions of technical terms this text uses frequently.

Whereas writing in the late age of print is a mostly linear affair, writing in the information age will rely more and more on multimedia blended with hypertext into what is called *hypermedia*. If we could have, we would have constructed this book as a hypertext. That is, we acknowledge that writing community members need not start on page one and continue through to the very end. Depending on the technological context of your school, the computer literacy of your learning community members, and the length of your semester, most will find it difficult if not impossible to complete every single activity of every single project in the book. In fact, we've designed each chapter and project to be comprehensive enough so instructors can pick and choose which ones are most appropriate for their learning community and the goals of the course. So, for instance, if most class members have fairly sophisticated and advanced word-processing and E-mail skills, you may want to start with Part II and launch right into the writing projects. And if your community decides from the very beginning you will use portfolio assessment and your school's access to the World Wide Web will allow you to create Webfolios, you might decide to start with Project 2 but then jump to the last project dealing with constructing Webfolios.

We welcome you to cyberspace and wish you luck as you begin writing the information superhighway.

ACKNOWLEDGEMENTS

First, we'd like to acknowledge each other. This project emerged from an exchange of E-mail messages in which both of us agreed that this was the textbook we'd write if we were ever to write a textbook and that we'd only write such a book if we could write it together. So we did. From start to finish, we've shared the conception, the development, and the sheer work of drafting and revising equally. So, while the publishing world demands that one of us be listed as "lead author," we want to state, here, that no such figure exists with regard to this text. In fact, we flipped a coin to determine which of us would be "lead author" in the eyes of the publishing industry and the Library of Congress. In subsequent editions, if we're fortunate enough to need them, we'll take turns.

Both of us also wish to thank several people without whom this book probably would not exist, and certainly would not have taken the shape it has. Joe Opiela is first among these, our editor at Allyn & Bacon, who knew when to push, when to give us some room, and when to seek some outside opinions. Our colleagues, whom Joe recruited, and who gave us always solid advice: John M. Clark, Bowling Green State University; Ray Dumont, University of Massachusetts, Dartmouth; Lisa Gerrard, University of California, Los Angeles; Marcia Peoples Halio, University of Delaware; and Christine Hult, Utah State University. We are grateful for their generous input; they helped this book work. We'd like to thank Kate Tolini of Allyn & Bacon and Merrill Peterson of Matrix Productions for their work in bringing our manuscript so quickly into print. Doug Day and Lisa Kimball, both of Allyn & Bacon, offered sustaining encouragement and advice along the way. Julie Steiff, an ECB colleague, prepared the index and provided support as we brought this project to a close.

We are also fortunate to belong to a number of real and virtual communities, all of which helped us immeasurably in ways we could not begin to acknowledge properly. Our colleagues at the English Composition Board literally kept us going with their encouragement and their willingness to listen to our ideas and to respond with gentle, helpful criticism. Our colleagues in the Computers and Writing community and on E-mail lists such as Megabyte University (MBU-L), and ACW-L (a list for the Alliance for Computers and Writing) kept us aware of the latest ideas and the latest in technology; thanks to them, we always knew what the stakes were and how high the community's expectations would be. At heart, we are all teachers, and the fact that we had so many good teachers surrounding us, literally and virtually, as this book developed helped us keep the focus where it belonged—on what happens as writers write and writing students learn.

We also need to thank some people individually.

WAYNE: I want, first, to acknowledge the contributions of all the student pioneers in a class called (what else?) *Writing the Information Superhighway* who helped develop *that* course and chart *the* course down the infopike. Special thanks to Irfan Murtuza and Stephen Chim, both stellar members of that learning community, for their invaluable research assistance. In addition, Dr. Rebecca Rickly, an ECB colleague, collaborated with me on current versions of the course. Becky's ideas influenced much of what appears in the book. Hugh Burns, Locke Carter, Fred Kemp, Nancy Peterson, John Slatin, Paul Taylor of the Daedalus Group—my first travel companions on the info highway— deserve thanks and much, much more for their past and current intellectual and emotional support and inspiration. Finally, I thank my wife, Sara, and my children, Alexis and Ian, whose love, patience, and good humor remind me the info highway can only take one so far.

BILL: So many people have provided help, inspiration, and courage as this project developed that I can't thank them all. But to A. D. van Nostrand, who really opened my eyes to a world of rhetoric and composition; to Rich Larsen and Carl Brucker, who helped get me started thinking about computers and writing; and to others along the way—Cindy Selfe, Gail Hawisher, Matthew Barritt, Martin Rosenberg, Susanmarie Harrington, Michael Joyce, Fred Kemp, Ann Green, Eric Crump, Trent Batson, Lisa Gerrard, and many others—who encouraged me, who unaccountably thought a lot of my ideas and were generous enough to spend time thinking *about* them, when asked; to all these valuable colleagues, thanks. My greatest thanks go to my wife Pat, who has always been my bluntest and most useful critic, and to my children Jennie, Maggie, Nick, and Misha, who have always lifted my spirits and given me many interesting things to do instead of writing.

In closing, we both freely admit that this book took shape amid many and varied influences and that we would have to write *another* book in order to acknowledge them all. Many more people than we can mention sent us advice, URLs, encouragement, and so forth. We could not have undertaken, let alone finished, this project without the support of the computers and writing community.

W. B.
B. C.

P A R T I

PRODUCING AND ACCESSING DIGITAL TEXTS

Chapter 1
Manipulating Text

Chapter 2
Communicating on the Internet: One on One

Chapter 3
Communicating on the Internet:
Accessing Virtual Communities

Chapter 4
Gathering Information on the Internet:
Reaching Out and Bringing Back Resources

Chapter 5
Constructing Texts On-Line

AN INTRODUCTION TO COMPUTER-AIDED WRITING ACTIVITIES AND THE TOOLS THAT FACILITATE THEM

On one level, writers write, and text is text. That is, no matter the medium, we writers strive to communicate meaning to readers, to convince readers, to inform and entertain readers. In carrying out this mission, we use whatever devices we have at our disposal. And that's where computers can help. Technology cannot help a writer write; computers cannot reason, and they cannot make or even understand meaning. No computer can think.

Can you tell the difference between these two statements?

The roast is ready to eat.

The tiger is ready to eat.

A computer can't!

But computers can help locate resources to establish the context for a piece of writing. And once you have something to say, the technology can provide a highly efficient tool for putting that meaning into text, for revising and editing the text, for illustrating and annotating the text, and for creating visual effects that, before desktop computers came along, were impossible for all but the professional printer. Finally, the computer can serve as the medium for new *kinds* of text—principally multimedia and hypertext, increasingly delivered through the World Wide Web—that are becoming increasingly significant tools in business, industry, government, and education. These new texts take full advantage of the computer's capabilities, and they are only readable/displayable on the computer because they contain features that cannot be printed, such as sound recordings, links that allow readers to jump around in a text or among texts, and full-motion video. In all these types of writing and kinds of text, the hardest part of the work—making the text *mean* something—still belongs to you, the writer. But as you work, the computer can provide a broader palette of options, a greater range of devices and strategies for making your writing clear, organizing it, and presenting it in a form that is friendly to both the eye and the mind.

As writers, we look for ways of using technology to become more productive, more efficient, or just more successful. In that effort, the first thing we have to realize is that writing with computers is different for everyone. Some of us will be novices. Some will have mastered word processing but never used an E-mail program. Some will be "power users" who can use any type of application on any type of computer. Furthermore, how computer technology is integrated into a writing course's curriculum will vary depending on the number of computers available for instructional use, the teacher's level of expertise, the range of services available to students on a particular campus, and so forth. So, for example, a great many writing teachers may want students to word process their papers and use the Internet to gather information for research papers, but because their school has no dedicated computer classrooms, they can only request that students use the tools of the information superhighway outside class, in public computing sites. In addition, the educational computing world includes personal computers such as Macintoshes and IBM-compatibles and mainframe computers that permit access via workstations or terminals. And each of these types of hardware can run scores of different brands of word processors, E-mail programs, newsgroup readers, and so on.

Because of this extreme range of possibilities, Part I is designed to be flexible. Novices might rely on every section, beginning with the activities on word processing and moving along through each section, adding capability as they go. Anyone who is comfortable with word processing but is an E-mail novice can skip to that section, and E-mail users who feel comfortable with "netiquette" but want to learn advanced techniques for doing research on-line could skip the other sections and move on to that one. In different places, using different software and hardware, writers will nevertheless pursue these same activities:

- Manipulating text
- Communicating on the Internet, one on one
- Communicating on the Internet in virtual communities
- Gathering information on the Internet
- Constructing texts on-line

As tools change, the descriptions can change; the activities will, most likely, remain constant. You will almost certainly pursue all the activities mentioned here, if not in your current writing course, then in other college courses. You will go on to pursue many of these activities in the workplace. In each of these settings, the technology and technological methods available for manipulating text or accessing the World Wide Web or sending electronic mail will differ, perhaps widely. Later in this book, you and your classmates will have an opportunity to explore the ways your campus provides for pursuing these activities and to explain those methods to each other. This book can help as you think about the activity, and it can provide advice about the *capabilities* of the different functions listed here. It can't, of course, provide a manual for every conceivable system or every item of software.

As writers, you will constantly be moving from one set of expectations to the next. As you enter college, for example, you meet expectations about inquiry, analysis, and argumentation that you probably did not encounter in high school. As you move into courses in different fields of study, you also find differing expectations, different ways of thinking and writing about knowledge. So you have to become expert learners, writers who can attune themselves to the texts being produced in the field and who are able to adapt to the expectations readers have for those texts. You learn, in a typical first-year college writing course, how to inquire, analyze, and argue. In later courses, you will adapt those activities to the ways practitioners in different disciplines inquire, analyze, and argue. The same is true for the ways computers support writing. With this book, you'll learn how to carry out these activities, and you'll explore the ways these new tools allow you to communicate meaning to a reader, support and clarify your assertions, and organize and develop your ideas. Later, you'll have to learn how to adapt these activities in different technological settings.

The following chart shows what kinds of writing activities you can accomplish with what kinds of application, with special considerations on what each application does best.

Activity	Common Applications	Special Considerations
Word processing	• Microsoft Word, Works, Office • Macwrite • WordPerfect • Writenow • Nisus	• Flexibility for generating and organizing text • Formatting, fonts, stylistic effects, graphics (tables, figures, still pictures, etc.)
Desktop publishing	• PageMaker	• Highly specialized formatting options • Professional printers' functions • Built-in templates for brochures, newsletters, advertisements, etc.
Hypertext	• Storyspace (Macintosh) • Guide (IBM and compatibles) • HTML editors	• Nonlinear composing and reading • Rhetoric of links and pathways • Inclusion of nonprintable resources (sound, video) • On-screen reading environment
Multimedia documents	• Most standard word processing applications • Standard desktop publishing applications • Specialized multimedia applications (MediaText, Macromind Director, etc.)	• Inclusion of nonprintable resources (sound, video) • Rhetorical effects of nonprint resources • Nonlinear composition and presentation • Rhetoric of linking to and displaying video and sound

ACTIVITY 1: Internet Literacy Inventory

In the traditional writing classroom, one can only speculate as to the relative abilities of all those who arrive on the first day of school. Similarly, potential members of the computer classroom writing community will arrive with all levels of computer literacy, from total novice to experienced "power user." One of the first things the burgeoning community needs to learn is its collective level of computer knowledge. To navigate successfully in cyberspace, furthermore, we need to know more than just the technology itself. As anyone who has entered cyberspace for the first time knows, it is a place, with its own language. Although cyberlanguage uses English words and letters, it often resembles an alphabet soup of acronyms. To some cybernauts, the sentence "To set up a homepage on the WWW, you need to create an ASCII file using HTML, and then you need to tell all your friends your URL so they can check out your GIFs" makes perfect sense. To others, it's intimidating: Oh, no—letters that don't spell anything!

The following activity taps into the superhighway metaphor and works well during the first class meeting. The goal of the activity is to create a knowledge inventory of many of the acronyms, terms, and concepts community members will come across as they navigate the Internet or some other part of the information superhighway. Once community members (including the teacher!) complete the inventory, they are to tally their scores and determine into which category—driver, navigator, or passenger—they fall.

Writing the Information Superhighway Computer Experience Survey

Directions: Below you will find a list of acronyms and terms you will probably come across as you use computers to navigate the information superhighway. For each of the terms, write on a separate piece of paper 1, 2, or 3 based on the following assessment of your recognition of the term:

> 1=I know nothing or almost nothing about this.
> 2=I have heard of this, but I don't have much experience with it.
> 3=I have considerable experience with it.

After you have assigned a score for each of the items, add them up to determine your level of knowledge as you begin your journey on the information superhighway.

	1	2	3
1. RAM	1	2	3
2. ROM	1	2	3
3. CPU	1	2	3
4. DOS	1	2	3
5. Windows	1	2	3
6. UNIX	1	2	3
7. modem	1	2	3
8. LAN	1	2	3
9. WAN	1	2	3
10. CMC	1	2	3
11. FAQ	1	2	3
12. Internet	1	2	3
13. E-mail	1	2	3
14. bbs	1	2	3
15. usenet	1	2	3
16. listserv	1	2	3
17. telnet	1	2	3
18. IRC	1	2	3
19. MOO	1	2	3

20. FTP	1	2	3
21. Fetch	1	2	3
22. Archie	1	2	3
23. Veronica	1	2	3
24. gopher	1	2	3
25. WWW	1	2	3
26. browser	1	2	3
27. hypertext	1	2	3
28. http	1	2	3
29. HTML	1	2	3
30. URL	1	2	3

Add your scores and categorize yourself:

Passenger: if you scored between 30 and 45
Navigator: if you scored between 46 and 75
Driver: if you scored between 76 and 90

Follow-Up Activity

The community can use the results of the inventory in a number of ways. Immediately after the inventory results are in, members can introduce themselves to the community by going around the room and saying, "My name is Monica Ruppert, and I am a _____ (passenger, navigator, or driver). My lowest score was on _____, and my highest score was on _____. The three items I would like to learn more about are _____, _____, and _____. By the end of the semester, I would like to become a (passenger, navigator, or driver)." When everyone has introduced themselves, the whole community will understand the level and range of Internet literacy.

The follow-up conversation can be extended by going through each of the items, asking who circled "3" for each item, and asking those people to explain what the acronym means, what it is used for, and how they use it. The categories can be used also during later activities to form working groups consisting of members of each category.

1

MANIPULATING TEXT

This section focuses on the individual writer, working at an individual computer, and it considers how that writer can use the computer and the kinds of text available to reach an audience.

Although word processing clearly evolved as a better, easier way to type, a word-processing application is far more than a fancy typewriter. Many writers first turn to the computer because of the ease of typing up a written draft. Fewer actually use the computer to aid in arranging and presenting that draft. Fewer still take full advantage of the computer's ability to provide a powerful, flexible tool for composing texts. A word processor does, of course, greatly ease the activity of typing up a text, but used from the outset, it can also provide the writer with a range of options for coming up with something to say, incorporating evidence for major assertions, putting those assertions into the most effective order, altering sentences to create the needed rhetorical effect, and controlling formatting so that the writer's meaning is as accessible to the reader as possible.

Used as a word processor, a computer can help a writer *generate* ideas, organize those ideas, and present them most effectively. We'll consider each of those stages of the writing process and the degree to which the computer accommodates a central fact of writing: that writing is a recursive process. Writers don't just come up with one idea and move on to the next. They move back and forth in their texts, tinkering with what they have already said in order to come up with more to say, for example, or making earlier statements more precise in light of the discoveries the writer makes later in the text. The ability to change words, sentences, and paragraphs instantly and infinitely supports this recursive method.

Word processors are well suited for composing, for easing the process of getting ideas from the rough, disorganized state in a writer's mind to the finished, well-ordered structure of a class paper, lab report, business memo, or other written material. *Editing,* in word-processing terminology, includes the actual typing of a manuscript, moving around in it, moving text from place to place, searching for and replacing parts of the text, and so forth. The "editor" is the program's feature that enables all of this. As you think at the keyboard, cut and paste until your ideas are in the right order, and correct any problems you may have included in your text, you are using the program's editing function.

Formatting is carried out by a program's "formatter" feature that reads any commands you have inserted in the text and turns your file into something that your printer will print according to your specifications. Thus, when you enter text into the word processor's editor, you are not, in fact, typing; you are sending instructions to your printer, instructions that you can change at any time to suit the requirements of your assignment or just to satisfy your sense of what "looks good." So, if you specified (while using your editor) that some text should be **boldfaced** when it is printed, the formatter will read your command, and when the file goes to a printer, the formatter will tell the printer to begin and end boldface as you specified. Of course, most word-processing programs do not distinguish among these three functions, so you don't see the moment when you move from the editor to the formatter, and you don't have to worry about the difference. All you have to do is learn how to take full advantage of the word processor to make your writing experience easier and more rewarding.

Basically, when you use a word processor, you are engaged in one of three activities:

- generating text
- revising text
- formatting text

COMPOSING

Generating Ideas and Putting Them into Words

Beginning any writing project can be tricky. Few things in life are so universally intimidating as a blank sheet of paper—or a blank screen. But you can make the process easier by remembering just what you're trying to do as you sit down (or walk around, eat a pizza, or whatever else you may do) to decide what to write. In working on this problem, you can use to your advantage the fact that text is cheap on a word processor—that is, you don't use up a lot of paper or, for that matter, a lot of time. Just open a new file and make notes in it. If the notes turn into an essay, then that can be the file you actually write in. But chances are the file will be messy, disorganized, maybe even outrageous, so that once you get what you need, you can open another file and begin writing the actual paper there. Here are some ideas for using the "text is cheap" factor to get started on a writing task.

Finding Something to Write About

In most writing classes—in fact, in most classes that involve written assignments—you will have some ability to select or even originate a topic. Given a set of options or the ability to come up with your own topic, you might begin by typing some likely or possible topics into a word-processing window. As you develop the list, add notes about prospective topics to find out what you already know about the topics on the list. Don't worry about making sense or sounding good. Just get some ideas about the topics on-screen. Write about what you *might* write about, in an unfocused way, just to discover more about what you know the most about or might be the most interested in. Just write to yourself; give yourself advice about what topic to choose. These notes will help you sort through your ideas, sift your knowledge about the different possibilities, and help you discover which topics you are more interested in pursuing. That knowledge, in turn, will make choosing a topic easier. You can use this process to discover which topic interests you most and on which topics you already know enough to allow you to write (or at least begin to write) intelligently about them.

Example

Abortion

> right to life vs choice. Polarized. Lots of nuts on both sides. Rape and incest exceptions. Most people support abortion, but the minority is really vocal. How much do I know about all this? Conception vs viability? How much should I, as a man, have to say about it anyway?

Are computers good for us?

> Do we spend more time out of touch with people? Yes and no. We spend time on-line, connected with people. E-mail puts many people in touch more cheaply than phone can. Can share work or collaborate across time and over distance more easily with computers. Do computers help us work better? Probably not, but they might make us more productive. Can't make me smarter or better, but might allow me to do more. Work smarter, rather than harder?

Contrasting these two brief examples reveals that the writer knows more and asks more interesting questions about computers than about abortion. This writer should probably write about computers.

Finding What You Know

Sooner or later, you'll want to read more about your topic, but for the purpose of deciding on a topic, you will most often focus on what you already know—from lecture, class notes, your textbook, your own experience, and so on. You may not realize it, but you have a considerable store of knowledge already, and you can use the keyboard to uncover it. This section presents several techniques for generating ideas, for getting some words onto paper. One or more of these techniques, all of which take advantage of at least one of the word processor's features, will help you start your next paper.

Electronic text is far more fluid—more changeable, less permanent—than text on paper, and this general fact has made word processing, which started out as a way to make business correspondence more efficient, attractive to writers in general. And as the demand for word processors expanded beyond the office, the applications themselves have become easier and easier to use, making them even more advantageous to writers of all kinds, from beginning and developing writers to professionals of every kind. So, when you're ready to begin, open a file and use it to do one or more of the activities explained next, all of which take advantage of the ease of producing and revising text in a word processor.

Focused Freewriting

Most of you, at some point, have probably done some freewriting, so the process is not new. You just sit and write for a given period of time, often five or ten minutes, and the point is to keep writing, keep the pen moving on the page, even if you have to write the same word over and over because you can't think of anything else to write write write write. Sooner or later you will think of something more, and at any rate you'll write *some*thing that you can work with. Once the freewriting period is finished, you can review what you've written, looking for anything usable as the basis for a paper. Again, the computer aids in the process, principally in four ways:

- Writing with a computer is easier on the hands—you won't tire as quickly.
- You need not worry about correctness. You can just focus on typing quickly, so you can put a lot of text on-screen.
- You can darken the screen if you like, so that you won't be distracted by what you've written. If you can't see what you're typing, then you can focus more directly on what you're thinking—on what to say next, rather than on what you've said last.
- What you type into a word-processing file is easier to use. You can just delete anything you don't want, or you can easily copy what you do want into a new file, and you can use the cut-and-paste function to rearrange what you've chosen to keep.

ACTIVITY 1.1: Freewriting on Computer

Whatever the topic you've chosen or been assigned, type it in at the top of your file, take a moment to concentrate on that topic, take a few deep breaths, and just type for five or ten minutes. Type about that topic, if at all possible, but whatever you do just keep typing, keep the characters appearing on the screen. Type in a stream of consciousness, ignoring correctness, paying no mind to whether you are making sense. Just get as much out as you can in the time you allot yourself. Pour whatever you know about the topic onto the screen, in whatever order it happens to come to you. If you find yourself stopping to look at what you've typed, then use the computer to trick yourself out of doing that. Just darken the screen or turn off the monitor so that you can't see what's on it, and continue to type in what you're thinking. Then read back through the file and select what you find useful. You may be surprised at how much material is there.

Example

Are computers good for us?

> I think they are, since I use them a lot, for classwork and for other stuff. I E-mail my parents and my friends. I think I keep in touch better with E-mail than I would with pen, paper, and stamps. I wonder why? Is it the convenience? I contact people from the same keyboard where I do my work—no running to the post office. No stamps. I'm lucky to have this account—glad the college provides students with them. I wonder what other services cost? This is expensive, now that I think of it. Computer—$2,500. Network connection—how much? Modem is $200–300. On-line services run $6–10/hour, I've heard. So maybe this isn't as cheap as paper and stamps, but if the stuff is available, the costs are hidden in other stuff—like tuition and usage fees. Still, I write more. If I had to do this on my own money—money I could see come out of my pocket specifically for this—would I do it? I hope so, because I like being in touch with home and with friends who, like me, are away from home at other colleges. I don't feel so isolated here when I can chat with them over the Internet whenever I want. Somehow when I send out a message, I feel better, even before anyone answers. I feel like I'm in touch. Like I've contacted someone. Even though I don't even know if the person's read the message. I wonder why that is? The act itself seems satisfying. Like I've done something about my loneliness (if that's what it is). I like that.

Think about the ways the preceding paragraph might be converted into an outline for an essay on computers and communication. Look at the subtopics, at the places where questions indicate insights, and at the questions that indicate a need for more information. This paragraph could easily be cut-and-pasted into a framework for an essay:

E-mail—Better than the phone or the P.O.?

> I use computers a lot, for classwork and for other stuff. I E-mail my parents and friends. I think I keep in touch better with E-mail than I would with pen, paper, and stamps.

I wonder why?

Is it the convenience?

I contact people from the same keyboard where I do my work—
no running to the post office.

No stamps.

I'm lucky to have this account—glad the college provides students
with them.

I wonder what other services cost?

This is expensive, now that I think of it.

Computer—$2,500.

Network connection—how much?

Modem is $200–300.

On-line services run $6–10/hour, I've heard.

So maybe this isn't as cheap as paper and stamps, but if the stuff is
available, the costs are hidden in other stuff—like tuition and
usage fees.

Still, I write more. If I had to do this on my own money—
money I could see come out of my pocket specifically for this—
would I do it? I hope so, because I like being in touch with home
and with friends who, like me, are away from home at other colleges. I don't feel so isolated here when I can chat with them over
the Internet whenever I want.

Somehow when I send out a message, I feel better, even before
anyone answers. I feel like I'm in touch. Like I've contacted someone. Even though I don't even know if the person's read the message. I wonder why that is?

The act itself seems satisfying.

Like I've done something about my loneliness (if that's what
it is).

I like that.

See? A little focusing, a little organizing, and the writer is on the way to a
draft. Now this writer could gather some more information, use this text
to trigger more thinking, write about examples of the claims about E-mail
and keeping in touch, and so forth. One five-minute freewriting session at
the keyboard *can* provide a whole essay!

Brainstorming

If freewriting isn't your style, try brainstorming (or do one after the other,
dredging up more and more information as you go). Brainstorming and word
processing make a natural match because the computer eases the processes of
producing text and selecting the items you want to keep. You can make your
list, arranging some items as you go. Because you can move your cursor around
at will, you can enter items and then return to them to list more items that you
feel are associated with the earlier ideas. Once you have finished your session,

---

How-to: Cut, Copy, and Paste

Most word processors accomplish this function in slightly different ways, using different keystrokes or commands, but the basic process is similar:

1. Highlight, or select, the text you want to cut or copy. Selecting text most often means placing your cursor at one end or the other of the text you want to cut or copy, holding the mouse button down, and dragging the cursor to the other end of the block of text. Other programs may use arrow keys or other function keys to reach the same end: highlight a block of text on the screen. Check your manual or the on-screen help to find out precisely how your word processor does this.
2. **Cut** or **Copy** the highlighted text. Again, most programs allow you either to use a keyboard command (Control-X or Command-X to **cut,** Control-C or Command-C to **copy**) or to use the mouse to pull down a menu (usually the **Edit** menu) and select **Cut** or **Copy.**
3. Place the cursor in the location where you want the block of text to appear.
4. **Paste** the text by using a keyboard command (most frequently Control-V or Command-V) or by pulling down the appropriate menu (again, usually called **Edit**) and selecting the **Paste** command.

---

you can use Cut, Copy, and Paste to arrange your items into categories, into groups of items that have something in common. You can do this in your original file, or you can copy the items you want to use into a new file, where you can arrange them into the order you think best. As you work, you'll not only be incredibly impressed with the workings of your own mind—and with how much you already know—but you'll begin to see how your topic might be organized. Your ideas will begin to take shape, and the categories you create will help you decide what you can say about all this information.

ACTIVITY 1.2: Brainstorming on Computer

The process is probably familiar to you. Focusing on your topic, make lists of anything—*anything*—that comes to mind when you look at the topic or at any of the items on the list you produce. Keep the items brief, if possible, and focus on thinking of everything you possibly can. Then, when you think you've run out of ideas, focus on the more general items and make lists about those items, and so forth, until you finally *do* run out of ideas. Don't worry about whether the items are useful or even make sense. Just play the "association game" to its fullest. The point, as with freewriting, is to put everything possible down on paper. Sorting and selecting can go on later. This process can take about as much time as you can devote to it— fifteen minutes to several hours—so give it time to work for you. Allow each item to act as a "trigger" to inspire more items, so that your list will become a record of all your ideas about the topic, of all the possibilities for filling those pages you have to write.

Example

Reach out and touch someone—uses of E-mail

Keeping in touch at home
> Mom's insane need to know how I am, what I'm doing
> Dad's compustion to offer advice
>> Good filter—can keep or delete
>> They get to write me, I don't have to "listen"—skim-and-delete!
> Send money!!!!!
> Get the news about home, sibs, cousins, nieces, aunts, the whole bunch

Who else do I keep in touch with?
> Pat at Hollins
>> Ooh! Long-distance love
>> Whenever I sign on, I read her and write her.
>> We never sleep! I miss her voice, but her messages keep me alive
>> We'd never afford the phone bills

Rich at Colgate
> Best friend—no one like him
> Knockout sense of humor—definitely ROFL at least once per message
> Sports—need I say more? Woofin' about the home teams!
> This guy will listen to anything—*anything*—I say. And vice versa.

Liz in Hong Kong
> Seems weird to have a pal half the world away.
> We'd never talk on the phone—too many time zones
> She's my best reader—always send my drafts to Liz
> Always read hers, too.
> Sympatico, even so far away.

The gang at Cheers (that's what my swim team called ourselves)
> The whole bunch has E-mail
>> Big schools, small schools, in-between
>> Famous schools, total unknowns
>> 4-year, 2-year, community college
> We all use an address list to write everyone at once.
> Just like sitting in some virtual locker room—except for the smell. ;-)

Why do I write all these people?
> It's there
> It's fun
> It makes me feel good

It helps me keep from being homesick—or at least *as* homesick
I get good advice
I don't feel so completely on my own
I feel connected
I feel that others care, even when people I meet here don't
seem to.
I don't have to give up one place and set of friends just because
I'm someplace else for four years.

You get the idea. This list could go on for several pages (or several days) until the writer has enough information or just enough inspiration for a draft, for prose.

Now you try it. Think of a topic, and brainstorm for a while. Then take a break and come back to the list to add stuff. If you can, sleep on the list and return to it the next day. Just keep pumping items into the list. Once you've finished your list, use the computer's Cut and Paste capabilities to help you rearrange the items in your brainstorming list into clusters or categories. Play with different combinations. Experiment. Think about how the different combinations lead to differing focuses for an essay, and make the choice of focus carefully. Once you've decided on a focus, delete the items that are no longer relevant, and use Cut and Paste to arrange what's left into the order you think you want to use in your draft.

Heuristics

Freewriting and brainstorming are extremely useful when you are starting from nothing. If you are supposed to come up with your own topic and define or narrow it yourself, then these methods, which allow your thinking to range widely, work well. However, college writing most often demands a response to a fairly narrow topic. You might be asked to describe the life cycle of a moth, or to discuss the major causes of a historical event, or to compare two major sources on an issue and articulate your own position. You may also be asked to write up your observations or research within a preestablished format, such as a social science research report or a science lab report. In these cases, freewriting and brainstorming are less useful, because you have less intellectual room to work. They may help as you try to solve a particularly difficult problem or as you weigh your own decision about a given issue, but once you begin to write the paper, you may find that the heuristic method allows you to focus more profitably on the task you've been assigned.

Heuristic—comes from the Greek word *heurisis* (to discover), and it's where we get *eureka!* It's just a fancy word for a standard list of questions you might ask yourself or prompts you might respond to about any writing project, a routine that will get you started writing about your topic and allow you to use the writing process itself to educate yourself about your topic. Many computer programs have been developed to aid the rhetorical process of invention. These products are extremely useful, even though the heuristics they employ are often generic—not tailored to a specific topic, occasion, purpose, or genre of writing. But you don't have to depend on commercial products. You could easily type up your own heuristic by generating a list of questions or prompts based on your writing assignment: break it into parts, turn each part into a question, and answer the questions individually.

The following subsections describe three examples of this process. First, we've provided a heuristic to help you define your purpose in writing an essay. The second set of questions help you consider the needs of your audience. Then we offer a set of general questions based on the teaching of classical rhetoric. We've also provided a heuristic for writing the first draft of an argumentative essay, such as you might write in many different classes, particularly in humanities classes.

Heuristic 1: Deciding on a Purpose.   One of the easiest ways of sneaking up on the beginning of a paper is to think about the purpose for the piece. In the case of a paper for a class, you are writing because you have to, because a paper is due and you'll get a grade for what you do. But if you can get beyond that reason and write some notes about why the topic is significant, why you want to know more about it, why others need to know more about it, and *what* they need to know about it, then you'll have taken the first important steps toward writing an interesting, effective paper. Even within the context of writing for a class, there's a *reason* to write, a reason you chose the subject you did, and a reason people besides you should be interested in it. Writing about that reason can be a good way to discover more about your topic.

You might complete this sentence:

I think (my subject) is important because...

Then go on from there, explaining your reasons as fully as possible. The activity will allow you to focus your ideas more precisely, and it will give you a head start on building a context for your paper.

Again, because text is cheap, you don't have to worry whether your ramblings are polished. They shouldn't be. This process involves, literally, thinking on paper, getting your intentions out where you can see them, shape them, choose among them. Remember, if you make a mess, you can always delete anything that is not helpful, and you can always open a new file and begin working on the pieces of your ramblings that seem most promising. You can even copy those pieces into the new file, so that you can look at them in a more focused way. At any rate, knowing *why* you're writing is the next best thing to knowing *what* you want to write.

ACTIVITY 1.3: Deciding on a Purpose

This activity will show you how to create a generic word-processing file that you can use every time you sit down to write a paper. To do so, complete the following procedure:

1. Open your word processor and create a new file.
2. In that file, enter the following text:

   - Why am I writing about this topic?
   - Why is this topic important to me?
   - Why am I interested in this topic?
   - Why is this topic important to other people (readers)?
   - Why should other people be interested in this topic?
   - What is the single most important thing I want other people to know or realize about this topic?
   - How do I want to affect readers? That is, do I want to entertain them, explain something to them, analyze something for them, or persuade them?

3. Save the file on your diskette and and give it a name you will remember, such as "Purpose Template."
4. Now, go back and respond to all the items in as much detail as you can. You need not respond to them in the order they appear, and you can jump back and forth among them as your response to one leads you to think more about one you responded to previously.
5. After you've responded as much as you can in this sitting, use the **Save As...** function and give the file a new name that describes the topic or the assignment on which you are working. For example, if you are working on the first writing assignment your teacher has given you, you might save your file as "Purpose Proj 1."
6. If you used Save As, your diskette should now include the generic **Purpose Template** file and your **Purpose Proj 1** file.

When you have another writing assignment in the future, you can return to the Purpose Template again and repeat steps 4 through 6.

Heuristic 2: The Audience as Heuristic. Of course, practically speaking, your teacher is your reader, but writing to a teacher is the second worst choice of audience you could make (the worst is yourself). If you try to write to someone who you know is already an expert in the field, you will leave out a lot of the "boring details," and, as a result, your ideas won't be as complete or connected as they need to be—for either your reader or, more important, you, as you write.

So choose someone to write to, and make your choice as real as possible. If you know someone who is or ought to be interested in your topic, actually write to that someone; if not, choose a general audience, someone of about your age, background, and level of education. You could write to your room-mate, for example, and then ask her or him to read the paper to see whether you have done your work well.

ACTIVITY 1.4: Audience Analysis

Use the same procedure described in *Activity 1.3* to create an Audience Analysis template with your word processor. To do so:

1. Create a file and type in the following questions:
   - What do I know about my readers in terms of age, gender, values, beliefs, etc.?
   - Will my readers know more, less, or about the same amount about my topic as I do?
   - Will my readers share my beliefs, have opposing ones, or have no opinion on my topic?
   - Why would they care about (the topic)?
   - What does (the topic) mean to them?
   - Why *should* my readers care about this topic?
   - What do my readers think I know about the topic?
   - How do they think I know that?
   - What do they need to know about the topic?
   - What should they think or believe about the topic?

2. After entering these questions, save your file using the name **Audience Template.**
3. Respond to each of the questions as thoroughly and in as much detail as you can.
4. Use the **Save As** function to give your audience analysis file a name that relates to the assignment you're working on.

Once you've used the heuristic to develop the information you need, write an essay that answers those questions as fully as you can. The answers will give you information about your topic, and they will help you remember that you are not writing to someone who already understands what you have to say. Instead, you are writing to someone who needs to know what you know and needs to make the connections you have made with regard to the information available to you and your reader.

Heuristic 3: Classical Invention.   The notion of using heuristics for the purpose of invention derives from classical Greek culture. For example, Aristotle divided rhetoric into three parts:

1. *logos,* which is essentially what you have to say, the evidence that you claim supports your position;
2. *ethos,* which is whatever quality you possess that makes you the right person to say what you are saying—special expertise, unique experience, exceptional honesty, and so forth—and
3. *pathos,* which is the appeal to the audience's emotion, that part of the topic that they can relate to on the level of emotion or feeling.

ACTIVITY 1.5: Classical Invention

Here are a few general questions, based on Aristotle's concepts of *logos, ethos,* and *pathos,* that you can use for almost any writing assignment. Use procedures similar to those in the Defining Purpose and Audience Analysis activities to create for yourself a **Classical Invention** template.

- What am I writing about (topic, or *logos*)?
- Why am I writing about my topic (purpose, or *ethos*)?
- What knowledge do I have that makes me the right person to write about this topic (*ethos*)?
- What am I trying to say about my topic (controlling idea, which comes from a blending of all three concepts)?
- What evidence best supports and clarifies my controlling idea (*logos*)?
- Why should my reader(s) be interested in my controlling idea (*pathos*)?

As you learn more about writing and you develop your own writing process, you will encounter quite a few heuristics. When you find one that's useful, copy it into your own heuristics file. That way, when you encounter a similar writing situation, you'll have a strategy for responding to it.

Heuristic 4: Argumentation.   Here is a general heuristic you might use if you were beginning an argumentative essay. Open a word-processing file and copy in the steps for the following heuristic. Then use a similar process as in the first three heuristics as you fill in the "answers" and use **Save As**, and so forth.

ACTIVITY 1.6: Inventing an Argument

This exercise will guide you through the prewriting, organizing, and drafting stages for an argumentative essay. The procedure is not exhaustive—that is, there is more to inventing an argument than you will do here. But this format will give you a foundation from which you can build.

For the present purpose, we shall define an *issue* as a point on which reasonable people can disagree. Thus, that the Earth is round is a fact, not an issue, but whether computers do more to bring people together or keep them apart is an issue.

Step 1

List three issues that concern you (or, more realistically, that your assignment asks you to think about). Try to list three issues about which you have both knowledge and strong feelings.

Example

Computers for the homeless
Taking care of our own problems vs helping others solve theirs
Harsher penalties for drinking while driving?

Step 2

Think about each of these issues carefully. Decide which one you know most about and which one you care most deeply about. Then choose one of the issues as the subject of your essay. Then write *one* sentence—one *complete* sentence—that states your position on the issue. What you will write is your gut feeling about the issue, what you would do about it if someone appointed you ruler for a day. Your response needs to be a complete sentence because you need to make an assertion about your topic, and a sentence is the smallest grammatical unit that can contain an assertion. You need to have a subject, a verb, and a predicate to make the statement you need here.

Example

We need to do what we can to help all those in need.

Step 3

Now write at least three *complete* sentences, each of which clearly and fully expresses a separate, distinct reason you believe the position you have taken is the right one.

Example

We're all human beings.
Those who have plenty owe a duty to those who have less.
The Good Samaritan provides a useful example.
Unless everyone sees progress toward solutions, there could be
     trouble—war, riot, etc.
The U.S. brags that it can feed the world—let's prove it!

Step 4

Study your five sentences and think about how you will turn each of them into a paragraph supporting your position. Make notes in your file, on a separate sheet of paper, or in a separate word-processing file. Use the computer's Cut and Paste capabilities to arrange these sentences into the order in which you will use them in your essay. This ordering provides you with a topic outline for your essay.

Example

The Good Samaritan provides a useful example.
     Who is my neighbor? If I "take care of my own" first, how can
     I know who is "my own"? Samaritan saw someone in need and
     helped him. That example lay at the center of the Christian
     faith, and it has its equivalents in most of the world's most
     prominent religions—Hinduism, Buddhism, Islam, Judaism.

Those who have plenty owe a duty to those who have less.

> The primary lesson is this. I have what I have by accident of birth—born where I was, to the parents I got, etc. I can't believe in the Good Samaritan *and* believe that I should keep what I have all to myself *or* that I should refuse to help someone because the other person is different from me.

The U.S. brags that it can feed the world—let's prove it!

> We keep hearing about all our surpluses, about the U.S. as the world's breadbasket, about the Land of Plenty. If we put our minds and our backs and our pocketbooks to it, I wonder if we could feed the world?
>
> Probably, partially by providing food—combination of selling and granting, depending on the country or the situation—and partially by selling it, like to countries or people who have the means to buy, but not to produce (no arable land, famine, etc.).

We're all human beings.

> When you get right down to it, our differences are not as great as our similarities.
>
> Our differences don't justify our treating each other like dogs, just because of an unequal distribution of resources.
>
> As the world comes closer together—air travel, computer networks, TV and radio, etc.—we are closer to our more distant neighbors.

Unless everyone sees progress toward solutions, there could be trouble—war, riot, etc.

> Sharing is in our interests, too.
>
> Those who are without food and hope may decide to take both from those who do have them.
>
> Wars begin because of a grossly uneven distribution of resources.

We can solve problems by evening out resources and by "teaching them to fish."

> Begin by extending the helping hand—get them on their feet.
>
> Continue by helping them achieve self-reliance.

Step 5

Now think for a moment about what the points you listed have in common and how they relate to your gut reaction from step 2. Is there a sentence that organizes all those statements into a neat package *and* that expresses your gut reaction? (If not, you may want to eliminate or replace one or more of your sentences—or change your gut reaction.) Write that sentence at the top of your list of sentences. It will become your controlling idea, the statement that will *control* your response to your topic. All the other assertions in your paper will support or clarify this one idea, this one assertion.

> **Controlling Idea:** As transportation and communication technologies bring people closer together, those of us who have plenty must recognize our duties toward those who do not.
> The Good Samaritan provides a useful example.
> Those who have plenty owe a duty to those who have less.
> The U.S. brags that it can feed the world—let's prove it!
> We're all human beings.
> Unless everyone sees progress toward solutions, there could be trouble—war, riot, etc.
> We can solve problems by evening out resources and by "teaching them to fish."

Step 6

The last step before beginning to write the first draft is to think of what someone whose gut reaction is totally opposite from yours would think of your controlling idea and your reasons. This task is vitally important to writing an argument, for you will have to pay some serious attention to responding to what others might think or do about the issue you have chosen. To make certain you take other positions seriously, then, pretend you actually do hold a position opposite from the gut reaction you wrote earlier, and write a sentence that expresses what that person's position would be and why (again, list at least three reasons). If you can't pretend, then think of an actual person whose position is different from yours, because that will make the reasons easier to think of and more realistic.

> **Controlling Idea:** If everyone took care of the needs of their own people, the world would be much better off.
> When we send aid to faraway places, too much of it ends up being wasted.
> Different cultures need to make progress in their own ways, according to their own values.
> Trying to save the world from hunger and want will only result in bankrupting ourselves.

Step 7

Now write your essay, using your controlling idea and reasons as the basic outline. But remember that somewhere in the paper you must acknowledge the other points of view you listed in step 6 and explain why your views are preferable to them. Take time to think about how you will organize your argument into sections and paragraphs. Then write the essay.

As you can see, this general heuristic contains the gist of an argument—it helps you establish a context for your argument, lay out the issue, develop and state a position, use evidence to support and clarify that position, acknowledge other points of view, and reason your way to your conclusion.

As you move through your course of study, you'll find that you'll write a number of arguments, so this general heuristic will be useful more than once. Take care as you use it, though, because you'll find that from class to class, discipline to discipline, the form of the argument you're asked to write may differ. The central features are the same, but the way the argument develops will change with the kinds of questions you're asked to address, the kinds of evidence that the particular discipline uses as support, and the kinds of issues that matter in a given field of study.

Similarly, you'll find more genres—more kinds of papers—as you move through courses in the humanities, natural sciences, and social sciences. As you read assigned materials in these areas, be on the lookout for formats, standard structures, and common characteristics in the writing that might help you come up with effective heuristics for those genres also. In Chapter 11, for example, you'll find a heuristic for a social science–style research report (a form that, with slight alterations, also works for lab reports in science courses).

Arriving at a Controlling Idea

If you've followed any of the methods outlined here, you've done a fair amount of writing about your topic already, and you may know the point you want your paper to make. Or you may not yet know that. Instead, you may have a question that you hope your paper will explore or even answer. So now's your chance to discover ways to use the computer to help you find (or state) that idea, the statement or question that will control your response to your topic (hence *controlling* idea).

Stating it is important, because you can't really focus all your ideas without knowing what your goal is, and that goal is stated in a controlling idea. You might think of that idea as a statement or as the answer to a question; in either case, it must be a complete sentence (a sentence contains a predication, a verb that states a relationship between a subject and a predicate—and it's that relationship that gives you something to say). So here are a couple of procedures you might follow to arrive at a controlling idea:

Beginning with a Statement

1. Ask yourself what your basic, informal feeling is about your topic. What would you do about it, for example, if you ruled the world? This need only be a "gut" reaction, stated as simply and briefly as possible. For example:

    I think mountain bikes should be banned from trails in most state parks.

2. Now think of ways to make your personal response more objective.

- *Ask yourself why you feel as you do.* Give reasons that might attach to your original statement. For example:

    Mountain bikes tear up the trails in much the same way as motorcycles and off-road vehicles do.

- *Think about any qualifications you might want to make to your statement.* There is already one qualification in it. Can you find it? Yeah, that's it: *Most,* not *all.* The qualification means that there should be places where mountain bikers can go to ride through the woods—to *bike* in the *mountains*—just not everywhere. So your position does have a limit, a point beyond which your position becomes unreasonable. Are there any others? How about some *if*'s, *when*'s, *unless*'s, or *until*'s?
- *Do any conditions govern your response?* Is there a common occurrence that makes you say what you do? For example:

    As long as bikers and hikers must use the same narrow trails, having them use the same trails at the same time will be unsafe.

- *Is there more information you want to include as you present your idea to a reader?* Are one or two pieces of information simply crucial to your idea, without which it will seem arbitrary or illogical? If so, write those ideas down and plan to include them in your opening paragraph(s).
- By now, you may be ready to write a draft of your opening paragraph(s), the one(s) that will contain your controlling idea. *But first, in light of the thinking you have just done, rewrite the controlling idea in a more comprehensive, objective form.* For example:

    As long as bicyclers and hikers use the same trails, bikers will not only endanger hikers but also detract in other ways from the experience hikers come to the woods for; therefore, mountain bikes should be banned from most trails in Michigan's state parks.

As you can see, the statement is now longer, and it contains several clauses (the parts before the semicolon) that establish the major reasons for the proposed ban. The sentence is longer, but it says more to a reader and, more important, to the writer. If we were to go on to write this essay, the controlling idea would act as a guide, letting us know what we set out to do. In fact, we could copy it into a new file and keep that window constantly in view as we write the essay in another window. Then we wouldn't be as likely to stray from our original idea.

Responding to a Question

1. Here the challenge is to find a really *good* question, one that asks the major issue you want to explore and that takes account of as many as possible of

the lesser included issues. The best way to begin is simply to type out as many questions as you can think of from the notes you've made and the thinking you've done so far. Here is an admittedly carefully constructed example, but it will show you how this process can work to give you a place to start—and more. Your own work will be messier than this, but don't let that bother you. This is a book, after all, so it ought to look nice.

Topic: Clean water

List of Questions
Do motorboats pollute the water in lakes and reservoirs?
Do fishermen dirty the water they fish in?
Do sailboats, even though they don't use motors, pollute the waters they float in?
Should the city's waterworks reservoir be opened to recreational use?
Does recreational use of lakes and reservoirs add to the pollution of the water in those lakes and reservoirs?
Is it necessary to keep a city's water supply absolutely clean and pure?
Are there treatment methods that will remove the pollutants added to the water supply by recreational use of reservoirs?

2. Rearrange the questions into an order—a hierarchy, if possible—of most significant, general, or abstract to least significant, most specific, or most concrete. As you go, you will find that some of the questions fit together in groups. Use the indenting function to show that relationship. (You can also use your word processor's outlining feature to develop these questions into an outline. See your word processor's manual or use the built-in **Help** file to find out how the **Outline** function works). Here's how our list about the reservoir might look:

The Issue: Should the city's waterworks reservoir be opened to recreational use?
Does recreational use of lakes and reservoirs add to the pollution of the water in those lakes and reservoirs?
Do motorboats pollute the water in lakes and reservoirs?
Do fishermen dirty the water they fish in?
Do sailboats, even though they don't use motors, pollute the waters they float in?
Is it necessary to keep a city's water supply absolutely clean and pure?
Are there treatment methods that will remove the pollutants added to the water supply by recreational use of reservoirs?

You can see that answering these questions, in the order in which they are now asked, would yield the draft of an essay. But before you do that, you might want to add questions. For example, the section about whether recreational uses pollute contains several lesser included questions. There might be lesser included questions for the other main questions too. So take some time to expand your own question "outline" so that writing the paper will be easier and faster.

All these strategies are possible on paper, but they are much simpler on a computer, where text is easier to produce, where text is easy to rearrange, and where text produced in one file can easily be copied into another file. The computer, in other words, supports the heightened deliberativeness of college and workplace writing. It also supports a writer's need to try out ideas and explanations, to work with the actual words until she or he finds what works best, what is clearest and most effective.

Perhaps the most important principle to remember is that a word processor is an extremely flexible tool. Perhaps you will find that one of the methods we have described is perfect for the way you think and write. If so, by all means use it. More likely, one of our methods will show you a way to adapt the computer to your composing style and process(es). In that case, take advantage of the tool. As we said in the beginning of this section, the computer is more than a fancy typewriter. If you think about what you do as you write, you will find ways of using the computer to support that process, to enable you to work more easily or efficiently in the way you like to work.

EDITING

Arranging the Text on Paper

For the most part, dividing writing into different stages—thinking of it as a set of separate steps—is unwise. Writing, as we've said before, is a single recursive process. Obviously, as that process begins, we are more concerned with what Aristotle called *invention*. We struggle to come up with something to write about, something to say. Later in the process, when we know, more or less, what we want to say, we focus on shaping the content, on arranging it into the best order. Still, that stage also includes making sure the ideas are developed fully, that all the information a reader will need to know is on the page. So even as we proceed through Aristotle's stages of *arrangement* and *delivery*, we continue to invent. And as we arrange, we're always thinking about what the finished product will look like—always focusing on delivery, too. Only from the outside—in order to talk *about* writing, not in order to write—do we break up the writing process into stages.

That said, we turn now to the "stage" after invention, to what writers do after they've put some words onto paper: revising and editing. Most writers probably associate editing with checking a piece of writing for grammar, spelling, and punctuation. And editing certainly includes those steps. But a word processor's editor—not the person, but the tool—begins functioning as soon as you've entered characters on the screen. Once you've put text onto the screen, you can begin using the editor to manipulate that text. Thus, we move from a look at the ways writers use a computer as an aid for composing to a look at ways writers use computers in the editing stage of writing. In this chapter, we'll focus on some of the simpler ways, assuming that you may not be very experienced yet with using a word processor. We might be wrong about that, though—you may be very experienced. If you are, then you'll also be interested in some of the strategies we'll deal with in Chapter 6, "Assessing Writing," in the section on self-assessment.

Organization

We can think of organization as the stage of deciding what comes first and what comes next. Some of these decisions—perhaps the most important of them—happen during composing. Many of these decisions, though, occur after the first complete draft is finished. Here, too, the "text is cheap" aspect of writing on a computer helps writers develop the sense that no piece of writing is ever truly finished. It can always be revised. However, before the advent of word processing, the cost of revision was relatively high: retyping the revised draft. Using today's tools, writers can easily change what they've written, even markedly change it, and not have to worry about making the heavy commitment in time and effort that retyping an entire essay would require.

Among your primary tools for changing the organization of a piece of writing are the word processor's Cut (or Copy) and Paste functions. With these functions, you can rearrange your writing at will, trying out different orders until you find the one that you think will communicate your ideas most effectively. The precise set of commands for cutting and pasting will be different for each word-processing application, but in general the process works as shown in the following How-to Box.

How-to

- First—and most important—*save the file before you start rearranging it!* Then, if you make a huge mistake, you can always start from the point at which you last saved your text.
- Second, decide what portion of your text you want to move, and decide where you think that portion would be more effective.
- Third, select (highlight) the text you want to move.
- Fourth, use the Cut command to remove the text from its current position.
- Finally, place your cursor at the point where you want the cut portion to appear, and select the Paste command.

Now read the rearranged passage to decide whether you think the new order is, in fact, better than the old. If it is, you can keep it. If it isn't, you can always change it back to the original or relocate the passage to yet another position.

Consider, for example, the very different arguments you might construct using the following sequences of assertions, for which we've used **Cut and Paste** to put in their differing orders:

Progress is achieved only through the confrontation of the old and outworn with the new and revitalizing.

New ideas are disconcerting; they challenge our preconceptions and threaten our settled and comfortable view of the world.

Galileo shook the very foundations of theology when he disputed the validity of the Ptolemaic universe.

There is no question that new ideas can be dangerous to the smooth and orderly running of a state or social institution.

Thomas Paine and others throughout history roused the demon of social unrest and showed the way to bloody civil revolt.

Social progress is almost always painful since it is achieved through the downfall of earlier attitudes, beliefs, and social institutions.

Progress assumes the freedom to dissent from established ideas and institutions.

Suppression of dissent is the quickest route to social stagnation and eventual decay.

The free expression of ideas is essential to any healthy society.

New ideas are disconcerting; they challenge our preconceptions and threaten our settled and comfortable view of the world.

Galileo shook the very foundations of theology when he disputed the validity of the Ptolemaic universe.

Social progress is almost always painful since it is achieved through the downfall of earlier attitudes, beliefs, and social institutions.

There is no question that new ideas can be dangerous to the smooth and orderly running of a state or social institution.

Thomas Paine and others throughout history roused the demon of social unrest and showed the way to bloody civil revolt.

Progress is achieved only through the confrontation of the old and outworn with the new and revitalizing.

Progress assumes the freedom to dissent from established ideas and institutions.

The free expression of ideas is essential to any healthy society.

Suppression of dissent is the quickest route to social stagnation and eventual decay.

—from *Functional Writing,* 1st ed.

The only difference between the two sequences is the order of their assertions; the assertions themselves are identical. And yet each sequence works toward a different conclusion, using a different progression of ideas. And you could probably come up with additional sequences for this set of assertions. So, using **Cut and Paste**, you can actually change the character and purpose of an argument, even when it is already fairly carefully laid out. Use this function, then, to work with your ideas, even when those ideas seem well developed. The computer allows you to find better, more effective arrangements of your ideas (as they are contained in your sentences, paragraphs, etc.) so that you can make your writing better and more effective.

Working On-Screen and on Paper

Using the computer's functionality to its fullest, a writer might well reorder an entire essay, leaving no paragraph untouched, in a relatively short period of time, and then use a simple **Print** command, and, *voilà*—a printout. Even this most simple of features—the ease of producing printed copy—provides powerful support for a writer in the editing stage. Most writers find that working back and forth from screen to paper is the most effective strategy for revising their writing. Working on two versions of one text helps the writer see the text afresh, in a different form. Thus, writers catch different problems on-screen from the ones they catch on paper. On-screen, writers tend to see their texts from their own points of view. On paper, they tend to react more as readers will, seeing the gaps in the argument or the weaknesses in the evidence, or even just the errors in sentence structure, spelling, or word choice that are so easy to miss on-screen.

The most effective strategy, then, typically involves working on a piece on-screen until it seems finished or until you reach a point at which you can't really see how to continue, and then printing the file. At that point, you can read and mark up the printed copy, changing words, phrases, sentences, paragraphs; drawing arrows to note how to rearrange the order of sentences and paragraphs; making notes about text you may want to insert here or there; and, if you've stopped midessay, jotting an outline for the rest of the piece, or at least for the next section. Then you can go back to the screen, make the changes and additions, and work the piece over until you feel you've done all you can to it—at which point you print it out again and repeat the process. This movement back and forth from screen to paper to screen continues until you decide the draft is in its final state or until you have to hand it in, whatever its condition.

Finding and Correcting Mistakes

In short, computers support revision. They cannot revise for you, because they cannot read and evaluate your text for you. But they can support ways of seeing your text that, like the move from screen to paper, help you perceive ways to change your text. This point is particularly true in the final stages of revision, when you are most concerned with whether your text obeys the conventions of standard written English. Here are some more suggestions that can help you find errors that may have escaped your notice during earlier stages of composing and revising the text:

1. Change the font and/or font size in the whole piece, so that the words literally appear in different places on the page. This small change can make you look at the piece more objectively—the first step in *re-***vision.**

How-To

Select (highlight) all the text in your essay. Then follow the directions for changing fonts and font sizes in your word processor.

---

2. Scroll to the bottom of your text and read it backward, sentence by sentence, to check for errors. If you can resize your word-processing window so that you can see about one sentence at a time, the process will be even more effective. This strategy is best if you use it near the end of your writing process. It's an invaluable aid to proofreading, especially if you have a history of making mistakes that you really do know how to correct—if you can find them before your reader (or teacher) does.

Again, in Chapter 6, "Assessing Writing," you'll find some more advanced strategies for using features of your word processor to help you see errors.

As you become more adept at word processing, at manipulating text on a computer screen, you will undoubtedly discover more tricks for helping organize what you want to say. The computer offers many variations on the suggestions we've made here, all of which help you see your text anew—at a distance, so to speak.

When you can achieve a kind of critical distance from your own writing, you can more easily see it as a reader will see it. This kind of *re*-vision helps you discover ways to communicate more effectively with your reader, persuade your reader, or help your reader identify with you. Use the computer's functions to help you literally see your text in new and different ways.

FINAL EDITING: ENSURING CORRECTNESS

Once you have achieved the ordering or sequencing you want, and once you have developed your ideas as fully as they need to be developed, you can turn to the surface features of your writing. That is, once you've put the most effective content into the most effective words, you can pay attention to whether the words, phrases, and sentences are correct. Punctuation, spelling, grammar, mechanics, diction—all these can help make your writing *pleasing* to a reader. The first and most important job is to make your writing communicate effectively to your intended reader(s). Once you believe that you've achieved this most important goal, once your rhetorical purpose is fully and effectively expressed, you can strive for polish.

Word processors often supply several tools that, used with caution, can help you achieve the kind of polish that will please a reader and help you achieve your goals for the piece of writing. The most common of these is the spelling checker, and most modern word processors also come with a variety of other tools such as a thesaurus and dictionary that can also help you add polish and ensure correctness. Even a grammar checker—used very cautiously, because even the best are inherently inaccurate—can help you look more closely and more objectively at your own prose.

Spelling Checkers

There is no substitute for a careful proofreading of your own words. If you have enough knowledge of spelling, grammar, and mechanics that you can read, correct, and polish your own writing, then you'd be foolish to turn that job over to a machine that can't think. And yet, even the best speller misses a misteak here and there (see?). So, after searching out all the errors you can find, by all means run the spelling checker in hopes that it will find the rest. In fact, the most efficient procedure is probably to run the spelling checker at the point at which you feel the paper is completely finished, and then to reread the piece, carefully, looking for any words that you have misspelled into other works (see?). Remember, a spelling checker can't think; it doesn't know what words mean.

Knowing how the typical spelling checkers work will allow you to make the best use of this boon to poor spellers and inefficient proofreaders. Typically, a spelling checker "looks" at a word—a string of characters between two spaces—and strips out the vowels (except for initial vowels in words such as *opossum* and *initial*). It then compares the resulting string of consonants with strings of consonants in its built-in list. Most standard word processors have about 100,000 strings in this list, representing far more words than the average person's vocabulary (approximately 30,000 words). If the string doesn't match with a string in memory, then the computer identifies a "mistake." It may stop there and merely prompt the writer to decide whether the word really is misspelled and to make a correction. Or it may create a list of words from strings that are close to the one being checked and generate a list of words from which the writer can choose the intended word. The catch comes in the fact that the string may be from a word that the computer doesn't "know," a string that isn't in its list. As extensive as a list of 100,000 words is, it won't contain most surnames, and it will balk at even mildly specialized terms, let alone the kind of discipline-specific jargon most college-level writers quickly take for granted.

Put simply, there is no free lunch. No computer can truly check your spelling, but it can identify and help you correct obvious misspellings of common words, and it can help you correct typographical errors—as long as neither kind of misspelling has resulted in a legitimate word. That means that spelling checkers won't catch a plural that should be singular, a superfluous *-ed* on a verb form, or even a common typo such as *tow* in place of *two*. Like most tools, when you use it wisely, spell chick is a boon (oops—it missed another one!). Rely on it too heavily, though, or use it carelessly, and yew well comb too grief.

Dictionaries and Thesauruses

Whether they come as built-in features of a word processor or as stand-alone software, computer-based dictionaries and thesauruses can be invaluable resources for writers—if, as with spelling checkers, they are used intelligently by a writer who is aware of their limitations. Their advantages are speed and flexibility. Writers can check a definition in the dictionary or find synonyms, antonyms, or related words in the thesaurus by entering the word—or even just by selecting it on the screen—and clicking a button or pressing Enter. No flipping of pages, no thumbing back and forth from index to entries—just a fast, efficient process of entering or selecting words and following paths until the writer finds just the right word. And the tools are generally highly flexible (the stand-alones are even more flexible than the built-ins), allowing writers to choose from an array of options. They allow writers to find the standard synonyms and antonyms, of course. They also provide the option to choose words that are simply close in meaning, continuing that process until the right word comes up, and allow the writer a menu-based backtracking feature, so that when the trail turns cold the writer can always go back to the last promising option and follow a different path. And, finally, many dictionaries and thesauruses allow the writer simply to click on a button to insert the chosen word into their text.

The limitations of these features, as with the spelling checkers, is that they are not as complete as their paper-based counterparts. Dictionaries may have only half as many words as a standard desk reference dictionary, and they generally provide fewer and shorter definitions than a paper version would. Similarly, the computer-based thesaurus lists fewer alternative words, and it usually does not provide as much information about the words it does list, nor does it sort words by part of speech (noun, verb, adjective, etc.) as print thesauruses typically do. These limitations mean that writers should view the software versions of dictionaries and thesauruses as initial resources, to be used as a convenience but not to be considered as definitive. Writers who cannot find the word they want on-line should by all means take the extra time and trouble to consult the more robust, extensive paper versions.

Grammar Checkers

Perhaps the most problematic resource ever invented for the computer is the grammar checker. These applications promise a writer's dream. Automatic correctness. Ease. Surety. It sounds too good to be true, of course, and it is, for three main reasons:

- *First, these tools are not very accurate.* They typically identify *to be* helper verbs as passive constructions. They often mislabel many verb constructions, verbal phrases, gerunds, and other verb forms. They do not allow much variation in style, nor do they handle common grammatical inversions well (*nor do they,* for example, would cause most grammar checkers to flag an error). So grammar checkers can mislead writers, causing them to make corrections where there is no error—and, often, in doing so, to *create* an error out of a correct word, phrase, or clause.
- *Second, the applications do not* correct *the grammar.* They identify possible errors, and they may even suggest a "correction" (see the preceding point), but the writer still has to make the decision and effect a change—if, indeed, the passage calls for a change. In a sense, then, the grammar checker is an illusion, a fake. Writers who have a good feel for grammatical and mechanical correctness are better off relying on their own instincts, and writers whose grasp of grammar, syntax, and punctuation is more tenuous are easily misled—and often forced into errors they would otherwise not make.
- *Third, grammar checkers allow for only a narrow range of diction and usage.* They are typically set to gauge effective business prose, for example, so they are not particularly effective or appropriate in college writing, creative writing, or situations that involve writing about specialized subjects or for an audience of academic peers.

Given all these limitations, then, are grammar checkers at all useful? In general, they are helpful only if the output they generate can become the focus of peer review or if the writer can consult a teacher. Most grammar checkers "flag" potential errors. That is, they insert some sort of symbol into the text to identify the problem, so that the writer can make a decision about a change at a later time. This feature can prove extremely helpful. All the research in learning writing says that writers learn grammar best if they work within the context of their own writing. Indeed, the research demonstrates that studying grammar *outside* that context has no effect on the quality of a person's writing. The grammar checker's ability to mark potential errors presents an opportunity to learn more about grammar within the context of the writer's own prose. Looking over that output—especially in a peer review group or with a teacher—can help a writer learn about the errors she makes. Evaluating the flags that the grammar checker has inserted involves the writer in making deliberate decisions about changes, and engaging in a conversation with peers or teachers about those decisions is a golden opportunity to improve one's ability to write more grammatically to begin with. In this context, and perhaps in this context only, using a grammar checker makes sense.

FORMATTING AND PRINTING

Once the text is finished, you can think about how you want it to look on the page. These cosmetic features may not seem to matter, but they often help or hinder a reader's ability to comprehend a text. Consider, for example, the texts presented below:

I.

A composition textbook that uses the resources available on the Internet and explores new modes of electronic communication has a different audience profile than would a traditional rhetoric. Traditional composition textbooks offer teachers, who in comparison to the student have a comparatively high level of expertise, a supplemental resource to their own teaching. The teacher, therefore, uses the textbook to help her teach the students. In the past we could assume that the vast majority of teachers would have more knowledge than would the students. However, technology has altered this relationship between teacher and student. Although the English teacher will still know more about rhetoric, style, grammar and usage, writing, and composition pedagogy than the students will, in most cases the students, as members of a generation who grew up amid technology, will likely have more positive attitudes toward technology and far more experience with it.

II.

A composition textbook that uses the resources available on the Internet and explores new modes of electronic communication has a different audience profile than would a traditional rhetoric. Traditional composition textbooks offer teachers, who in comparison to the student have a comparatively high level of expertise, a supplemental resource to their own teaching. The teacher, therefore, uses the textbook to help her teach the students. In the past we could assume that the vast majority of teachers would have more knowledge than would the students. However, technology has altered this relationship between teacher and student. Although the English teacher will still know more about rhetoric, style, grammar and usage, writing, and composition pedagogy than the students will, in most cases the students, as members of a generation who grew up amid technology, will likely have more positive attitudes toward technology and far more experience with it.

The second font is attractive, but it is also fancier than the passage seems to call for. You might use the second font in a formal invitation, on a poster, or in a piece of writing in which you wanted to emphasize the aesthetic quality of the text—to present the text as itself an object of beauty. So although it might be appropriate for a poem, the plainer, clearer font in the first passage seems more appropriate for writing that intends primarily to explain, inform, or clarify.

Playing with fonts can be fun, *but too much of that sort of fun* **can interfere with communication.** See? Even though all those fonts are readable, changing from font to font is distracting. It directs the reader's attention to the font rather than to what the writer is trying to say. The same holds true for other effects: margins, indented lists, graphics, tables, and so on. Each device, no matter how simple or complex, has two effects:

- First, it has to communicate. It has to carry the meaning the writer intends to convey to the reader.
- Second, it should reinforce the writer's meaning, add to the impact of or enhance the communication.

The simple indented, bulleted list, which we've used often in this text, is one example of this dual function. Indenting sets the items off from the body of the text, adding emphasis. The bullets emphasize the beginning of each item, adding clarity and reinforcing the number of items the reader is being asked to consider. Finally, hanging the bullets into the margin helps the reader know when one item is over and the next is beginning.

> When you want to heighten the rhetorical effect of a list or of another kind of passage, you can consider indenting it.

And if you want to add even more emphasis, you could put it in a box, by adding a border.

You can also change the font style or size. Most word processors allow you to take advantage of **bold,** *italic,* <u>underlined</u>, outlined, or shadow styles, for example. The first three are useful within the text, whereas the others come into play in titles, posters, flyers, and other places where a writer uses a large font size and wants to call attention to particular words. Most novice writers think that manipulating fonts and font sizes is simply fun. More experienced writers think in terms of designing their documents. As you become more accustomed to the tools the word processor allows you to use in your writing, you will become more attuned to the rhetorical effects of these tools. You will find ways of using them to enhance what you have to say, without allowing them to interfere, to make your text look gimmicky. The point bears repeating:

> Change fonts, font sizes, font styles, and margins for a *reason,* not just because you can. Think about the rhetorical effect you want to create with these tools.

Tables, Graphs, and Graphics

The same basic advice that holds true for the simple effects—fonts, styles, sizes, and so forth—also applies to more complex effects. In this book, for example, the tables that appear near the start of each chapter are there, in part, because as word processors have become more powerful, they have allowed writers to create such effects easily. More important, though, is the fact that the table lays out the content of the chapter, helping the reader know what to expect and conveying information that the text will explore in depth. We chose a table because it was the *best* tool available to us, not simply because it was there. We might have conveyed the same information in list form or in paragraph form, for example, but the former would have been more confusing than the table, and the latter would have required far more space than the table does. Overall, then, the table allowed us to convey information clearly and economically, and it helps readers understand what they are about to read. Those factors make the table a good choice. The table looks good, and it was fun to do, but those factors do not, of themselves, justify its use.

> In document design, function comes first, and form follows function.

Reasoning with Numbers

Often, particularly in business, the natural sciences, and the social sciences, evidence comes in numerical form. You may, for example, want to convey the change in profits during the first half of the 1990s. You could use a table:

Profits 1990–1995 (in millions of dollars)

1990	1991	1992	1993	1994	1995
4.57	3.78	4.44	5.67	6.78	7.75

However, you could choose to present the same information visually, by using a graph. Here, for example, is a line graph that presents the same numbers:

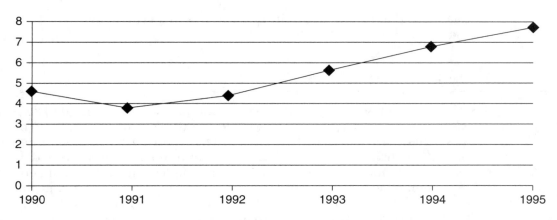

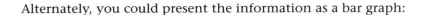

Profits 1990–1995 (in millions of dollars)

Alternately, you could present the information as a bar graph:

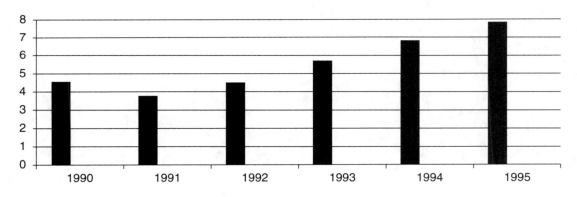

Profits 1990–1995 (in millions of dollars)

Each of these formats communicates the same information but in different ways, and each has a different impact on readers. All three formats show the variation in company profits for the years 1990–1995. The first conveys the information textually—in numbers printed on the page. Thus, if the reader needs the numbers, the chart is a good layout to use, because it presents the numbers in a way that allows the reader also to draw conclusions about trends. However, in many circumstances, the reader has no real need for exact figures but wants to understand the trends. The other two formats use a pictorial representation of the numbers to convey the trends in profits. The visual information is that profits dipped in 1991 but rose at a healthy rate after that, and that the trend is still upward.

PARTING THOUGHTS

This chapter has presented some basic considerations that writers need to deal with as they write with a word processor. Most of the considerations, though, are ones writers need to deal with no matter the tool. All your efforts as a writer are focused on presenting information in the way your reader needs to read it, in a way that will make the information easier to understand or the argument easier to comprehend and accept. The tools we've described so far, and the ones that we'll deal with in later chapters, all help you achieve those writerly goals—if you use them wisely. So do that.

2

COMMUNICATING ON THE
INTERNET: ONE ON ONE

As part of the purpose for generating text, writers use text to *communicate* with each other. Of course, the whole basis for writing is to communicate, writer to reader. Most communication in school or in the workplace occurs face to face or, in the case of a telephone conversation, one on one. Before electronic mail and other means of communicating via computer, the parties to such a communication had to be located in the same place or set aside the same block of time for the communication to occur. However, when one party works at company headquarters in New York and the other represents the company's interests in Hong Kong, time and space make one-on-one communication difficult or slow. Communicating via an electronic computer network alleviates the difficulty, but in doing so, it creates another "place," another medium for the writer to master.

In addition to needing to communicate in the course of school, business, or work, writers of all kinds have always valued communication with other writers, and computers can make that communication faster than traditional mail service and more permanent than a conversation on the telephone. Given a computer and an electronic mail account, writers can send text back and forth; they can read, react to, and give feedback about each other's texts. As was the case with generating text, this section covers one kind of activity that is by no means new but that the computer makes easier to accomplish. However, as with generating text, the benefits of communicating via computer are accompanied by complications to which writers must adjust if they are to write effectively. Just as the face-to-face communication has its own rhetoric and its own etiquette, so does the one-on-one electronic form. Ignoring the new rhetoric or the new etiquette can interfere with the writer's ability to communicate.

MOVING BEYOND THE DESKTOP: STEPPING INTO CYBERSPACE

Chapter 1 focused on what a writer can do using a stand-alone computer—a computer that is not connected to other computers via a network. Making that connection enables a variety of direct communications, the most widespread of which is electronic mail. Almost any network, whether it consists only of the computers in a single classroom or hooks into the Internet, potentially extending to more than one hundred million readers, electronic mail (or E-mail) is the most basic and heavily used medium for communication. Most of us come to computing already accustomed to two principal kinds of participatory communications technologies: letters and telephone conversations. With E-mail, writers enter a medium that seems to resemble these already familiar genres but that has its own technological and rhetorical demands. This section will address those demands. Focusing on the activity of one-to-one contact via electronic networks, we will explore what current tools enable, in a generic sense, writers to use these tools to promote effective exchanges.

ACTIVITY 2.1 Getting Started: Scavenging for Directions

Before we can move on to the most effective ways of communicating via electronic mail, we need to be sure that we can *use* E-mail. Because no two systems are alike, an exploration of your local system and its resources is necessary. Your teacher may have prepared some instructions for you already, and your school or workplace may provide workshops on electronic mail. In addition, someone, somewhere, has the documentation for your electronic mail system. And your most important resource may be each other—some of you may already be adept at using the system. What you need to do is find out how to use this technology on your your system and at your site specifically.

Listed here are crucial information and instructions that you will need as you begin to communicate via E-mail. If your class carries out Projects 1 and 2 in Chapter 7, you'll have a chance to put all this information in some sort of organized, written form that can be handed down to the next class that takes this course. For now, though, you need this information to

Activity	Common Applications	Special Considerations
Reading and writing electronic mail	Pine, Pegasus Mail, PowerTalk, Eudora, VAXmail, and many, many other mainframe-based E-mail systems or desktop mail handlers	• Rhetoric of the screen—formatting for readability • Netiquette: accommodating a reader's needs in a new medium

use your electronic mail account. So gather the information you need from whatever sources you can find, and compile all of it into an E-mail guide that you can keep handy. You might want to put all of the information you collect—handouts, notes, documentation, and so on—into a single folder or notebook so that you can refer to it easily as you have the need.

Using E-mail: What You Need to Know

- The hardware (the computer) where your electronic mailbox is located
- How to access your mailbox from class, your dorm room, home (probably via a modem), public computing sites, and so forth
- The software you use to read your E-mail (e.g., Pine, Pegasus, Eudora, VAXmail, etc.)
- Instructions for using both the hardware and software that allow you to read your E-mail
- How to sign on or log on to your E-mail system and open your mailbox
- How to access on-line help
- How to retrieve and read your incoming mail
- How to compose a message
- How to edit a message
- How to set line lengths and word wrap, if necessary (Note: More and more, systems automatically include these features, but if yours doesn't, then you could send out some strange-looking messages unless you find out how to specify and change these settings.)
- How to send or post a message
- How to reply to a message
- How to forward a message
- How to save and retrieve a message
- How to delete a message, either before or after you've read it
- How to download a message to a text file
- How to manage your mailbox so that it does not cause problems from being too full
- How to include the text of one message in another when you are replying to or forwarding a message you have received
- How to attach or include word-processed text in the text of a message
- How to include a signature line, including your E-mail address, at the end of a message
- How to keep track of and/or manage your computing account, including how to keep track of account funds and establish and maintain files in institutional storage "space"
- How to sign off or log off your E-mail system

All this information is important, and all of it should be available, in one form or another, at your institution. Unfortunately, it may not be readily available, and, like much computer documentation, it may not be very readable. That's why this exercise is important. Once you have compiled this basic information and made every effort to understand it, you will be equipped to handle the physical aspects of using electronic mail. Don't worry if, at first, you have to check and recheck the instructions you have compiled. The technology can be complex, and if you are new to electronic mail, you may need a few weeks of heavy use for it to seem even remotely as natural as licking a stamp or dialing a phone. But you'll get there!

ONE-ON-ONE E-MAIL: THE RHETORIC OF THE SCREEN

In some ways, E-mail seems like speech. E-mail is direct. It involves an exchange of messages. The messages are often short, like the turns we take in conversation. Messages generally elicit a reply, so that an E-mail exchange, in its entirety, seems like a conversation. Because we send E-mail over wires, an analogy that comes to mind is the telephone conversation, especially because, when we use a modem, we *do* place a call to initiate the "conversation."

In other ways, E-mail seems like writing a letter. We write the message, for example, and many systems use the command **Post.** And, after all, it's called electronic *mail.* The name itself reinforces the analogy to the kind of mail we put into envelopes and take to the post office.

However, *E-mail is neither speech nor letter.* Instead, it is a new and different communications medium, one that partakes of some elements of earlier media but has its own genres, rhetorical demands, and set of embedded assumptions about how writers and readers behave. Like most guidelines, these apply generally, so that any number of individual situations warrant breaking them— and may even reward breaking them. However, any breach of these guidelines should happen consciously, so that a reader can know why the breach has occurred and see that the violation is necessary. In any other case, we ignore those assumptions at our peril.

Here are some guidelines, some of the basic, obvious and not-so-obvious aspects of E-mail that help us as we try to communicate with readers using this new medium:

1. *The basic unit of communication is the screenful.* In writing, we work in pages and paragraphs. In E-mail, we work with the amount of text a screen will hold. Generally, that means that we communicate in the amount of text that can fit into twenty-four lines of text, each of which is about eighty characters wide. Once we write more than that, we ask the reader to scroll down or page down. If what we've written on the first screen isn't sufficiently interesting or worthwhile, most readers will delete rather than scroll. Thus, when writing E-mail, *get to the point.* The medium encourages brevity, conciseness. Readers pay, literally, for the time they spend reading, and even today reading on-screen text is neither as comfortable nor as convenient an experience as reading text on paper. Long messages—more than two screenfuls, say—must

need to be that long. The content must justify the length. Readers also pay physically, by sitting at the terminal and reading on a computer monitor, for the time they spend reading their messages. So, again, be concise.

2. *One message, one point.* For whatever reason, E-mail readers most often focus on one point in a message. Often, if a message contains two requests, the reader will only respond to the first. This is especially true if the message is longer, so that the second request comes in screen two of the message. Thus, whenever possible, make one point or one request per message, and *use a pertinent subject header*. Focus is the key. Print invites us to extend our ideas, add to them, combine them, elaborate on them. E-mail invites us to get to the point. Again, the reader goes to some amount of trouble to access his E-mail and pays for the privilege by the hour. In such an environment, wasting the reader's time is not an effective rhetorical move.

3. *Formatting is part of the rhetoric.* In Chapter 1 we explored some ways that formatting has rhetorical effects in word processing—in electronic documents that are destined, for the most part, to become paper texts. In E-mail—an electronic document that probably will remain an electronic text—formatting has an even greater rhetorical effect. First, the screen is analogous to the newspaper column. There's not much space for text, so short paragraphs and white space help make the text more readable. Second, the way the writer breaks up a message conveys the message's structure. This is especially important for longer messages, but even short messages can benefit from strategically placed white space. Consider this example, which is part of an E-mail exchange on defining plagiarism:

Cases I can recall:

1. A Washington Post reporter plagiarizes bits and pieces of actual stories about kids who are heroin addicts. In her pastiche, the addict becomes a three-year-old. Story wins Pulitzer, only when some reporter attempts a "where is he now?" followup—well, reporter loses her Pulitzer, her job, her career.
2. A Dean of Communications at a major university publishes a textbook. One chapter seems familiar to a number of readers. For good reason. It's plagiarized from another textbook. He loses his job, his career—and probably his royalties.
3. A graduate student, under the gun and extremely intimidated by a big-time prof, turns in a paper that is copied in toto from a little-read journal. Unfortunately, the big-time prof reads that journal, and this straight-A student is out of the program.
4. A student includes in his portfolio the lyrics from a song on a popular album, claiming that they are his own and that he had gone through a great deal of anguish and revision to get the poem just right. A portfolio reader recognizes the lyric. The student's admission to major university is revoked.

I think all these cases sound the same, and that all constitute plagiarism. I sympathize, I guess, with the urge to downplay plagiarism—it's really an infrequent occurrence that receives far too much attention. But I don't get why so many folks on this list are trying to define plagiarism out of existence, just because it is OK in some contexts and not in others. So's belching.

On-screen, that message is much more inviting, more reader-friendly, than the following:

Cases I can recall: A Washington Post reporter plagiarizes bits and pieces of actual stories about kids who are heroin addicts. In her pastiche, the addict becomes a three-year-old. Story wins Pulitzer, only when some reporter attempts a "where is he now?" follow-up—well, reporter loses her Pulitzer, her job, her career. A dean of communications at a major university publishes a textbook. One chapter seems familiar to a number of readers. For good reason. It's plagiarized from another textbook. He loses his job, his career—and probably his royalties. A graduate student, under the gun and extremely intimidated by a big-time prof, turns in a paper that is copied in toto from a little-read journal. Unfortunately, the big-time prof reads that journal, and this straight-A student is out of the program. A student includes in his portfolio the lyrics from a song on a popular album, claiming that they are his own and that he had gone through a great deal of anguish and revision to get the poem just right. A portfolio reader recognizes the lyric. The student's admission to major university is revoked. I think all these cases sound the same, and that all constitute plagiarism. I sympathize, I guess, with the urge to downplay plagiarism—it's really an infrequent occurrence that receives far too much attention. But I don't get why so many folks on this list are trying to define plagiarism out of existence, just because it is OK in some contexts and not in others. So's belching.

Both messages contain the same information, and both would be perfectly readable on a printed page. Version 1, though, is much more intelligible than version 2 *on-screen,* where most E-mail is read. The layout indicates the basic structure of the message (a list of examples), and the white space and numbers reinforce that structure. Finally, the short, focused items in version 1 accommodate the reader's desire for the writer to get to the point. Each paragraph is succinct, short, and concise.

4. *Try to write correctly, but develop a tolerance for error in others' messages.* In this regard, E-mail is like speech. That is, we rarely correct the speech of the people with whom we converse, primarily because we see speech as relatively informal, not governed by the constraints of correct grammar and usage to which we subject written texts. (However, if the speech is formal—an address to a group or some other form of presentation—then we do demand correctness.) E-mail is similarly informal "speech," even though it is written text, and most readers in most situations read right over minor errors as if they were not there. Most readers assume that the writer is composing on-line, without the usual advantages of time or the resources that a word processor would supply. For example, some E-mail systems provide an editable screen, similar to a word processor's; others make editing so difficult that most writers don't bother. Because most readers know that the writer may not have the ability to edit, the level of tolerance for everyone goes up. As always, this guideline depends on context. If you are writing to your boss or your teacher, or if you were sending an electronic memo to your staff or your colleagues, then you would certainly take more care with that text. In such a case, if your system does not provide a fully editable screen, you'd probably compose and edit the text off-line, in your word processor, and then copy it into the message screen or upload it in whatever way your system allows.

5. *Keep your head.* In the end, even though E-mail messages resemble speech in some ways, they are written texts, so the nonverbal cues that help us determine a speaker's tone are not available. In this way, E-mail is more like a letter, which is easily misinterpreted. From time to time, you may find a message offensive. Resist the temptation to "flame" the writer. Instead of firing off a response in kind to a message, ask yourself whether the writer really meant the supposed offense. Better yet, reply to the writer and ask whether the offense was intended or accidental. If you can't do that, then draft your response, but don't send it for a while—for at least a day—so that you can reconsider your reaction. Anything you can do to respond rationally and calmly will help you in the long run. You'll avoid embarassment in situations in which the writer intended no offense, and you'll seem extraordinarily mature in situations in which the writer was in fact intending to offend you.

6. *Use nonverbal signals to indicate tone.* Whenever you think that readers might misunderstand your tone, you could use an *emoticon*—a little icon you can create to embellish a message—to establish the tone you want. The situation that gets writers in trouble most often is the attempt at humor, irony, or sarcasm. Perhaps because E-mail involves using mysterious, expensive machines, perhaps because the reader is paying for the time, or perhaps for some other reason, E-mail is a serious medium, one in which most readers, most of the time, focus on communication. They often miss the written cues that indicate a shift to humor, so the writer needs to provide those cues in the text. The easiest way is by making up an emoticon that mimics the expression the writer's face might display in a face-to-face conversation. Thus, if you don't want to be taken too seriously, use a smiley face. The symbol :-) or just :) is commonly used for a smiling face. (If you have trouble seeing it, tip your head to the left.) Or a symbol like ;-) can indicate irony (it's a winking smiley face, made by using the semicolon for the eyes instead of the colon). Here are some examples of emoticons, taken from Electronic Frontier Foundation's *The Unofficial Smiley Dictionary,* which you can find on the World Wide Web at http://www.nova.edu/Inter-Links/bigdummy/eeg_286.html (more on this http gibberish later):

:-)	Your basic smiley. This smiley is used to inflect a sarcastic or joking statement because we can't hear voice inflection over E-mail.
;-)	Winky smiley. User just made a flirtatious and/or sarcastic remark. More of a "don't hit me for what I just said" smiley.
:-(	Frowning smiley. User did not like that last statement or is upset or depressed about something.
:-I	Indifferent smiley. Better than a :-(but not quite as good as a :-).
:-D	User is laughing (at you!)
:-X	User's lips are sealed.
:-C	User is really bummed.
:-o	Uh-oh!
:-/	User is skeptical.
8-)	User is wearing sunglasses.
B:-)	User's sunglasses are on head.
::-)	User wears normal glasses.
B-)	User wears horn-rimmed glasses.

7. *Use capital letters sparingly.* Putting words in all capital letters IS THE TYPOGRAPHICAL EQUIVALENT OF SHOUTING, and most readers consider it rude or stupid (like, I mean, learn where the caps lock key is, doofus!). Capital letters can be useful to emphasize a word or to indicate a title or heading. You can also surround a word or phrase with *asterisks* to add emphasis.

All right, now that you know how E-mail works and you've had some introduction to the rhetorical situation of the medium (but keep learning—there's no teacher like experience), what can you do with it? As one writer to another, quite a lot. Here are some activities that you can use in one-on-one communication with your classmates or anyone whom you can engage in a conversation about writing. All the activities are geared to provide feedback on your writing from an actual reader.

ACTIVITY 2.2: E-Mail and Invention

If you have been assigned or are working on a common topic, use an E-mail conversation to help you come up with something to say.

- One partner starts by posting what seems like the most significant question involved in exploring the topic.
- The other responds by revising the question, suggesting an alternative question(s), or attempting to answer the question.
- The messages continue until the writers are exhausted, out of time, or confident that they have enough information to begin a first draft.

ACTIVITY 2.3: E-Mail and Peer Review

The most valuable resource for a writer is a careful, critical, yet tactful reader. When you find one, marry him (her). Seriously—no regrets. In the meantime, you can both give and receive help with your writing via E-mail, from a classmate, from local or distant friends (remember, you can reach all sorts of places instantly with E-mail). But take some care. Remember, when you send a draft to someone else, you've violated some of the assumptions people have about E-mail. In particular, the message will most likely be far longer than one or two screens, and you'll probably be asking for more than one kind of help. So give your reader/reviewer some help.

- Determine what kind of feedback you want. What worries you most about your draft? Are you concerned that the introduction doesn't work? Do you wonder whether the sequence of paragraphs is logical? Do you think the conclusion is weak or off the topic? Do you want some suggestions for adding content to the paper? Make some notes about what you'd like a reader to pay most attention to as she reads the paper.
- Make a list of questions you want the reader to answer. This list will help the reader focus on the important points, and it can serve the reader as a kind of checklist.
- Compose a *very* nice, polite, short message asking the reader to help you.
- Copy and paste (or type, if your system won't allow you to copy and paste) the list of questions into the message.
- Skip a couple of lines and then copy and paste (or append, upload, or whatever your system allows) your draft into the message, just below the list of questions.
- Conclude with one more remark: "Please write three questions that I need to answer but that you feel I have not yet answered in this paper."

This structure will help you focus the reader's attention on the points you worry most about, and it will allow the reader to respond to all your concerns. And the final list of questions will give the reader a place to respond to problems you may not have anticipated.

ACTIVITY 2.4: E-Mail and Collaborative Writing

Initially, the main purpose for establishing the ArpaNet (the earliest version of what has become the Internet) was to foster collaboration among scientists working in different locations but on similar projects. Today, that use is still paramount. E-mail can help us all keep in touch with a wide variety of people, for a wide variety of purposes, but it's principal value is that it enables us to work with each other more or less without regard for constraints of time and space. Studies that examine the role of writing in the workplace reveal that collaborating over distance via electronic mail is increasingly the way people work. We have laid out here the outline of a process for such a collaboration. You'll probably carry this one out with a classmate, but your instructor may have arranged for a collaborative project with a student or students on another campus. Either way, you can begin to orient yourself to the on-line workplace.

Step 1

- One partner starts by posting what seems like the most significant question involved in exploring the topic.
- The other responds by revising the question, suggesting an alternative question(s), or attempting to answer the question.
- The messages continue until the writers are exhausted, out of time, or confident that they have enough information to begin a first draft.

So far, this process ought to seem a little familiar (see Activity 2.2). The invention process for a collaborative essay won't differ much, if at all, from the collaborative invention process outlined earlier. Once you begin to collaborate on a draft, however, there is one additional piece of technical information you need to have. You need to be able to attach a formatted file to your E-mail message. Some mail handling software (Eudora, Pegasus Mail, and others) allows you to do this easily. Other environments (VAX-mail, many mainframe systems, etc.) require you to encode the file first, upload it to your E-mail account, and then attach it to the message. If your class completed Activity 2.1, you'll already have the instructions for doing this. If not, then you need to find out before you continue.

Step 2

- Negotiate how you want to arrive at a first draft. Many options are possible. One of you might rough out an outline and post it to the other, who could revise the outline and write the draft. Or the two (or three, or however many) might divide the project into sections, so that each participant writes a section. Or you could use an exchange of E-mail messages like the process described in step 1 to draft a solid introductory paragraph or section, so that all the collaborators know what the essay will accomplish, and then work on sections or in turns from there.
- Once you have a rough draft, pass it back and forth via E-mail. From this point on, you'll need to send formatted word-processing files back and forth, so that each writer, in turn, can work with easily editable text. Each writer makes changes to content, organization, sequencing of ideas, and so on, until both (all) are satisfied that the piece effectively says what it needs to say.
- Pass the piece back and forth once or twice more—or as many times as you need to—focusing this time on editing, formatting, and so forth. Correct the grammar and spelling; work on style and usage; attend to margins, headings, font, and so forth.
- Once all agree that the piece is finished, the last person to have the file posts a copy to each group member and the teacher.

3

COMMUNICATING ON THE INTERNET: ACCESSING VIRTUAL COMMUNITIES

Writers communicate one on one, and they also communicate in *electronic communities*. The renowned rhetorician Kenneth Burke uses the metaphor of the parlor, where a group of people are gathered for conversation, to illustrate the kind of community that, today, we often find on-line. In this portion of Part I, we consider electronic communities—virtual parlors, if you will, that in some ways resemble Burke's metaphorical parlor. In that parlor, people casually chatted about topics of common interest or discussed issues of import to the group. Typically, we gain access to such a conversation by invitation, because we are known to and valued by the host, who owns the parlor, or because that person believes we will fit in with the others in the group or circle of acquaintance. Such a gathering has its own etiquette, its own sense of order and decorum. Violate those rules, and we are not likely to be included the next time the group gathers.

Electronic communities, like their real-life counterparts, exist because the people who write to each other there share common interests. Groups form around topics, and they continue because enough people find the topic sufficiently engrossing to keep that channel of conversation open. Teachers "gather" on electronic mail lists such as ACW-L, for example (a list sponsored by Texas Tech University and the Alliance for Computers and Writing), to discuss topics ranging from their shared topical interests to teaching methods, from advice about computer applications to information about new or particularly useful resources. Other groups gather on other lists to discuss sports, medicine, movies, games, politics—literally tens of thousands of electronic mail lists, bulletin board services, on-line chat rooms, Usenet forums, MUDs, MOOs, and so on. If you have an interest, a question, or an ax to grind, somewhere an electronic parlor awaits your participation.

Unlike their real-life counterparts, however, virtual parlors are generally open to whoever drops in, and participants cannot see each other. And these parlors may have hundreds, even thousands of attenders, a few of whom post messages, and most of whom read and learn. The sheer volume and variety of participants creates a need for a new kind of etiquette, often called *netiquette,* so that the discussions remain manageable and civil. Breach one of these rules—a general one such as sticking to the list's topic or keeping private messages off the list or a list-specific one regarding, say, the care one takes in writing a message—and the consequences can range from being criticized on-line to, in the most extreme case, provoking some hacker into changing your credit rating, altering your school or work records, changing your medical records, or worse. Knowing how to enter and how to participate in these electronic communities—knowing both the rhetoric and the netiquette for these new venues—can mean the difference between a positive, enriching experience and a nightmare.

As the table indicates, on-line communities divide into two distinct kinds, asynchronous and synchronous, each of which has its own constraints, as well as its own advantages.

Activity	Common Environments	Special Considerations
Reading and writing electronic mail (asynchronous communication)	Listserv, listproc, bulletin board service (BBS), Usenet groups	• Rhetoric of the screen—formatting for readability • Netiquette: accommodating a reader's needs in a new medium • Netiquette: conforming to group purposes and expectations
On-line, synchronous messaging	Internet relay chat (IRC); on-line chat rooms; multiuser dungeon (MUD); MUD, object oriented (MOO)	• Immediacy of experience—real time, but virtual space • Environment constructed with language • Netiquette: accommodating a reader's needs in a new medium • Netiquette: conforming to group purposes and expectations

ASYNCHRONOUS COMMUNITIES

In this kind of community, all the members have access to all the messages, but the participants are not on-line together at the same time. The communication is therefore *indirect* and *extended over time.* The message you post today may elicit a response in tomorrow's E-mail, or it may start a discussion that lasts for days or even weeks. It is also multivocal; that is, all the members of the community could comment on any given topic. If they did, of course, the community would rapidly become dysfunctional, since most of these groups involve several hundred participants. A list that is at all active will usually pursue several strands of discussion at once, with other, shorter exchanges intermingled in a day's traffic.

Typically, an individual member comments on messages that directly interest him or on topics on which the individual possesses some special knowledge or expertise. Most members "lurk"—they almost never post a message, but they read the discussion to gain the knowledge being shared. This kind of community, then, is a cross between a print resource such as books, journals, and magazines, in which general knowledge and recent thinking is available to the reader, and a constructive, participatory environment for thinking new thoughts, making new knowledge, in a collaborative setting. In the latter environment, the thinking tends to be cutting-edge, preprint. The best of on-line thinking finds its way, eventually, into print. But because conventional printed resources generally involve a lag time of two or more years, the thinking in even the most up-to-date journals is already stale by the time it reaches its audience. Thus, members of on-line communities can gain access to the future, in a very real sense—they can often find out today what will be in books and journals two years from now.

The most common forms of asynchronous communities fall into three groups: mail lists, bulletin boards, and Usenet groups. Each has its own form of access and its own netiquette.

Mail Lists

One computer acts as the host so that a message sent to a single address can be delivered to all the people who have subscribed to the group. Thus, a single message to acw-l@ttacs6.ttu.edu would be delivered to all six hundred or more subscribers to the list. This is a great convenience, because without the listproc or listserv software, reaching that many people who are interested in a given topic would be practically impossible and prohibitively expensive. The postage alone, for six hundred letters, would be $192.00 (at 1996 rates). Subscribe (i.e., put your name on the mailing list—there's no money involved, outside what you have to pay to access your own E-mail) to MAPS-L and you could join more than one thousand people who are interested in maps and aerial photo systems. Or, on the other extreme, GIGGLES is described as "The House of Laughter, Jokes, Stories, and Anecdotes" (TILE.NET/listserv: the reference to Internet discussion groups, http://tile.net/lists). Mail groups are self-defined audiences and, for the most part, self-organizing and self-regulating structures. The list members subscribe voluntarily because they are interested in the list's topic. Thus, those who post to the list can make certain assumptions of interest and expertise (or at least the pursuit of expertise) that are different from the assumptions writers can make about most readers. In addition, as long as the messages remain on topic, writers don't have to worry whether their readers are interested.

These lists are controlled by software, so that little human intervention is needed. The three kinds of software used to operate most E-mail lists are called majordomo, listserv, and listproc, and though they use similar commands, each operates a little differently. When you subscribe to a list, the software automatically sends you instructions for posting mail to the list, setting several options for receiving your mail, accessing archived messages, and sending other commands to the host computer. *Do not lose that message!*

To subscribe to one of these lists, you would send a one-line message, with no subject header, to the listserv, majordomo, or listproc address, depending on which software the site is using (listserv is more widely used, but the move to listproc, which is UNIX-based, is gaining momentum). Let's look at a sample sign-on, just to familiarize you with the process. To subscribe to SGHOST-L, a (fictional) list run with listserv and devoted to discussion of episodes of *Space Ghost,* you'd send the following message to listserv@correct.domain.address:

```
subscribe sghost-l yourfirstname yourlastname
```

To send mail to the list, you'd use the address

```
sghost-l@correct.domain.address
```

Commands that control how or whether you receive mail from the list always go to the listproc or listserv address and include these:

- ACK or NOACK (to specify whether the listserv should acknowledge receipt of your message);
- REPRO or NO REPRO (to receive—or not—copies of your own messages to the list);
- MAIL and NOMAIL (to turn the flow of mail on or off, without unsuscribing from the list); and
- DIGEST=ON or =OFF (to receive all a given day's messages in one long message, or to receive them as separate messages, the way the other participants send them).

When you subscribe, the listserv or listproc automatically sends you a long message about these commands. Again, *save that message.*

Netiquette
As you participate in mail lists, be aware of the special netiquette that exists for these lists, in addition to the rules you learned earlier for E-mail in general.

- *Know the list.* Lurk (just read messages, without posting any of your own) a while before you post. Find out whether this really is the list you thought it was, and discover how widely the discussion can range. Some lists are *very* specific, basically question-and-answer resources. Other lists have a

garrulous quality about them, allowing the conversation to range sometimes far afield from the specific list topic. Some lists are intolerant of all
but the most highly polished prose; on other lists, subscribers make fun of
people who seem to write too carefully and correctly. Some lists are moderated; that is, your message goes to a single person (the moderator) who
decides whether it's good enough or sufficiently relevant to post to the list
members. Other lists are wide open, allowing even nonmembers to post
messages there. You'll find participation much more fun if you learn a little about the list before you actually post a message to it.

- *Get the FAQs.* Frequently Asked Questions, that is. One message you can
  post right away is a request for the list's FAQ file, if it has one. This list will
  give you most of the information you need to keep from making a fool of
  yourself when you begin to post messages to the list, and it'll keep you
  from having to ask the kind of "newbie" questions that longtime list members can tire of answering over and over again.
- *Stick to the topic.* Unless you know that off-topic messages are welcome,
  always stick to the list's topic in messages you post to the list. Remember,
  the list exists because the subscribers are interested in its announced topic.
- *Know when to respond.* If every member of the list responds to every message, then no one will be happy. Respond when you have knowledge that
  others don't seem to have, a point to make that moves the discussion
  along, or some new insight. Remember, each message you post goes to
  hundreds of recipients, creating a message that they have to read. Make
  that reading seem worthwhile.
- *Read all the messages in your mailbox before you respond to any.* The conversation, remember, is asynchronous. By the time you read a question, someone else may have answered it. If you also answer it, that's an unnecessary
  duplication of effort—a waste of your time and everyone else's, too, since
  they have to read your message. Similarly, you may want to comment on
  a message, but you'll find, if you read all your messages, someone else has
  already made that comment, or the discussion has taken a turn that you
  didn't anticipate, so that your comment is irrelevant. You can prevent all
  these problems by reading first and only then responding.
- *Identify yourself.* Always sign your E-mail, or include a brief (four-line maximum) signature line that indicates your name, address, position, affiliation, Internet address, and so forth.
- *Reference the context.* If you are responding to something someone else said
  on the list, then include *that part of the message* in your response. Do not
  merely include the whole previous message, because that takes up time
  and space for recipients and wastes listserv capacity.
- *Remember that there is no such thing as private E-mail.* Any message you send
  to a list goes to hundreds of people, any of whom might well decide to forward it to another list or another person and so forth and so forth and so
  forth. Many people, over the years, have been embarrassed to find that a
  message they posted to a friend has ended up being circulated widely.

(Note: Such forwarding is, in itself, a breach of netiquette; you should always obtain the author's permission before you forward anything that is not clearly a public announcement.) Messages that are appropriate in one context may seem tactless in another context. Don't say anything that you'd be ashamed to acknowledge if it appeared on the front page of tomorrow's newspaper. E-mail, especially an E-mail list, is a public forum.

- *Self-reveal, up to a point.* If you're new to the list and posting for the first time, say so. Then, if you violate some tacit understanding among the experienced members, they'll be kind. If you are not sure whether a message is relevant or appropriate, say so. Apologizing in advance allows other list members to ignore the message if it truly is inappropriate, and if it is appropriate, they'll still have a kindly feeling toward you. If you're worried that a message will be taken wrong, say so, and explain how you want readers to understand it. E-mail is a context-poor communications environment; anything you can do to help the communication along is wise. However, *do not post personal information to the list,* unless you're awfully sure of the list members. This is not *Oprah,* but it is a public medium. Gripe about your job, boss, teacher, Dean, spouse, and so on, and your message could end up being forwarded to your target's mailbox. That can be embarrassing. Also remember that any personal information you reveal could end up in the hands of someone who can make unscrupulous use of it. So, as *Hill Street Blues*'s Sergeant Esterhaus used to say, "Be careful out there."

- *Know when to "take it off-list."* If you just want to thank an individual for a particular message, or if you merely want to say "I agree with X," use private E-mail, not the list. These are nice actions to take, but in most cases these messages do not have to go to the whole list. Also, when a strand of the discussion is really being dominated by only two or three people, those people should realize that their discussion is not of general interest to the group. Out of courtesy to the others, these people should continue the discussion off the list, via private E-mail.

- *Do not "flame."* "To flame" is to make an unnecessarily hostile, negative criticism of someone else. Discussion lists are supposed to be constructive, and they depend on a level of civility. Criticize ideas, not people. Calm down before you respond—or don't respond at all—to a message you find offensive, stupid, or inflammatory. Respond to others as you would want others to respond to you.

- *Manage your E-mail account.* If your mailbox fills, it will start generating error messages to the listserv, causing someone, somewhere (often the list owner) to have to take action to remedy a situation created by your negligence. If you are going to be away for a while, unsubscribe from your lists or set them to "nomail." Then, when you return, you can resubscribe. And, above all, don't subscribe to more lists than you can keep up with. If you find yourself falling behind in your E-mail reading, unsubscribe from lists you find less useful, or set your lists to the "digest" mode, so that each day's messages come to you at once, usually in one long message. If you change E-mail accounts or addresses, unsubscribe using the old address and then re-subscribe from the new one.

ACTIVITY 3.1: Joining a Virtual Community

Find an E-mail list that covers a subject that interests you and subscribe. Follow the list for a week or two, at least, to decide whether you will continue. You can obtain a list of E-mail lists via the World Wide Web by setting your browser (Mosaic, Netscape, Lynx, etc.) to http://tile.net/lists/ or by looking up addresses of common lists in a guide to the Internet, available in your library or local bookstore.

Bulletin Board Service (BBS)

The oldest, once the most widespread, still the most individualistic kind of asynchronous on-line community is the BBS. Almost anyone with a computer, a phone, and a little expertise can run one. Basically, the BBS is run on a single computer, often a desktop computer, hooked up to a dial-in modem. The user dials the number, connects to the host, and finds a menu of messages. The operative metaphor is the literal bulletin board, so the BBS tends to be fairly intuitive. Users read the subject headers of messages and select which ones to read. Also, of course, readers can leave messages for other users to read. The BBS is probably on its way out as an active technology—its heyday took place before the Internet became the mainstay of computer networking—but there are still a number of BBSs around, and they are still the grass roots, so to speak, of the networked computer world.

The rhetoric and the netiquette are basically the same for a BBS as for E-mail, with the exception that you don't have to worry about managing your own account. Because you download only the messages you want to read, and because they don't come to you as electronic mail, you don't have to worry about your mailbox overflowing. And because users access only those messages they want to read, you don't have to be as careful about what you post. Do identify yourself in your messages, though, because that's often the only way other users can know who you are, to answer your questions or respond to your comments; and be sure to use succinct, descriptive headings for your messages. And try not to post a lot of messages, because other users have to scroll through them to find the messages they want to read. Basic consideration for other users—acting the way you'd want them to act toward you—is the central guideline for BBS netiquette.

Usenet Groups

Usenet is a cross between the mail group and the BBS. And Usenet is huge—more than ten thousand Usenet groups exist, on any subject you might imagine. Like a mail list, Usenet operates by subscription—users decide which groups to receive automatically and which to browse occasionally. Also, the managers of your Internet node can decide which Usenet groups to support, blocking out those deemed undesirable or useless. Finally, users send messages via E-mail or by using software that allows for Usenet access. However, like a BBS, Usenet messages don't come to the user as E-mail; instead, the user signs on to a group and reads the subject headers in order to choose which messages to read. Nuntius, for the Macintosh, and *Trumpet,* for the MS-DOS/Windows machines are the most commonplace Usenet readers, but new readers are being developed all the time to provide simpler, easier interfaces between Usenet's UNIX-based operating system and a desktop computer.

Usenet groups are named according to rules that describe the content and the level of seriousness of the group. So *rec.humor,* for example, is a recreational group that focuses on humor. Go here to find new jokes but not to have an academic discussion of humor in eighteenth-century Scotland. *Alt.gopher* provides useful information for new users of gopher (see Chapter 4 for more about this information-retrieval system). *Comp.infosystems.gopher* is for the more expert user. How do you tell the difference? The prefixes *alt* (alternative) and *comp* (computers) tell you that the former is "alternative," informal, open to anyone, whereas the latter is more technical, more of a comprehensive guide to information systems using gopher.

Usenet demands the same netiquette as a mail group or BBS, but be aware of the fact that Usenet has far more readers and browsers than any other form of asynchronous electronic communication. *Anyone* who can get access to the Internet can browse a Usenet group. So your potential audience is huge—some groups have more than 1.5 million subscribers. That size is an advantage and a disadvantage. Each message you post can reach a very large audience, so the information you share or the insights you post can affect many, many people. On the other hand, anything you post on Usenet is, in effect, on a billboard by the side of the road. Don't post a message you'd be sorry to have your grandmother, boss, best friend, or worst enemy read.

Usenet's size carries one more set of constraints on your writing. Usenet is an international network. Your readers access Usenet groups from all over the world, from all language groups. Thus, the usual E-mail netiquette rule to keep language plain, concise, and precise holds even more true for Usenet. If you use irony or sarcasm, if you use too delicate a nuance, if you fill your prose with colloquial phrases and metaphors, if your sentences are long and complex, then your message is likely to be difficult to read, even for native speakers of English (the lingua franca of almost all newsgroups), and it will be even more difficult for readers whose native language is something other than English. Similarly, references to places, events, people, and so forth, may not carry the weight or the clarity, for the international readership, that they do for your conationals. Common references in one culture (e.g., using the suffix *-gate* to liken something to a major political scandal) may not carry meaning in other cultures. Plain-speaking, simple prose and straightforward language should be the rhetorical watchwords in composing posts to Usenet newsgroups.

Before you post a message to a Usenet group, review the section on E-mail netiquette in Chapter 2.

ACTIVITY 3.2: Accessing Usenet

Part II contains several activities for using asynchronous communications, so if you want to know and do more, see those chapters for more activities. For now, though, you need to have some information at your disposal, just to be *able* to access these electronic parlors. So you need to find the information you need, given your hardware, software, and local computer systems. Here are some questions you should be able to answer by contacting your computer support office, consulting the documentation your institution makes available, asking the more experienced user down the hall, and/or sharing what you know with your classmates (note: this list assumes that you've already found the information you needed to access your E-mail):

- What kind of software do you need to access Usenet from your computer?
- How do you acquire that software? The software is free, and most institutions that provide Usenet access also provide the software. If yours does not, then you can use FTP to get it, and you can FTP it through the World Wide Web as well. Set your web browser (Mosaic, Netscape, Lynx, etc.) to open the following location, for example, to retrieve Nuntius for the Macintosh: ftp://ftp.ruc.dk/pub/nuntius/.
- How can you obtain copies of documentation and other instructions for operating the Usenet software for your computer?
- How can you sign up for any Usenet workshops your institution may offer?
- How do you use a modem to connect to your institution's computing system from your dorm, home, or other out-of-class location?
- What modem settings does your institution's system require, and how do you set your modem and communications software?
- How do you change the settings for your modem and communications software to allow you to connect to various BBSs?

ACTIVITY 3.3: Joining a Usenet Group

Once you have located the above information, you should browse a few Usenet groups, just to get a feel for the kind of information that is out there, and to practice using the software you have acquired. Perhaps the best place to start is *news.announce.newusers*. As the name implies, it contains announcements relevant to new users. There you'll find several items that reinforce and augment the information in this section about Usenet:

- Tips for Usenet writing style
- "Emily Postnews," who answers questions about netiquette
- General guidelines for posting to Usenet groups
- A how-to guide for working with Usenet groups as on-line communities
- A general FAQ file about Usenet

You may have to "lurk" for a week or two before all of these items appear. Your local Usenet subscriber (your institution) probably deletes messages that are a week old, but these standard messages are posted regularly—at least twice a month. Starting here will help you safely enter the Usenet world, and the people who are regulars on news.announce.newusers are there because they want to help "newbies" learn to use the huge and sometimes bewildering resource called Usenet.

SYNCHRONOUS COMMUNITIES

IRC. MUD. MOO. MUSH. Chat room. These are the sites for perhaps the most exciting form of on-line communication, the kind that allows you to send messages back and forth to have a (written) conversation on-line, in real time. You send a message. Someone reads it and replies immediately. People move in and out of the group, joining and leaving conversations just as they would in an actual parlor or at some actual reception or cocktail party. Only *these* people may be located on different continents! Instead of driving up in their limos, they connect to the Internet, open a connection to a computer that may be halfway around the world, and talk with others who have similarly "gathered" in that computer's active memory (its RAM), taking advantage of the software described by the acronyms listed here:

IRC: *Internet relay chat.* Software that allows groups of people to chat on-line. IRC is the "wild and wooly" version of synchronous community. As many as ten thousand people at a time may flit among seven hundred to one thousand different groups, called *channels*. Some of these groups are pursuing serious topics; some are entirely frivolous. Some are raunchy; some are prim and proper. Some are friendly; some seem almost sinister.

MUD: *MultiUser Dimension (or Dungeon).* Software that was developed to play a virtual version of the once-popular Dungeons and Dragons game, it now also allows groups of people to gather in "rooms" to hold conversations, to interact electronically. Individual users have "characters" that they construct using a simple programming language, and they can "build" objects that remain for others to see and use. Still widely used for extended role-playing games, MUDs are also being developed for more serious purposes.

MOO: *Multiuser dimension, Object Oriented.* Like a MUD, only more user-friendly. Objects are easier to construct, and the programming language is more like natural language. MOOs are not generally game-playing sites. Instead, they are places people meet to accomplish work. In a biology MOO, researchers gather for an almost constantly ongoing scientific conference. In MediaMOO, researchers exploring topics related to communications gather for many different functions, from conferences and formal presentations to informal gatherings in the Technorhetoricians Bar and Grill, where Gus, the bartender, serves virtual beer. Several MOOs function as college campuses, complete with different buildings in which classes are held. Some MOOs serve as writing labs, where anyone can check in for a little help with a piece of writing.

MUSH: *MultiUser Shared Hallucination.* Another role-playing, text-based interactive gaming format that is being adapted for more serious uses as well. MUSHes allow you to meet and interact with people from all around the world, either under the theme of a game or for another common purpose.

MUDs, MOOs, and MUSHes all feature interaction in a text-based virtual "place," a physical environment created in text, using a set of relatively simple programming commands.

Chat room: A variation used on commercial service providers such as America On-line, the chat room is similar to a MOO, except there are no objects, nothing that attempts to mimic a physical environment. When you access the chat room, you begin seeing the messages people are exchanging, and you can join the conversation by sending a message of your own. The chat room most closely resembles IRC, except that it's nowhere near as wide open and flaky as IRC can be.

Accessing Synchronous Communities

Internet Relay Chat (IRC)

To use IRC, you will have to have an IRC client, a computer at your institution or at another location that allows users to participate in IRC, or a client program for your own desktop computer, if you have a direct Internet connection. If your campus doesn't have an IRC server or doesn't furnish an IRC client, use Telnet to reach a client machine. Most people can access IRC from the main prompt of their institution's mainframe computing system by just typing IRC<return>. As you log on to IRC, you'll be asked for your name and for a nickname you'd like to use while you're signed on. You can use the nickname

> You can get almost all the information you need for accessing IRC by pointing your World Wide Web browser to http://www.botree.co.uk/library/irc.htm

to reveal your actual identity (bcondon or wbutler, e.g.), or you can conceal your identity by making up a nickname that has no connection to your actual identity.

Once you're in, you'll find people talking on "channels." You can join a group by joining that channel. Here are some useful commands (you can find other commands by requesting instructions as you log on). Note that in IRC commands are preceded by a slash (/). The slash tells the computer that what follows is a command, not just an attempt to say something.

IRC Commands

/nick <nickname> Allows you to change your nickname at any point during a session.

/list Allows you to view a list of all active "channels." This list will scroll by very quickly. To stop it, use your system's interrupt command (for most, this is Control-S; that is, you hold down the Control key while typing the S key). The resume command (often, Control-Q) will start the scrolling again. Jot down channels you'd like to try out, because you won't be able to do anything else until the list finishes scrolling past.

/help Allows you to access IRC's help files, so that you can learn all the commands we don't have space to tell you about.

/join #<channel> Allows you to join a channel. Once you've joined, you'll see a list of the people in that channel, and you'll start seeing messages scroll past as other participants talk. To talk, just type a message (three lines or less) and hit the Return key at the end (note: do not hit Return at the end of each line, or you'll send your message prematurely). When your post appears, you won't see your own nickname, but all the others will.

/whois <nickname> Allows you to find the other participants' real names, which they gave when they logged on. They, of course, can do likewise, so even though you may be using a clever nickname, people can still find out your real name.

/leave #<channel> Allows you to leave one channel to join another. When one participant leaves, the others see a message to that effect on their screens.

/MOTD Accesses the Message of the Day, which typically tells you whom to contact if you are having trouble with others' inappropriate behavior.

/exit Allows you to leave IRC and return to the command prompt in your home computer system.

The rhetoric of IRC stems from the fact that all messages are short; the usual three-line maximum in a standard Telnet application means that you either have to compress what you want to say or you have to post in a series of installments, each three lines long. Some applications that have been developed especially for IRC allow messages of up to five thousand characters (700–1,000 words), but few users move beyond standard Telnet, for a variety of reasons. The emphasis, then, is on *chat*. Three lines don't allow a lot of room for more. Brevity also creates a sense of speed, a sense that the conversation is really moving along. On an active channel, messages seem to fly past, and strands of discussion (IRC is multivocal, too) sometimes shift so quickly that they are difficult to track. This medium, then, offers challenges, especially for anyone using it for serious discussion or debate. But it can also be a great deal of fun.

Enjoy yourself, then, but remember that IRC has a strong alternative, even avant garde feel to it. Insiders call it the "undernet." You'd do well to begin by joining #newbies (once you're logged on to IRC, type /join#newbies and press the Return key). That channel is generally filled with people who will be happy to answer questions about IRC and steer you toward some useful, interesting, or new channels. Another safe place to start is #friendly, a channel that lives up to its name.

MUDs, MOOs, and MUSHes: Virtual Reality without the Goggles

We've all seen or read about virtual reality, but relatively few people have telnetted into it. M**s began as interactive character-based games that often stretched over months at a time. Since about 1993, though, these virtual environments have been applied more broadly for educational and business use. They present a relatively easy, stable means of meeting on-line in a familiar environment. MUDs, MOOs, and MUSHes all use programmed descriptions of "spaces," usually rooms, where people who telnet into the host machine can gather to hold debates, discussions, or even standard lecture presentations, all, of course, in text form. The idea is to provide on-line discussants with a physical presence (their own character) inside something that resembles a real environment—unlike IRC, where the users just seem to hang out, disembodied, in virtual space. In effect, M**s have moved from the "undernet" occupied by IRC into more mainstream use.

Several MOOs use the classroom as the primary type of space. Others use the hotel conference area. The possibilities are endless. MUSHes include versions of Frank Herbert's *Dune* books, Tolkein's Middle Earth books, even an on-line version of Graceland, complete with a virtual Elvis. Beside these, the biology MOO, where researchers and professors gather for planned and impromptu conference presentations, may seem tame. However, such MOOs may soon provide a medium where new knowledge can reach the public at a much faster rate than the publishing industry can manage. And international collaborative research is much easier when the participants can easily and economically discuss their progress with each other on a daily basis. Some businesses, too, use MOOs for regular Directors' meetings. Gathering the honchos into a MOO is much cheaper than flying them in to the same location, and MOO technology allows for more frequent meetings.

MUD, MOO, and MUSH Commands.   Like IRC, you can access a M** by using Telnet, and the interface will look much the same. However, most people use an application such as MUDDweller, which provides easier access and a more understandable interface. Here is a sample sign-on using MUDDweller:

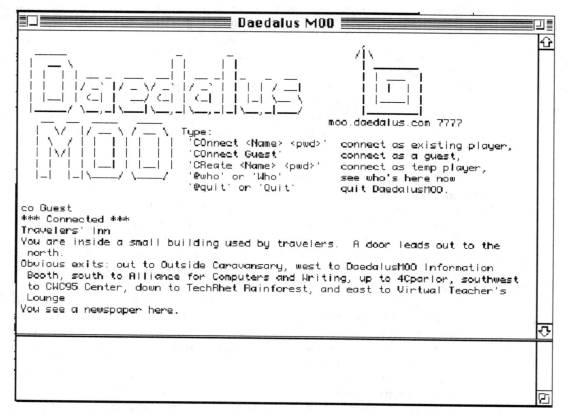

Note: DaedalusMOO is an educational site, which we're just using as an example. If you want to play around in a MOO, find another one. On the other hand, DaedalusMOO can be a good place for your class to go to find out more about how MOOs work.

As you can see, we connected as a Guest (co Guest) by setting MUDDweller to telnet to moo.daedalus.com 7777. As we connected, we were given a short description of the space, the entryway for this MOO. From here, we can use directional commands or the commands for the names of the different places to move around and find where others are in the MOO. Again, the idea is that the descriptions allow you to locate yourself in relation to others, so that you will feel more comfortable. You have reference points similar to the ones you have in real life, and the heightened comfort level allows for more productive, more enjoyable interactions.

Once you have entered the M**, you'll want to know how to get around and locate others. To do this, use command words, preceded by the @ sign. The common commands—the basics for survival—are as follows:

@who Gives you a list of all the characters signed on at the moment, with information about their location and recent activity.

@go \<placename> Takes you from where you are to the place you've specified. Some M**s don't support this name convention, so you'll need the number for the location, in which case the command is @go \<number>.

@join \<character's name> Allows you to join a character wherever that character is in the M**. This is an easy way to get around. When you use the @who command to see who is where, then you can @join someone who already is where you want to go.

@whois \<character's name> As in many on-line environments, people often use aliases. It's just part of the element of play in the activity. @whois will give you information about the real person behind the character.

@quit This one, of course, lets you leave the M**.

@linelength, @wrap, @pagelength Many M** accessing tools don't give you a very friendly interface. They don't wrap words, the text just scrolls endlessly off the screen, and the lines can run beyond the end of your "page." If you see any of these symptoms, you can use @linelength 75 (for most computers) to break the text up into lines that will fit on your screen; @wrap to turn on wordwrap, so that the words will break at spaces, instead of midword; and @pagelength 22 (again, for most screens) to stop the scrolling every twenty-two lines, or every screenful.

" Use quotation marks to "speak." You don't have to close the quotation. Just use quotation marks to begin what you want to say, and hit the Return key when you're finished.

:\<verb + action> Allows your character to "do" something. You might enter *:grimaces at Joe's joke,* for example, in order to produce the action *Bill grimaces at Joe's Joke.*

help Allows you to access help files. If you know the command you need help with, you can use help \<command> to access the specific information. Otherwise, start with help and follow the choices to the command you want.

look Repeats the description of the room you are in.

exam \<object> Gives you the description of an object.

page <character's name + message> Let's you send a message directly to another character, in another room in the M**. Only characters in the same room with each other can "hear" each other's conversation, so this is a useful way to contact someone in a different room.

mu <character's name + message> The whisper (or MUtter) command allows you to say something in private, to enter a message that only the recipient will be able to read.

Netiquette for M**s.   M**s have a sense of immediacy and play that no other form of synchronous on-line community enjoys. Even when people are working in a MOO, for instance, they are also having fun. That's the nature of the activity. M**s offer so many things to do, see, and try that experimentation takes place even in the midst of serious work activity. After all, if you stop to check out an object, you don't have to worry about missing someone's comment. It will appear on the screen, and you can read it when you're ready. Still, there are guidelines for M**ing, principles that make the experience more pleasant for everyone, including you.

- *Be nice.* There are real people out there, and they are seeing what you say as soon as you say it. The immediacy of M**s is a great advantage, but you have to respect it and others' feelings.
- *Be polite.* This is, in effect, a face-to-face medium, in the sense that everyone is in the same virtual place at the same real time. Use the same sense of decorum you'd use in face-to-face conversation. Also, because a M** is divided into rooms, think about the etiquette you'd use in moving around in someone else's house.
- *Respect others' privacy.* Page someone before joining them. Don't "shadow" another player, following from room to room, especially if that player does not want you to follow.
- *Respect others' property.* The rooms and objects in a M** may be constructed of text, but someone constructed them, and the process may have taken a great deal of time and effort. Don't go into someone else's room without permission. Don't take an object or modify an object that does not belong to you. Exception: If someone leaves an unwelcome object in *your* room, you can get rid of it, preferably by putting it back where it came from. Also, most rooms in most M**s are public space, where anyone can enter (but review the preceding point).
- *Respect others' rights.* Freedom of speech is important in M**s, as it is generally on the Internet. However, players quickly lose respect and patience for those who use obscenities or threats, who are violent, or whose behavior is obviously and generally offensive. Harassment of any kind is likely to result in your being thrown out of the M**.
- *Respect each others' culture.* Any on-line community can, and often does, involve interacting with people from a variety of countries and cultures.

That's one of the greatest advantages of this technology. Having access to that advantage brings with it the responsibility to respect others' customs, beliefs, and so forth, even when they may differ markedly from your own. Do everything you can to avoid offending another player.

ACTIVITY 3.4: Accessing Virtual Communities

I.

As with the other kinds of community discussed in this chapter, you'll need to know a few things before you can gain access. Later, in Chapter 9, you'll have an opportunity to reflect on this technology, analyze your experiences, and critique them. Here the purpose is merely to find the information you need to know to gain access to a M**.

- What software is available for accessing MUDs, MOOs, and MUSHes?
- How can you acquire that software? (It may be in a local archive, or you may need to FTP it or retrieve it through the World Wide Web, etc.)
- How, at your institution, do people connect with M**s?
- What documentation and/or help is available for using the software?
- How can you set up the software to allow the most convenient use of a M**?

II.

Try it out! FredNetMOO is a good place to start. It provides an easy MOO to explore and a great deal of support. You can telnet to fred.net 8888 and jump right in, using the instructions listed earlier, or you can point your World Wide Web browser to http://www.fred.net/cindy/frednet.html first, where you'll find good instructions on how to use MOOs, create your own character, behave on a MOO, and so forth. FredNetMOO provides an excellent hands-on tutorial. By the time you finish exploring it, you'll know all you need to know to enjoy MOOing.

On-Line Chat Rooms

The on-line chat rooms on America Online have become an extremely popular feature of that service, and they are likely to pop up on other commercial providers as well. Basically, the chat room is a version of IRC, though it has a better interface—interaction is easier there, because the screen is better organized for both reading and writing than the typical IRC interface. The chat room provides the defined space that a M** provides, but there are no objects, no physical markers—just other people chatting.

The netiquette demands of the chat room are similar to those for the MOO, with the additional constraints that accompany using a commercial service provider. Thus, everyone's paying for time on-line, so don't waste it. And people are not paying their hard-earned dollars just to be offended, outraged, verbally assaulted, or harassed. Behavior like that can result in a suspended account. Be nice. Be polite. Consider others' feelings. Chat rooms have all the immediacy of IRC and MOOs, so use the same guidelines and exercise the same restraint.

4

GATHERING INFORMATION ON THE INTERNET: REACHING OUT AND BRINGING BACK RESOURCES

THE DOCUVERSE: PART I

As we saw in the last two chapters, computer networks offer a sometimes bewildering array of on-line communities that can help writers find information, pique their interest in a new topic, critique their ideas as they are taking shape, and offer the kind of support and encouragement that writers need as they struggle to fill up all those blank screens. Communities are not the only kind of resource networks offer. An often bewildering array of resources is out there, too, waiting for us writers to explore and discover—a huge, sophisticated, incredibly varied library that comes to our desktops via electronic networks. So, in addition to communicating via wide-area networks such as the Internet, writers can gather information on the Internet, reaching out and bringing back resources.

Just after World War II, President Truman's science adviser, Vannevar Bush, imagined something he called Memex (you can read Bush's essay on-line at http://www.isg.sfu.ca/~duchier/misc/vbush/). Memex was a microfilmed compilation of huge numbers of documents, all indexed and cross-indexed so that an individual scholar or researcher could jump from one location to another at will. Eventually, by inserting links, researchers would find all the connections among these documents and establish pathways that readers could use to find the information they needed quickly and easily. By 1957, a Stanford University computer scientist named Douglas Englebart had created a computer model for Bush's vision. In 1964, Ted Nelson called it *hypertext*.

Nelson envisioned a docuverse, a universe of all the documents in the world, residing on millions of computers that were networked so that information on one computer could easily be transferred to another. For more than a decade, people thought Ted Nelson was a kook, an impossible dreamer. Then along came the Internet, the network of networks that does indeed link millions of computers all over the world. And along came some information retrieval capabilities that, if they did not amount to Nelson's docuverse, showed at least that it was possible. File transfer protocol (FTP). Wide-Area Information Server (WAIS). Gopher. Finally, in 1993–94, the World Wide Web emerged as the latest step toward the docuverse. Fully hypertextual, the Web potentially links documents on any computer with those on any other computer, making Nelson's crazy dream a reality.

This chapter deals with the earlier tools—FTP, WAIS, and Gopher—and with the Web as a tool for accessing information. Chapter 5 will look at the Web as a site for writing, communicating, and collaborating. Here, though, we introduce the world of information retrieval, which is the function that gives the information superhighway its name. Files of information on a wide variety of topics, not to mention computer software and other useful resources, are available via FTP, for example. The Internet also provides a home for WAIS and Gopher servers, which supply text-based information on almost any subject from agencies and institutions around the world. And the World Wide Web furnishes "point-and-click" access to books, discussion, news, commerce, audio and video clips—all the raw materials a writer might wish for in order to compose conventional texts, multimedia documents, or hypertexts.

Of course, as in each of the other areas of activity, there are drawbacks. As the network of information becomes more and more extensive, the problem of reliability becomes more and more significant. Basically, anyone with a personal computer and an Internet connection can place information in a Gopher server or on the World Wide Web or make it available for retrieval via

Activity	Common Applications	Special Considerations
Transferring whole files and or documents from a distant computer to your own	File transfer protocol (FTP), wide area information server (WAIS), fetch (Macintosh), Rapid Filer (Windows)	• Sheer quantity of available information • Reliability of information • Difficulty of retrieving and decompressing files
Searching for files by keyword	Gopher, Turbogopher	• Sheer quantity of available information • Reliability of information • Limitations on kinds of information (text only)
Searching for information on the World Wide Web	Lynx, Mosaic, Netscape, Internet Explorer	• Sheer quantity of available information • Reliability of information • Rhetoric of hypertextual, multimedia documents

FTP. **Most people who go to the trouble of making information available in that way are acting in good faith and are reliable. But many are not, and *their information may be intentionally or unintentionally unreliable—false or corrupt.*** "Cruising the 'Net" for information, then, becomes an exercise in critical thinking, as the seeker of information must be sufficiently resourceful to find what she's looking for and sufficiently rigorous to test and confirm what she finds.

> **Note:** More and more, the World Wide Web has taken over all the information retrieval functions listed here, and the Web provides easier access to the information than the earlier tools do. If your institution provides access to the Web, then you probably do not need to learn FTP, WAIS, or Gopher, because the same files can be accessed and more easily retrieved from the Web. If you do not have Web access, then you will want to learn about these earlier, more universal tools.

FILE TRANSFER PROTOCOL (FTP)

FTP is the most rudimentary form of file transfer that we have to deal with today. Originating as a mainframe-to-mainframe procedure for copying files across the Internet, FTP retains all the complications of earlier interfaces and methods. Unfortunately, in some places, FTP is still the only game in town, so we have to learn something about it. Besides, FTP can still be useful, because not all the hundreds of archives have converted to other forms of access. Far more files are available via FTP than are on the Web, WAIS, or Gopher. And FTP moves whole files, so you can transfer documents—text files—and transfer applications, programs, multimedia resources—literally any file or application that a computer can use.

These files come in two basic flavors: ASCII, or plain text; and binary, which includes everything from fully formatted word-processing documents to large applications, or programs. In addition, almost every file is compressed, so that it will take up less space where it is stored and take less time to transfer from one machine to another. So, in addition to knowing how to access and retrieve the files, you must know how to decompress them. There are applications that help in all this, but still, it's a complicated affair.

The Basics

FTP is a client/server method. That is, you use a client program to send commands to a distant server. Those commands allow you to telnet to another computer and run programs there or to bring back files stored on that distant computer. Most FTP clients reside on a mainframe computer, one where you have to login to your own account and then run FTP, typically by entering *ftp* at the system prompt. All these client programs use somewhat different commands, which adds to the confusion. In addition, there are desktop clients, for people who can connect to the Internet using a high-speed modem and something called Point-to-Point Protocol (PPP) or if you have a Serial Line Internet Protocol (SLIP) connection to the Internet. *Fetch* is one example of an FTP client, one that allows you to transfer files directly to your own personal computer rather than to your mainframe account and then downloading from there.

FTP is not a good tool for exploring or cruising the 'Net. Before you can FTP a file, you have to know where it is—what computer it is on. Each file takes quite a while to download, using your own account funds and a significant amount of the source computer's processing power. And each file must be decompressed. So browsing around, downloading this program or that file just to see whether it *might* be useful, is not a practical way to operate in FTP. Instead, you need to know what you want, and you need to know where it is at least likely to be stored. Then you can use FTP fairly economically.

ACTIVITY 4.1: The Different Part

It's time to explore again, time to find out how your local institution provides for FTP. Before we can explain the uniform part, you have to gather information about the different part, information that will allow you open an FTP connection to another computer. So here is a list of questions for you to answer. Again, dividing this task and gathering the information collaboratively may make the task easier and faster.

- What FTP client does my institution use?
- How can I acquire or access that client?
- What information does my institution provide about FTP? What documentation is available to me, and how can I get it?
- How do I launch that client? That is, how do I run it on my computer or from my mainframe computing account?
- What are the commands used by that client? How do I use those commands from my computer or my mainframe account?
- How do I enter an FTP address, so that I can open the connection to the server I need to access?
- Once I have retrieved a file, how do I download it from my mainframe account to my personal computer?
- Once I have retrieved a file, how do I decompress it?

ACTIVITY 4.2: The Uniform Part

Once you've discovered what client to use and how to operate it, the rest is fairly uniform. Here's how it goes, step by step:

1. Once you've opened a connection to a remote site, that computer will ask you to log on. Because you are unlikely to have an account on that machine, you'll do what's called "anonymous FTP." Just type in *anonymous* instead of the usual login ID.
2. If the server allows anonymous FTP, and most do, it will ask you for a password, usually your complete E-mail address (so know it!).
3. Once you've entered a password, you'll see a system prompt. To get a directory of files, type *dir. Dir* tells the server to display the directory of files available on that machine.

> **Hint:** If you type *help* at any of the prompts, you'll see a list of the available commands.

4. The first level you see will probably be a set of folders (in the Macintosh environment) or directories (in the DOS/Unix environment), not the actual files. So you'll need to change directories (using the *cd* command) until you see the files you want. The proper form is

```
cd <directory>
```

> **Another hint:** Usually, the files available via anonymous FTP are in a directory labeled *pub* or *public.* So if you type *cd pub,* chances are you'll see what you want.

> **Yet another hint:** FTP servers are case sensitive; that is, they pay attention to whether a command or a filename is capitalized. So if you are sure you have the right command or filename, but nothing is happening, look to be sure you're using upper-case and lower-case letters correctly.

5. Once you see the file you're after, use the Get command to retrieve it:

```
get <presentfilename> <filename I want to give it>
```

Thus,

```
get lincoln lincoln.doc
```

would tell the server to send me a file named *lincoln* (note: not *Lincoln*), and it would tell my client to name the file *lincoln.doc,* once it has arrived.

> **One last hint:** FTP operates in two modes, text and binary. Text files are in text, usually with a .doc or a .txt file extension. Programs and formatted documents have to be transferred in binary mode. To change modes, just type in the command *text* or *binary* just before you enter the command *Get.* If you forget which mode you're in, type *status* and the computer will tell you.

6. When you are finished, type *quit* to log off the server. Now you're ready to decompress and use the file!

That's all there is to basic FTPing (we say, with a wink ;-)). And the one netiquette consideration has to do with processor time. FTPing uses a lot of power, and the archives are maintained out of the goodness of people's hearts (there's no profit in it!). So be considerate. Get files after working hours or on weekends, when the demand for processing time is low. This may be a little inconvenient for you, but it'll help the people who maintain the archive a lot.

WIDE AREA INFORMATION SERVERS (WAIS)

WAIS takes FTP a couple of steps forward, in both ease and economy of use. WAIS uses something called TCP/IP to connect clients and servers in such a way that you can search files using keywords, and you can more easily retrieve files from the list your search produces. However, WAIS only works for documents, not programs, though it does allow transmission of formatted texts and multimedia documents. You can find movie reviews, bibliographies, recipes, scientific papers, and so forth, so WAIS answers a range of needs. The basics of using WAIS go like this:

1. You launch your client on your own computer.
2. You enter the keyword(s) you want to search for—words that are central in the topic you're researching.
3. WAIS searches its more than 450 databases for any documents that contain those keywords, and it returns to you a list of the documents.
4. You select which documents you'd like to see, and WAIS sends you a copy of each.

ACTIVITY 4.3: Using WAIS

To use WAIS, you have to find out whether your institution supports the service and how to get and use a client. Go do that, alone, or in teams. And, just to make the job easier, we can give you a head start. If you have

Web access, and if your institution supports WAIS, you can point your web browser to

```
http://cnidr.org/welcome.html
```

to download freeWAIS from the Clearinghouse for Networked Information Discovery and Retrieval.

GOPHER

WAIS was an important step along the path to Gopher, an information retrieval process pioneered at the University of Minnesota (hence the name Gopher, after the Minnesota mascot). Gopher, in turn, is a half-step between WAIS and the World Wide Web.

Gopherspace is huge, allowing access to tens of thousands of servers worldwide. And Gopher is searchable by keyword and using Boolean search techniques. That is, you can ask Gopher to find documents that contain the words *writing* and *computers* but *not* the word *fiction*. The "search engines," then, are as powerful as their names are whimsical (they're named Archie and Veronica, after the comic book characters). These search engines are built in to most large Gopher sites. You may have to surf a few sites to find one, or you can find them on the University of Minnesota's site, which you can access from almost any other Gopher site. At the end of the search process, you have a list of documents that you can easily download or just read on-line.

In addition, and unlike WAIS, Gopher is browsable. You can hop from server to server, following pathways that seem interesting or logical, until you find some useful information. So, if you know you want information about Egypt, you can jump from your home Gopher server to "Other Gopher Servers" to "All the Gopher servers in the world" and thence to "Egypt," following a set of file directories that, eventually, lead you to all the gopher servers in Egypt.

For the most part, Gopher is easy to use, because you use a client that resides on your institution's computing system, and because you can easily use either of the search techniques or just browse Gopherspace. If you do happen to have a connection that uses point-to-point protocol (PPP), or if you have a serial line Internet protocol (SLIP) connection to the Internet, you can use Turbogopher, a fast and nifty application that puts a graphical interface onto Gopherspace, so that all the directories look like folders, and you can maneuver around using the graphical interface's point-and-click technology.

ACTIVITY 4.4: Using Gopher to Find Information

You must have a paper to write by now! And any paper is improved by some solid source material. So, if you find the answers to the following questions, you should be able to connect with Gopher and find some good source material for your paper:

- Does your institution support Gopher?
- How do you access Gopher from your classroom, dorm room, home, and/or a public computing site?
- What instructions or documentation are available to you?
- How do you get help using Archie and Veronica?

WORLD WIDE WEB (WWW)

A general note about this section: Even as we write this chapter, the Web is beginning to offer access to virtual communities (e.g., hypermail and Usenet archives) and to introduce actual conferencing capabilities. By the time you read this book, such systems may be totally operational and widely available. So, in addition to the Web's offering new ways to share information, it is also becoming a platform for computer-mediated communication (CMC). In essence, it is about to do for CMC what it did for FTP.

The newest and most convenient way of finding information on the Internet is the World Wide Web. Like Gopher, it is browsable and searchable, and there are many, many search engines on the Web, so searches are extremely flexible. Worms and Web crawlers look for keywords in both titles and documents, Yahoo! adds subject area searches to keyword searches, or you can just follow links, browsing until you find what you want. The advance over Gopher is that the Web is fully hypertextual. Each document has links in it, words or phrases or graphics that you can click on in order to jump to another document or another location. In other words, Gopher provides links from file to file, from directory to directory, but the Web links individual documents—even words and phrases within individual documents. Whereas Gopher's pathways are more or less similar, the pathways users can follow on the Web are infinitely variable. In addition, the built-in links give the Web a different rhetoric, a rhetoric of the page, which we will explore in the next chapter. For now, though, we will look at the Web as a tool for finding information.

The client/server formula still applies here, though the servers are almost infinite in number, and the client applications are called "browsers." These browsers allow you to locate and download individual documents by using an addressing system called a uniform resource locator, or URL (sometimes pronounced *"earl"*). Each document has its own URL, so documents are easily located. And each link contains the URL for the next document, so you don't have to know the URLs to find the documents. And you don't have to wade through a lot of directories—the URL or the link takes you directly to the document you want. Sound too good to be true? There's more. You can use your web browser to telnet, to FTP, to access Gopherspace, to read Usenet, as well as to read Web pages.

To use the Web, you have to have a PPP or SLIP connection, or what is called level 3 access to the Internet. If you have any one of these kinds of connection, you can use a Web browser. These come in three varieties:

1. *Line-mode*—primitive command-line interface that operates much like FTP. If this is the only browser you can use, you're better off with WAIS and Gopher and FTP.
2. *Full-screen*—Lynx is the "default" full-screen browser in use, for both mainframe access and desktop use. Here you see a whole Web page, and you can use the arrow keys to move from link to link and <Return> to select the link. Full-screen or nongraphical browsers deliver text only, so you will miss the graphics, sounds, video, high-concept page designs, and so forth.
3. *Graphical*—Point-and-click access to everything the Web has to offer. You can see the graphics, movies, and text. You can hear the sounds. And you navigate using the mouse. Mosaic and Netscape are the dominant graphical Web browsers, for both Macintosh and Windows environments.

Most colleges and universities that supply Web access also provide a common browser, so you'll want to find out what's available where you are. Internet providers are increasingly pressured to offer Web access too, so you're likely to be able to browse the Web in all its glory (graphically, that is).

Once you have a browser, you need to know something about URLs, the addressing system for locating the document you want among the literally millions that are out there. A URL has two parts, as you can see from the example below:

```
http://www.lsa.umich.edu/ecb/infohighway.html
```

The first part—the part before the colon—tells the browser what method to use in accessing the document. URLs for Web pages all start with *http,* indicating that the document is in HyperText Transfer Protocol. That first part could also be *FTP:* or *file:,* allowing the browser to access a document via anonymous FTP. It could also be *news:* (to access Usenet newsgroups), *gopher:,* or *telnet:,* allowing the browser to access any of those resources. The rest of the address, the part after the colon, is the sequence of directories that lead to the document itself, which is the last name in the string. So the document address here points to a web page on the WWW server of the College of Literature, Science, and the Arts at the University of Michigan, and it's in a folder named *ecb.* The document itself is named *infohighway.html.* This addressing system allows each document to have its own, unique address, so linking them becomes relatively easy.

Ironically, this most brilliant basic concept—the addressing system that allows the Web to work—is virtually invisible to the average user. Sometimes you will start with a URL you've found somewhere, but usually you will arrive at your destination via a search of one kind or another, without ever needing to see a URL.

ACTIVITY 4.5: Getting Started on the WWW

In Part II you'll have a chance to look critically at Web Sites and to analyze (and use) the rhetoric of the Web. Here we just want to find the information you'll need to get to the Web and explore the information there. As usual, there are some basic answers to find:

- Does your institution provide Web access?
- What browsers are available? How do you obtain them? How do you install them or otherwise access them?
- Do you have an ethernet, PPP, or SLIP connection, so that you can use a graphical browser?
- How do you connect from class, a public computing site, your dorm or home?
- Are there workshops on using the WWW? How do you sign up?
- What instructions, documentation, and so on, is available for the Web and for the browsers your institution recommends?

ACTIVITY 4.6: Searches

Once you've found the information in Activity One, you're ready to open your browser and explore. When you launch the browser, you'll start at a "homepage." It may be your institution's homepage, Mosaic's or Netscape's homepage, or some other variation that has been set locally, by the folks who provide the browser. At any rate, links will be there, and you'll have access to common search engines, often just by clicking a button.

1. First, just browse for a while. Look at some documents. Select some links. Follow some paths that interest you. Become familiar with the "look and feel" of the Web and your browser.
2. Find the Web search engines (Lycos, Yahoo!, WebCrawler, etc.). Most graphic browsers will let you access search engines through a pull-down menu or a button on the screen. If yours won't, then try these URLs:

   To get to Lycos:

   ```
   http://www.lycos.com/
   ```

   To get to Yahoo!:

   ```
   http://www.yahoo.com/
   ```

Then follow the directions and search, more or less as you did in the section on Gopher. Most search engines provide an FAQ list or directions in some other form. Read those carefully to see what the engine searches and how to define the terms for your search.

The page here is Netscape's "Net Search" page, located at the address you see in the "Netsite" line in the status area above the actual Web page. Here are the many search engines you can use, and Yahoo! is featured. Note that Yahoo!, like many others, allows searching by keyword, Boolean techniques, and subject area. Also note that the underlined, different-colored words represent the links. Click once on one of these words, and you will call that document; the Web page at that address will download to your machine, and you will view it on your screen. Find out how to access these search engines on your Web browser. Then see whether you can find information relevant to the next paper you have due in any of your classes. Start using the Web as the information resource it is!

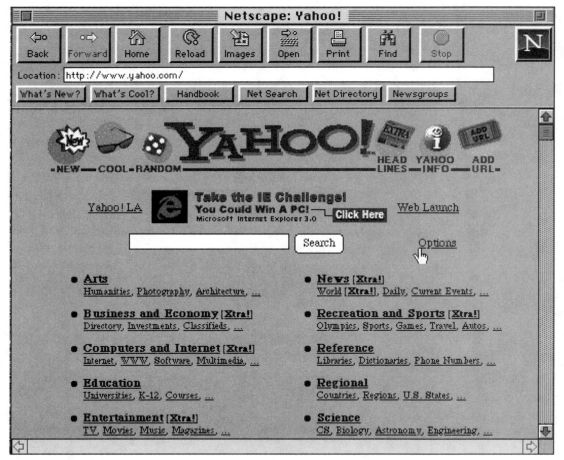

Netscape Communications, the Netscape Communications logo, Netscape, and Netscape Navigator are trademarks of Netscape Communications Corporation.

5

CONSTRUCTING TEXTS ON-LINE

THE DOCUVERSE: PART II

The availability of the extensive, varied resources of the World Wide Web brings us full circle, in a way, back to manipulating text, except that the kinds of text we will think about in this chapter are texts writers construct and share on-line, using the Internet as the medium for and the delivery of the text. As writing tools evolve, the Internet becomes more and more a site for writing. Writers can collaborate by sending texts back and forth, of course. In addition, the advent of the World Wide Web has created a virtual workspace where writers not only can give others access to their documents but also collaborate, with as large a group of other writers as they wish, in constructing documents. Moreover, hypertext markup language (HTML) provides a means of linking these individual documents—giving the reader the ability to jump from one to another with the click of a mouse—so that the individual document changes, in effect, because of its juxtaposition with other documents. This section discusses the world of on-line texts that writers can explore and participate in, using, again, constantly evolving tools.

Activity	Common Applications	Special Considerations
• Writing on the World Wide Web	• Plain text word processors • word processors with HTML filters • HTML editors	• Graphic design of Web pages • Rhetoric of the page • Juxtaposition of pages; montage • Rhetorical effect of links on page

Before we get very far, we need to set some parameters, some limits, for this chapter. First, the Web is a large and continually changing place, so we'll focus on giving you a sense of it, rather than writing on and on about specific features that will have been replaced by newer, better tools by the time you read this page. Second, composing on the Web is also a complex activity, though it's becoming simpler all the time. So, again, we'll focus on the principles involved, point you toward some good tools, and let you find out the specifics as you go. Finally, the one thing that won't change (for a while, at least) on the Web is its basic structure, its hypertextual nature. That has a set of constraints that are quite different from the word-processing concerns with which we began Part I. Here we can begin to think about the rhetoric of the Web, even as the Web itself is still taking shape.

If you have not yet read the World Wide Web section at the end of Chapter 4, this would be a good time to do so and to work through the activities. That section can give you an introduction to using the Web as a resource. Learning how the Web works and how to navigate it will provide a good foundation for beginning to construct Web pages yourself.

BACKGROUND: CHANGE IS CONSTANT (AND FAST!)

In 1989, Tim Berners-Lee, a researcher at the Particle Physics Lab in Geneva, proposed a hypertext-based system that would allow researchers to share documents over the Internet. Two years later, in 1991, the system was brought into being there. In 1992, the CERN lab's Web browser (one of those line-mode browsers we deplored in Chapter 4) went onto an FTP server. By January 1993, there were fifty Web servers. That number increased tenfold in just nine months.

Rapid change is the norm on the Web. Consider the fact that the very best book about the Web, December and Randall's *The World Wide Web Unleashed* (©1994), praises Mosaic, the first major graphic Web browser but does not mention Netscape, the browser that, just one year later, claims 80 percent of the market! So what we write here, if we get too specific, will be out of date by the time you read it. We can, though, focus on developing a sense of the Web's structure, of the way it works, that will help you as you move into this new medium for communication.

First, the Web operates on the Internet, and for the most part, it does for the Internet what the Macintosh did for the personal computer. That is, the Web covers up the complexity of the Internet, smoothes over the difficulties inherent in using FTP, Telnet, and other mainframe-based programs and services. In the mid-1980s, Apple's Macintosh showed the world that almost anyone could use a computer. Its object-oriented graphical user interface (GUI) and its point-and-click mouse technology made computers much more accessible to far more people. Similarly, the Web simplifies the process of navigating on the Internet and finding and retrieving resources there. This basic factor is exploited further by the graphical browsers, like Mosaic and Netscape, that bring point-and-click methodology to the Internet. People like that. They'll use it. With a graphical interface, the Internet becomes user-friendly, and users are flocking to it.

Second, the Web uses hypertext. Whereas Gopher provides a linkage among seemingly endless numbers of tables of contents, the Web links actual documents. Readers can reach these documents easily, often by merely clicking on a word or phrase on the screen. In the days of FTP, WAIS, even Gopher, the Internaut had to know a little about UNIX, the operating system of choice for linking computers together and for multitasking. UNIX is complicated, and the procedures require more effort, energy, and memory than the average computer user will expend. Not so on the Web. Navigation is easy. Readers don't have to remember file names or URLs. They can click on the results of searches or browse their way through documents until they find what interests them or use their browsers to set "bookmarks," so that they can always get back to locations they use frequently.

Third, the Web is a multimedia environment. It is grounded in text, of course, but a Web page is also a graphical document. And the ability to incorporate sound, animation, and full-motion video creates a medium that is potentially much more powerful than plain text. We suppose, instead of coming back around to manipulating text, as we suggested earlier, we've spiraled upward, so that we are exploring text as amplified by these other resources.

What does all this mean? The fact that the Web acts as a kind of GUI for the Internet means that the Web is everywhere—hence the name World Wide Web. The fact that the Web is hypertextual means that readers can navigate easily, as long as writers do their job by presenting intelligible links from document to document. And the fact that the Web is a multimedia environment means that its potential impact on readers is far greater than conventional printed text. If a picture is worth a thousand words, then how many words might a well-constructed Web page count for—one with pictures, sound, and video to reinforce, illustrate, and amplify the text?

COMPOSING ON THE WEB: THE BASICS

Webspinners use hypertext markup language (HTML) to construct documents that incorporate the kinds of resources we discussed previously and that link to other documents on the Internet. Presently, composing in HTML is fairly difficult, even with some of the HTML editors that have begun to appear. The concept, however, is simple. You take a page of plain text—ASCII text—and mark it up, much as an old-style printer might have marked up a document to set it in an appropriate typeface and format. HTML uses "tags," strings of characters that change the appearance of text or that serve some other function within the text but that do not show up on the finished page. Let's take a look at a portion of a fairly uncomplicated Web page:

Wayne Butler's Homepage

A Little Bit about Me

I was born on the 4th of July in 1957 in New York City. I grew up in the Mid-Hudson valley, about 50 miles north of the city. After high school it took me a couple of years to find my calling, so to speak, as I attended community college, worked as a travel agent, a stage hand at the Metropolitan Opera house, a cook in both diners and "fine" restaurants, and a waiter at various other establishments. By 1979 I had earned a bachelors degree in English Education at SUNY Oneonta in upstate NY. Upon graduation I toured Europe for three months, spending a significant part of that time exploring Joyce's Ireland and Hemingway's Spain. Upon my return I began teaching English at a suburban NY high school (Nyack) and then a middle school (Scarsdale). I embarked on my next journey when I accepted a teaching job at the American School in Mexico City. During the two years I lived in Mexico, I wrote poetry and fiction, climbed pyramids, did a little community theater, and collected masks and folk art. I also met my wife.

My desire to get an MA led me to Austin, TX, where I enrolled in the English Education program at the University of Texas, was first introduced to computers, worked in the University of Texas's English Department Computer Research Lab, and fell in with a crew of grad students and faculty members who would eventually dub themselves The Daedalus Group. I also became a father of a daughter and a son. In 1992 I earned a Ph.D. in English Education at the University of Texas. Upon the completion of my doctorate, I was hired by the English Composition Board at the University of Michigan.

Now let's take a look at the HTML version, the ASCII text and the tags that make the page look the way it does:

```
<HTML>
<HEAD>
<TITLE>Wayne Butler's Home Page</TITLE>
</HEAD>
<BODY>
<I><H1>Wayne Butler's Homepage</H1></I>

<IMG SRC="http://www-pcd.stanford.edu/gifs/line.rainbow.gif"><P>

<IMG SRC="Wayne.GIF"><H2>A Little Bit about Me</H2>

I was born on the 4th of July in 1957 in <A HREF =
"http://www.mediabridge.com/nyc/">New York City</A>. I grew up in the
Mid-Hudson valley, about 50 miles north of the city. After high school it
took me a couple of years to find my calling, so to speak, as I attended
community college, worked as a travel agent, a stage hand at the Metropolitan
Opera house, a cook in both diners and "fine" restaurants, and a waiter at
various other establishments. By 1979 I had earned a bachelors degree in
English Education at <A HREF = "http://137.141.153.38/">SUNY Oneonta</A>
in upstate NY. Upon graduation I toured Europe for three months, spending
a significant part of that time exploring Joyce's <A HREF =
"http://www.ieunet.ie/ois/iis/irish.html">Ireland</A> and Hemingway's
<A HREF = "http://sol.des.fi.udc.es/">Spain</A>. Upon my return I began
teaching English at a suburban NY high school (Nyack) and then a middle school
(Scarsdale). I embarked on my next journey when I accepted a teaching job at
the American School in Mexico City. During the two years I lived in
<A HREF = "http://info.pue.udlap.mx/mexico.html">Mexico</A>, I wrote poetry
and fiction, climbed pyramids, did a little community theater, and collected
masks and folk art. I also met my wife.<P>

My desire to get an MA led me to <A HREF =
"http://www.quadralay.com/www/Austin/Austin.html">Austin</A>, TX, where I
enrolled in the English Education program at the University of Texas, was
first introduced to computers, worked in the <A HREF =
"http://www.en.utexas.edu/">University of Texas's English Department Computer
Research Lab</A>, and fell in with a crew of grad students and faculty members
who would eventually dub themselves <A HREF = "http://daedalus.com/"> The
Daedalus Group</A>. I also became a father of a daughter and a son. In 1992
I earned a Ph.D.in English Education at the University of Texas. Upon the
completion of my doctorate, I was hired by the English Composition Board at
the University of Michigan.<P>

<IMG SRC = "http://www-pcd.stanford.edu/gifs/line.rainbow.gif"><P>
```

Text inside the < > is a *tag*. Tags are like switches. The first one turns a function on. For example, <H1> creates a large, boldfaced heading. The second tag turns off the function, so </H1> turns off the heading style and takes the text back to the default font, which for most Web pages is twelve-point Times. Some tags, such as boldface, headings, underlining, italics, and links (like <A HREF = "http://137.141.153.38/">SUNY Oneonta</A>), need both an "on" and an "off" switch. Others, such as paragraph breaks (<p>), only need one switch. In effect, they turn themselves off.

In the early days of word processing, tags were necessary to get the features we now take for granted as easy. Underlining, italics, boldface, changes in margins, centering text, changes in typeface—all these and more had to be accomplished by inserting tags into the text. All that changed with the advent of WYSIWYG (what you see is what you get) word processors. We expect that the same thing will happen with HTML. A couple of years ago, the only way to write HTML was to learn the tags and work in an ASCII word processor like SimpleText. Already, though, HTML editors allow us to insert tags automatically. Although they don't produce a WYSIWYG document, they do ease the process of constructing a Web page. Sooner or later, the capabilities of Web publishing will stop expanding exponentially, and we'll all be working with a stable set of tags and other devices. Within five years, then, HTML editors will probably allow for WYSISYG Web page construction, because the editors will evolve in much the same way as word processors, responding to similar pressures from Webspinners.

In the meantime, constructing a Web page is not too difficult, especially if you have access to a graphic browser and an HTML editor, many of which are available via FTP as freeware or shareware. Here is a list of several good editors that are available as we write this book:

    HTML Web Weaver
    HTML.edit
    HTML_Editor
    HTML_Pro
    simple-html-editor

As you read this book, however, you'll want to launch your Web browser and initiate a search, using the keywords "HTML editor." That search should lead you to several of the latest editors, which you can download with the click of a link.

Another simple way to create a page is to find one with features and a layout you like, and then use your browser's **View Source** command to copy the page, tags and all. Then you can simply substitute your own textual information and graphics. Finally, many word processors now offer HTML translators, so that you can easily convert word-processed documents into HTML. Although these translators are not very good today, by the time you read this, they may well be very solid and easy to use. Either of these techniques can provide a head start, at least—a way to avoid having to start from nothing. Then you can develop your pages as you learn more about HTML.

DESIGN

However you develop your Web pages, the main point to remember is that these documents are *visual* as well as textual. You still have to think like a writer, of course, but you also have to think like a printer. Lay the page out in your mind as you would a page in a magazine or a book that includes graphics. Where will you place the headers? Where will the chunks of text be most effective? How much "white space" will you need to set off text and graphics well? How will you divide your text up into chunks (the chunks may or may not be paragraphs) that help a reader both understand your point and see the organization of the information you present?

In addition, think about the rhetoric of the page. Just as E-mail operates by the screenful, the Web operates by the page. Readers can scroll, of course, so the page is potentially endless. However, readers don't necessarily like to scroll and scroll. Instead, they'd generally rather read one page and then jump to another page. So think about how your information breaks into larger chunks that you could present discretely, on separate pages that are linked at appropriate points. Then readers can find out as much as they want to. They can stop after reading the general information on your home page, for instance, or they can follow the links there to get more detailed information. Or they can follow links to other pages, where they may find out more about where your ideas originated. If printed books were hypertextual, we'd have a link for *The World Wide Web Unleashed,* because that book has affected our thinking about the Web. We'd also have links to Wayne Butler's Writing the Information Superhighway courses, because they acted as a kind of laboratory for this book. We can't do that, though, because books aren't hypertextual. But the Web is, and you can and should make links like that.

The Effects of Links

In effect, the Web is a literal representation of the fact that our thoughts, values, beliefs, and actions exist in a context, in a web of culture, society, family, school, and so forth. Linking our documents to others, then, helps us demonstrate how our ideas originated, what they have in common with the ideas of others, and how they may lead to new connections.

Links also have a simpler but no less significant effect. Links can bring far-distant documents together and put them next to each other in cyberspace, so that readers move from one to the other. This aspect of Web construction means that your web is a montage of pages. Some of the pages are your own, but some belong to other Webspinners. Your links bring your work into contact with theirs, and the connection creates meaning. You might, for example, create one link to a neo-Nazi Web Site containing claims that the Holocaust never happened. Then you could create another link to a Web Site associated with the Holocaust Museum in Washington, D.C. Placing those Web pages next to each other raises questions and issues that neither site raises by itself. The juxtaposition allows readers to compare assertions and evidence at both sites and to draw conclusions that you may not have to explain in your own text, because the conclusions will be self-evident. Linkages mean something, so you should think carefully about what links you make.

Design Resources on the Web

As always, the best resource the Web has to offer is its searchability. So run a search to look for the latest information on HTML basics and home-page style sheets. New information and new capabilities are emerging almost daily, so although the principles we've laid out here remain constant, the tools develop very quickly.

ACTIVITY 5.1: Your Own Homepage?

Before you can begin to construct your own homepage, you need some information (surprise!). So, singly or collectively, find the answers to the following questions (these are in addition to the questions in the Web section of Chapter 6):

- Does your institution provide a server on which you can place your homepage?
- Does your institution provide classes or workshops in HTML, constructing Web pages, and so forth?
- How can you gain access to a good HTML editing program on your campus?
- What instructions or documentation does your institution provide to help you construct your own Web pages?
- How can you (or *can* you) access these resources from class, public sites, dorm room, or home?

In Part II, you'll have more opportunities to think about and develop your own Web pages. The information here should be enough to enable you to begin; later on, you'll explore the possibilities in greater depth.

PART II

WRITING PROJECTS FOR THE INFORMATION AGE

Chapter 6
Assessing Writing

Chapter 7
Building Community On-Line

Chapter 8
Tales of Cyberspace

Chapter 9
Writing to Analyze

Chapter 10
Writing about Issues: Analysis and Argument

Chapter 11
Writing in the Disciplines

Chapter 12
Writing for the World Wide Web

Learning to write in a traditional writing course and learning to write in a computer-based course share certain qualities. To start with, the main goals are similar—to help you develop the necessary skills, habits, and techniques to master the various types of writing you might be expected to produce first in your academic lives and then in your professional lives. So, in both traditional and computer-based settings, you will need to learn concepts such as audience—who may read the texts and what are those readers' needs—and purposes such as explanation, analysis, and argumentation. In both settings, also, you will learn elements of style and which styles are most appropriate for which audiences and purposes. You will also need to learn the mechanics of punctuation and grammar usage. But on-line writing and communication are changing how knowledge is produced and learned in school and how people communicate in the workplace. So, although the general goals remain the same, the means have been altered.

In the computer-based writing community, your texts and social interaction remain at the center of the learning activities, but the mode of communication is computer mediated, which makes all the difference. Whereas in the traditional classroom you have to meet face to face to hold oral conversations about drafts or to exchange drafts and written feedback, in the virtual writing community, much of the social interaction can be conducted through computer-mediated communication (CMC). The very fact that you, your peers, and your writing teacher need not meet face to face to handle the logistics of collaborative learning creates opportunities to think of alternative ways of using class time to learn how to write effectively. And such changes in the ways you interact with your peers and your teacher also imply different roles and responsibilities for those who participate in virtual writing communities.

How you might learn how to write in virtual writing communities is not the only aspect of your education affected by virtual writing communities. What you write in cyberspace and how you write are also different. Writing courses typically focus on a number of genres (i.e., narration, exposition, argumentation), in various school activities such as using writing as a way to learn a topic or demonstrate knowledge. And the written products themselves are fairly predictable. For example, assignments in typical introductory composition classes will require you to produce five- to ten-*page* essays that conform to some acceptable academic standard as outlined, for example, by the Modern Language Association (MLA) or the American Psychological Association (APA). Such papers are typically double-spaced on 8½" × 11" paper, and the final product must employ traditional notions of unity, coherence, logical development; demonstrate an academically acceptable style; and use "correct" grammar and punctuation.

Communicating and learning to communicate in cyberspace share most of the goals, techniques, genres, and purposes of traditional writing and writing instruction. But as cyberspace matures and takes shape, new purposes for and forms of writing are developing. As a literate culture, we are entering a transitional phase. Most of us still need to know how to produce traditional, linear texts that would be easily recognized by any of our ancestors during the last five hundred years. On the other hand, some of us, and soon most, will need to learn how to communicate in ways made possible by the Internet. We will still need to be aware of our readers, our audience, but because of the immediate and broad "publishing" of electronic texts, our audiences are potentially wider and more diverse than those we might have written for when one could better predict who might read our texts. We will still need to be aware of purpose because we will still need to use writing as a way of learning, we will still need to inform or teach our readers something, we will still need to analyze the world around us, and we will still need to write persuasively to represent ourselves in civic discourse. And we will still need to use appropriately a range of styles that will best promote our purposes and connect with our audiences. How we will do all these things will change.

Our audiences will grow and become more diverse as we communicate in virtual communities in E-mail groups, on bulletin boards, and in newsgroups and as we "publish" on the World Wide Web. These readers, who will read on-line, will have neither the time nor the endurance to work through long documents. If an extended argument or analysis is to be offered and read, it cannot be a linear text for a reader to scroll through but rather a hypertextual document. And the form of communication need not—nay, will not—be mere text but will also include graphics, audio, and video, or what today we call *hypermedia*.

Despite all the publicity about the information superhighway, the majority of the world will not become totally hypermedia literate or dependent for at least another generation and, in all probability, not for several generations. While we are in this transitional phase, therefore, we cannot live by the expression, "Out with the old, in with the new." Instead, we will be better served to think of writing in cyberspace as yet another writing situation in which we need to consider the relationships among audience, purpose, style, and media.

The following set of writing projects are designed and arranged in a way that will lead you, your classmates, and your teacher—a community of writers—through community-building activities, introduce you to the information superhighway, and guide you through more and more sophisticated writing genres and media by writing both about and for the information superhighway and by using the resources of the Internet to write documents typically required in writing courses. Note our conscious use of the term *projects* instead of *activities* or *essays. Activity,* for example, can be construed to mean something that happens once and in isolation, often serving more as a lesson or an exercise (in much the way the activities in earlier chapters functioned). *Essays, papers, or themes,* traditional terms most associated with what you might produce in writing courses, tend to emphasize on the product—the thing. Both *activity* and any one of the terms synonymous with *paper* fail, we believe, to accurately label all the work that goes into generating a final product. For this reason, we prefer the term *project*.

A project is something that occurs over a period of time, one that requires planning and organization, time management, and formative evaluation—that is, evaluation of how the project is going while it is in progress. A *writing project,* too, should be considered a series of activities that lead up to a *text.* A writing project involves an invention process, one that might include social activities such as verbal or electronic brainstorming. The invention stage might also include engaging in some general background reading, a process that might very well, as we will suggest later, include writing about what you have read as a way of reflecting, evaluating, and recording your thoughts. Perhaps at some moment while you are talking through your ideas with peers, lurking on newsgroups, or participating in MOOs, you begin composing your text. You might freewrite for a while to see what you know and don't know about your topic and your perspective. You might then write a reflection, one separate from the formal text on which you are working, in which you reevaluate your purpose, analyze your intended audience, and conduct an internal monologue about what you have completed and where you need to go next. You might then compose a more thorough draft of the text in progress and share that with other writers in your class or somewhere on the Internet. Because of the cooperative pact you enter into with writers from whom you seek feedback, you also read and compose a written critique of their work in progress. After receiving and giving feedback, you might reflect again, in writing, on what you learned from the formative evaluation offered by your readers before you return to compose a version of your draft.

Finally, because the projects are arranged from the simplest to the more complicated in terms of both the genre and the type of media required, writing community leaders could conceivably use the assignments in the order represented throughout the rest of Part II as the basis of an entire course. We encourage teachers to adapt the projects in accordance to the technological realities of their settings.

6

ASSESSING WRITING

Why are you here, reading this book, taking this course? Why, to improve your writing, you say. And, perhaps, to learn more about using computers. Well, you're partially correct. Half credit for those answers. We want to suggest a more important reason. We want you to think for a bit about assessment.

Here is the critical statement, the provocative assertion we have in mind:

> If you leave this course dependent on the teacher to tell you what your writing needs, then this course has failed in its mission.

No writing course can be effective in helping you improve your writing if it does not, at the same time, equip you to know, yourself, what you need to do to make a piece of writing better, more effective, more communicative, more complete. You cannot accomplish those goals alone, and you are unlikely to accomplish them by writing for and communicating solely with a teacher. You need audiences—readers. You need to participate in a community of readers, one that will let you know when your writing communicates and when it does not, one that will tell you when you've answered the kinds of questions readers ask when they read, and one that will tell you when your writing meets the community's expectations for style, usage, and correctness.

This chapter, then, focuses on three principal objectives:

- Using computers to help individual writers self-assess
- Using computers to help develop and understand community standards
- Using computers to demystify the process of evaluation and grading and to make that process both rigorous and fair

SELF-ASSESSMENT

During this course, you will make several specific pieces of your writing better, clearer, more effective. As you do this, you should also develop some strategies, some techniques, for assessing any piece of your prose so that you can make that piece of writing serve its purpose for its intended audience and thereby reflect well on you as its writer. So, as you participate in peer review, of whatever kind, you need to develop an awareness of the key factors that have positive or negative effects on readers. Then you can steer your own prose toward the positive factors and away from the negative ones. Participating in activities that help define community standards for effective writing helps you develop your own "ear," your own sense of when and where you need to improve a piece of writing.

As we said earlier, a writing course is effective only insofar as it promotes sound self-assessment practices. What are those practices? They'll differ from one context to another, but in general they include at least these three elements:

- *Process.* developing a writing process or, better still, a set of processes that can serve you well in writing for different purposes, for different audiences, on different occasions, in different contexts
- *Consultation.* how to seek help from others, as well as how to give help to others
- *Re-vision.* seeing a piece as if you had not written it, gaining what some people call *critical distance*

We'll focus, in this part of this chapter, on how to use computer technology to develop these elements.

Process

Chapter 1 on word processing contains many suggestions for using computers to influence your composing process. Some of the strategies there will undoubtedly be useful. As you evaluate those possibilities, you might conduct a quick self-study of your composing processes by typing the following questions into a word-processing file and then writing answers to them.

ACTIVITY 6.1: Guidelines for Self-Assessment

1. What kinds of writing do I typically do?
2. To what audiences do I typically write?
3. Why do I write?
4. Where do I get the information for my different kinds of writing?
5. When I write, how do I typically begin?
6. What do I do next? How do I proceed from there? What are the steps, stages, or phases in my writing process?

7. How do those steps, stages, or phases recur as I write a draft or move from first to final draft?
8. When do I typically begin a writing project?
9. Do I like to share my thoughts and drafts with others? If so, with whom?
10. How many drafts, on the average, do I write?
11. What do I usually change from one draft to the next?
12. How do I know when a piece of writing is finished?
13. With what parts of my writing process am I most satisfied? Why?
14. With what parts of my writing process am I least satisfied? Why?
15. In what ways do I want to change my writing process?
16. How will I begin those changes?

Now look back at the activities and heuristics in Chapter 1 to find particular strategies that seem to fit with and support the process you've outlined in the notes. In addition, think about ways computers can help you carry out the plan you laid out in questions 12–15.

Consultation

Knowing how to give and receive assistance with writing may be the most valuable skill you can develop. As you move into a career, chances are that you'll work in teams, collaborating on projects that result in presentations or written reports, memos, and so forth. Even when you work alone, you'll find that your writing is more effective—and so brings more credit to your performance—if you seek advice from peers or supervisors along the way, before the final product is ready for distribution. Finally, if you can become the person others consult about their writing, then you will be indispensable to the office—virtually layoff-proof! Studies show that only the person who knows all about the company's computer system is less likely to fall victim to "downsizing." (After this course, you could be both those people!)

Learning to give and to receive assistance with writing means heeding some general guidelines about conduct and interpersonal relations, and it means developing some specific strategies—some questions to ask, some factors to consider, and so forth.

Guidelines for Seeking and Giving Help in Writing

1. In general, whether you are on the seeking or the receiving end, *say nothing that you would not want said to you.* This does not mean that you cannot be critical or that you have to give only positive feedback. Writers appreciate constructive criticism. They don't appreciate a put-down. So couch criticism in terms of improvement. You can say, "This part really stinks," or you can say, "I think this part would be better if. . . ." Which would *you* rather hear?

2. *Respond as a reader, not as a judge.* You can say, "This sentence is not very clear," or you can say, "I didn't understand what you meant to say in this sentence. Can you explain it to me?" Which would you rather hear? Which response is more likely to lead to improvement?

3. *Ask questions rather than state objections.* Asking a question is less confrontational (see point 1), and questions lead writers to explain what they meant, what they were trying to accomplish. Questions are more likely to lead to improved writing.

4. *Work* with *the writer rather than against the writer.* Always position yourself as teammate, as someone who is working along with the writer to help produce more effective writing. Be supportive of the writer, even when you have to be critical of the writing.

5. *Offer clear advice, or ask clear, specific questions.* Writers get more help if they can focus readers' attention on known problem areas. This strategy gives the reader permission to criticize, and it gets her talking about the writing. Once you start a reader talking, it's easier to keep her talking. Similarly, when you are a reader, offer specific advice. Writers may like to hear you say you like their writing, but if a writer has come to you for advice, you should be sure to suggest ways the writer can help you understand what he has written, and you should be sure that the writer understands what you are saying. Specific questions and specific advice serve to focus the exchange on the writing and to help the writer find ways to improve the writing.

6. *Be supportive.* Find something to praise. In fact, try to balance negative comments with positives. The praise will help the writer listen to the criticisms.

7. *Remember which of you is the writer.* As the saying goes, keep the *author* in authority. No matter how tempting, don't just rewrite the piece for the writer (exception: if you're working on a team project, then you are also the writer, so have at it). No learning is involved in that, and if you make a habit of being an in-house editor rather than an in-house peer tutor, you'll quickly become swamped with work.

ACTIVITY 6.2: Seeking Help with a Draft

In Chapter 2 on communicating one-on-one, Activity 2.3 sets out a useful process for seeking a response from a reader via E-mail. Turn to that exercise now, and send a draft to a reader, so that you and your classmates can begin to put these principles into action. You'll find that as you respond to your classmates' writing, you learn more about what readers need; in other words, as you become a better reader yourself, you'll also learn how to satisfy readers like you. And as you receive input from readers, you'll begin to find specific areas in your own writing where you can do a better job of addressing readers' needs; that is, when readers consistently misunderstand some of the ways you write, you'll begin to change those ways so that readers *can* understand you.

Re-vision

Everything this chapter has led you to think about contributes to your ability to revise your own writing—to see what needs changing and to make those changes. Revision—*re-vision*—is the way we make our writing better, in both senses. Revision makes a specific piece of writing better, and the learning we do as we revise makes us better writers.

ACTIVITY 6.3: Questioning Your Own Assumptions

Part of the process of revising is to look at your writing as if it were new to you, to gain a kind of critical distance that allows you to judge your own work in light of what you know to be the standards by which others will judge it. Computers are particularly useful in revision, because they offer easy ways to ask new questions about the text. As you read through your draft, you can easily insert questions, in a different typeface or type style, for example, focusing on the following general questions:

What do you think you know?
How do you think you know it?

Test your own ideas, in other words, as if you were a reader approaching them for the first time. The first question, "What do you think you know?" will help you identify your assertions, your claims. The second, "How do you think you know it?" will help you locate the ways you've supported your assertions, provided evidence for your claims, or incorporated information that helps a reader understand why the reader should value your ideas.

This part of revision is largely mental, and it is hardly technology dependent. However, the computer can help you see your text anew. You can literally change the physical appearance of your text in ways that help you see problems that you might miss if you were merely reading over the same old text, in the same old shape. In short, computers support revision. They cannot revise for you, because they cannot read and evaluate your text for you. But they can support ways of seeing your text that, like the move from screen to paper, help you perceive ways to change your text. This is particularly true in the final stages of revision, when you are most concerned with whether your text obeys the conventions of standard written English. Here are some more suggestions that can help you find errors that have escaped your notice during earlier stages of composing and revising the text.

ACTIVITY 6.4: Changing the Shape of Your Text

Use your word processor's Find/Replace function to insert two carriage returns after each sentence. This will create a copy of your file in which each sentence appears on a new line, with a blank line between each.

You'll be able to see the sentences individually, in sequence, so you'll be able to check everything from whether the sequence is correct, to whether the sentences are complete and correctly punctuated, to whether you've used varied sentence patterns and lengths.

How-To

Consult your word processor's manual or **Help** files to find out how to use the **Find/Replace** function and how to enter the special character for a carriage return. Tell the computer to **find** each period that is followed by two spaces. (This approach assumes that you are following the convention of putting two spaces after each period that ends a sentence, and only one after other periods, i.e., those that follow abbreviations, etc.) Then tell it to **replace** the period and two spaces with a period and two carriage returns. (Here you'll have to use the special character for a carriage return, because if you simply hit the <Return> key, it will start the **Find/Replace** process.) Macintoshes, IBMs and compatibles, and UNIX workstations, and their different word-processing applications, all will require slightly different processes and different commands to complete this operation. Here is an illustration of how the **Find/Replace** dialog box looks in Microsoft Word™ 5.1 on a Macintosh computer (Note: you can't see them, but two spaces appear after the period in the "Find What" box; ^p is MS Word's special character for <Return>):

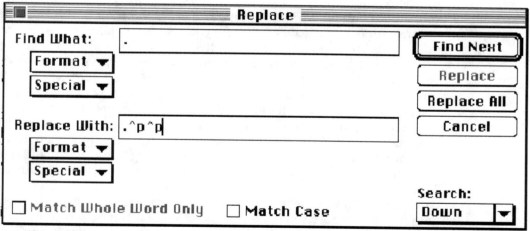

Screen shot reprinted with permission from Microsoft Corporation.

This process will turn the paragraph above the graphic into one that looks like this:

```
Consult your word processor's manual or Help files to find out how to
use the Find/Replace function and how to enter the special character
for a carriage return.
```

Tell the computer to **Find** each period that is followed by two spaces.

(This approach assumes that you are following the convention of putting two spaces after each period that ends a sentence and only one after other periods, i.e., those that follow abbreviations, etc.).

Then tell it to **replace** the period and two spaces with a period and two carriage returns.

(Here you'll have to use the special character for a carriage return, since if you simply hit the <Return> key, it will start the **Find/Replace** process.)

Macintoshes, IBMs and compatibles, and UNIX workstations, and their different word-processing applications, all will require different processes and different commands to complete this operation.

Here is an illustration of how the **Find/Replace** dialog box looks in Microsoft Word 5.1 on a Macintosh computer.

(Note: you can't see them, but two spaces appear after the period in the "Find What" box; ^p is MS Word's special character for <Return>):

As you can readily see, the passage uses sentences of various kinds and lengths, and reading each sentence for completeness and correctness is easier to do than it is when they are run together in paragraph form. Once you have completed the proofreading exercise, you can simply reverse the process. Again, call up the **Find/Replace** function. This time tell it to **Find** a period followed by two carriage returns and **Replace** it with a period followed by two spaces. Then, with the click of a button or a depressing of the <Return> key, the set of sentences will again become a paragraph.

ACTIVITY 6.5: Changing the Look of Your Text

Change the font and/or font size in the whole piece, so that the words literally look different and appear in different places on the page. Even this small a change can make you look at the piece more objectively—the first step in re-vision.

How-To

Select (highlight) all the text in your essay. Then follow the directions for changing fonts and font sizes in your word processor.

ACTIVITY 6.6: Changing the Way You Read Your Text

Scroll to the bottom of your text and read it backward, sentence by sentence, to check for errors. This is best done near the end of your writing process, but it's an invaluable aid to proofreading, especially if you have a history of making mistakes that you really do know how to correct—if you can find them before your reader (or your teacher) does.

ACTIVITY 6.7: Multiple Columns

Every full-functioning word processor allows you to reformat a document so that it prints out in multiple columns. This function helps make newsletters and brochures look more professional. You can use it to force yourself to see your text differently—literally. You'll have to find out how to format columns in your word processor (in Microsoft Word for the Macintosh, you'd use the **Format** menu and select the **Section** option; then you'd be able to specify a number of columns). Once you've done that, you can print your document in two or three columns, and you'll be surprised at how different the text looks and at how this simple change allows you to gain some critical distance as you read through your own writing. (If your word processor does not allow you to print in multiple columns, you can gain a similar effect by just selecting the whole text and narrowing the margins so that the essay prints in a column three or four inches wide.)

As you become more adept at word processing, at manipulating text on a computer screen, you will undoubtedly discover more tricks for helping you organize what you want to say. The computer offers many variations on the suggestions we've made here, all of which help you see your text anew—at a distance, so to speak.

When you can achieve a kind of critical distance from your own writing, you can more easily see it as a reader will see it. This kind of *re-vision* helps you discover ways to communicate more effectively with your reader, persuade your reader, or help your reader identify with you. Use the computer's functions to help you literally see your text in new and different ways.

All the tools described earlier can help you see how to improve your own writing—to self-assess. These tools provide mechanisms that allow you to gain some critical distance from your writing and see how you might make that writing more effective. The next step in developing as a writer is to begin to realize and understand what readers expect from you as a result of the community we all belong to. That community may be a class, a business, a town, a club, or even just you and a correspondent. However large or small your community of readers may be (and over your life as a writer, you'll belong to many, many such communities), your writing will be more effective if you attend to the standards that community sets, whether those standards are implicit or explicit.

COMMUNITY STANDARDS

All communities have standards and codes of behavior. Our notions of common courtesy and etiquette come from community standards, for example. These rules extend to the ways community members communicate with each other (it's no accident that the two words share the same root). They determine the accepted forms of communication (letters, telephone calls, E-mail, etc.), and they determine what we could call "thresholds" of communication: the minimums for how much a person has to say and for how well it has to be said for the community to accept the communication as real, much less as significant. These rules differ from situation to situation. Your friend will not care a great deal if your informal letters are not grammatically correct, unless the mistakes interfere with meaning. But if you send a mistake-laden business letter, your correspondent is likely to lose confidence in you. Every writing context has its constraints, and those constraints are set by the community, by the relationships and the values each community expresses.

This special property of communities, together with the fact that in using this book, you will move through activity after activity in which you function as a community, creates opportunities that the class can take advantage of come evaluation time. Given the nature of these tasks and the many built-in occasions for communication, collaboration, and implicit evaluation and revision, students and teachers actually collaborate in developing the means for assessing students' performances on assignments. As you pass work back and forth, and as you work together in groups, you will create a workshop atmosphere. You and your classmates will work together on many projects, and you will give each other feedback that will enable writers to improve their work. That feedback will be based on the collective standards for the class. At first, those standards will be implicit. You'll base them on individual and then collective senses of effective, correct writing, and you'll be guided by your teacher's feedback. Gradually, across all the projects and activities, a collective sense of standards will emerge. Collecting and codifying those standards can be an effective way to assure that grading in the class is both rigorous and fair.

Because the intellectual tasks this text demands are fulfilled in performance, we strongly believe that students should be graded in some kind of performance assessment. This kind of assessment requires the class both to generate criteria and make those criteria accessible to all its members. Here is an activity that can help generate such criteria.

ACTIVITY 6.8: An E-Mail-Based Writer's Workshop

Step 1: Exchanging Drafts

On a predetermined schedule, each class member posts a draft of an essay or other project to the class's E-mail group. Essays could be posted all at once, but the workload from this activity will be more manageable if writers post their essays in turn, spread out over a few weeks. Three writers might post on a Monday, three on a Wednesday, and three more on a Friday, for example, to spread out the work of responding to each essay. Readers can then respond to three essays on Tuesday, three on Thursday, and three over the weekend.

Step 2: Writing Responses

Each class member writes a one-page response to each essay and posts that response to the list. Thus, if the class has twenty-one people in it, each writer will receive twenty pages of feedback about the essay. And over a two- or three-week period, each member of the class will have the opportunity to post an essay and receive this kind of rich feedback. In addition, because everyone reads all the E-mail, class members can easily come to understand the community's standards and use them to improve their own drafts.

Step 3: Developing Criteria

Someone—the teacher or a team of students—reads through all the responses to all the essays and compiles a list of all the significant factors readers attended to in their feedback. Once the factors are listed, they can be arranged into categories in whatever way makes them most intelligible. For a typical essay, you'd expect, at the least, to have several clusters of factors:

- Overall organization and structure
- Organization and structure of the parts (paragraphs, sentences, etc.)
- Completeness (Does the essay contain enough information? Does the writer offer convincing evidence in support of assertions? Has the writer left out information or topics she should have addressed?)
- Voice (Is the writing too formal, too informal, etc.? Can you sense a human being behind the prose?)
- Clarity and fluency, in both language and structure (transitions among sections, paragraphs, sentences; readability; sentence structures that enhance the writer's rhetorical intentions; etc.)
- Significance of content (Does the topic matter? Is the information important? Does the writer show why the topic is significant to readers?)
- Correctness (grammar, mechanics, spelling, word choice, etc.)

Other kinds of writing might yield other categories. Thus, the categories you'd develop for the brochures you'll design in a later chapter may contain different characteristics. The point is to design the characteristics, or dimensions of effective writing, collaboratively, so that they incorporate the community's standards.

Step 4: Evaluating the Criteria

Use the list of dimensions to conduct a paired or small-group peer review of revised essays. Readers examine a revision of the original piece, using the list of dimensions as the basis for feedback. Because this list expresses the community's standards for effective writing, peers can point out where the writing meets, exceeds, or falls short of those standards. Writers will then revise once more in response to this feedback.

Step 5: Revising the Criteria

On E-mail or in a brief class session, the class members revise the dimensions again, in an attempt to make the dimensions as fair a tool for evaluation as possible.

Step 6: Using Criteria for Grading

The teacher uses the edited dimensions to grade the final revisions.

Of course, this activity can work in a traditional classroom as well. The technological version, though, requires less class time and far less paper.

AUTHORITY-CENTERED ASSESSMENT

Once you've finished a piece, the usual procedure is to turn it in for a grade. That means that your teacher will evaluate your performance and give you a grade on it, along with some advice for revision or improvement. Using computers in teaching and learning writing introduces some nontraditional concerns into the writing class, and it can lead to some nontraditional but highly effective methods for assessing performance in a course. Most obviously, students in courses that use computers centrally and extensively read and write more, and they deal with different kinds of text. Electronic mail, hypertext, multimedia documents, Web pages and Web Sites—all these and more introduce a different mix of texts and a different set of criteria by which to judge those texts. The traditional classroom presents few, if any opportunities to assess the following:

- On-line portfolios
- Collaboratively produced texts
- Hypertext and hypermedia documents and portfolios

- Participation in electronic conferences
- The rhetoric of design

All these new phenomena—new kinds of writing or elements of writing that have never been part of college composition—present difficulties for graders of student work. We want to suggest a way of deriving criteria and carrying out a process of evaluation that takes advantage of the amount of information the computer can bring to the writer and of the ways in which computers, thoughtfully employed, can foster collaboration and community. Here, then, is a kind of template exercise, an adaptation of the E-mail-based writer's workshop activity we presented earlier in this chapter, where we suggested some alternatives for deriving criteria for grading. Steps 5 and 6 address one way of translating community standards into grading criteria. We'd like to take a few pages now to suggest some more alternatives to standard grading practices.

ACTIVITY 6.9: Developing a Portfolio Method for Evaluation

This activity addresses grading by portfolio, but it could be applied to any new *kind* of document. It is especially useful as a means of grading documents that contain new elements—graphics, video, sound, and so forth. These new kinds of compositions, like portfolios, have more *parts* than traditional essays do, and the parts fit together in different ways. When teachers decide, alone, how to assess these new forms, we often miss important elements. Involving students' voices in the assessment process makes a great deal of sense. The students have had to figure out how to produce the documents, and so the students may be able to bring hidden factors to light—if the teacher simply asks!

Sample Portfolio Process

What follows is a sample portfolio-based evaluation process. Your class can adapt this process to fit the kinds of text you will produce, or you can refer to Chapter 12, where we guide you through the process of constructing a portfolio on the World Wide Web.

Step 1: Assigning the Portfolio

This class has two major foci. In writing about technology, in thinking about your own and your classmates' experiences as writers using computers and networks, and in writing about those experiences and about the important issues surrounding these emerging technologies, you will learn a great deal about the technology itself—how it works, how it alters personal relationships, how it affects global communications, how it changes our whole sense of "local," and so forth. The discoveries you make through your own experiences, the information and insights you share with your classmates, the research you do in the library and on-line—all this and more make up the content of this course. This body of information will take all term to develop fully, and the understandings you develop will emerge gradually. In fact, while you will think and explore and learn a great deal during this course, that understanding will continue to develop long after this course is over. Because the knowledge you will acquire in this course emerges from your explorations and takes shape over time, the evaluation of your work will occur at the end rather than along the way. Once your ideas, understanding, and knowledge have had a chance to develop, the written products in which you display all that will be ready for evaluation.

Of course, this class also focuses on your development as a writer and a thinker. That's why the class is also a writing class. That's also why you'll write a lot in this class and why you'll revise that writing. The only way to improve as a writer is to write; the only way to improve your writing is to revise it, work on it until it becomes better, and learn, in the process, how to make a given piece of writing better, more effective. As you work through the drafting and revising process on your writing assignments for this class, your writing will improve. For that reason, evaluation ought to take place later, rather than sooner, after you've had a chance to improve as a writer. That's why this class is evaluated by portfolio.

Your grade for this course will come from the portfolio you produce by the end of the semester. A portfolio-based grading system allows you to develop a *corpus* of work, a collection of different kinds of writing that, taken together, display a broad range of your abilities as a writer. Delaying grading your work until the end of the semester allows you to take full advantage of the opportunities this class presents for you to learn by drafting, sharing your writing with readers, and revising to make the writing address your readers' needs. It also allows you to take part in deriving the criteria for judging those portfolios. Portfolio evaluation preserves time—your time—for learning, developing, and discovering what to write, how to write. It provides you time to revise, to work over your ideas and the means by which you express those ideas. Delaying evaluation until the end of the term, and involving you in the process of developing the criteria for evaluation, allow for a fuller, fairer evaluation than would be possible if you were evaluated essay by essay, exercise by exercise, text by text, day by day. It also allows us, as a group, to develop a tool for evaluation that deals fairly with the complicated, sensitive subject matter you develop in your texts, hypertexts, E-mail groups, CMC communities, Web-sites, and so forth.

Your portfolio will consist of a selection of the writing you have done for the class, including both paper-based and electronic texts. Here is a basic outline for the contents of your portfolio:

Required Items
Your portfolio must contain all of the following:

Entire files of the electronic texts you prepared in this course (supply files on disk, or include a URL that accesses the texts)

All but two of the finished essays you produced, on paper, during the course

Reflective essay, two to five pages, containing your reflections about the course, the contents of the portfolio as a whole, your development as a writer, your goals for the future, and so forth

Optional Items
Your portfolio must contain at least two and no more than four items from the following list:

Any of your written peer review responses

Any collaborative writing product, such as group peer reviews, collaboratively written critical annotations, group CMC brainstorming sessions, and so forth

Any of your other writings for class exercises: your brochures, together with an explanation of their usefulness, for example; or your analysis of an issue or CMC community

Written description and critique of comprehensive hypertext or WWW archive of the class's work

Any essay(s) you did not include as Required Items

About three weeks before the end of the term, you will put together a draft copy of your portfolio. You will bring five copies of that draft portfolio and your electronic text files on disk to class. We will divide the class into Portfolio Review groups of four or five each. Group members will help each other improve the writing in their portfolios, and they will work together to help derive and perfect criteria that will be used in evaluating the portfolios and assigning grades at the end of the semester.

Step 2: Peer Review and Deriving Criteria

During the many peer review sessions and across the many opportunities you will have in a course like this to respond to your peers' writing, you will develop a sense of where individuals' strengths and needs as writers lie. In addition, you will form a strong sense of what the community's strengths and needs are and of what the community's standards for high, middle, and low performance are. You will use those senses, whether you developed them formally or informally, in carrying out the following step, using portfolio-based peer review sessions both to help each other develop stronger portfolios and to derive criteria for evaluating portfolios.

About three weeks before the end of the term, you will form Portfolio Review Groups of four or five members each. Then, during the first class meeting of that week, each member of a review group will provide copies of her or his portfolio (in draft versions, of course) to every other group member, and one copy to the teacher (see step 1 for guidelines on what to include in the portfolio).

Before the next class meeting, you will read through the portfolios of every member of your Portfolio Review Group and make a list of the strengths and needs you perceive in each portfolio you read.

At the beginning of class, readers will distribute copies of their list of strengths and needs to the group and to the teacher (the teacher's copy should be electronic—you can copy it onto the teacher's disk). Each group will spend about half an hour discussing their lists of strengths and needs relative to the draft portfolios in that group. The object of these discussions is to give writers a sense of where readers detected strengths in the portfolio and where they felt the writer still needed to work to make the writing more effective.

During the final hour of class, you will compile a list of strengths and needs based on the lists you provided and the discussions you've had in your portfolio review groups. Through discussion and revision, you will derive a draft of criteria to use in further peer review of portfolios and to refine on the last day of class. The teacher will then use that list of criteria in performing the final evaluations on students' course portfolios.

Step 3: Peer Response and Revising Criteria

You will respond to each other's draft portfolios, guided in your responses by the criteria developed in class (step 2). Again, analyze each group member's portfolio—and your own—for its strengths and needs, according to the criteria. You may go beyond the criteria, but please make notes when you do, so that the class as a whole may consider your additions or variations in making final revisions to the criteria. These responses, and the self-assessment, should be written, and you should hand one copy to the writer and one to the teacher. (You may also wish to include one of these responses in your own final portfolio.)

On the *final* day of class, the class should discuss any other revisions you want to make to the list of criteria, before they are used in evaluating the portfolios for your course grades.

This kind of process involves teachers and learners together in promoting self-assessment and in helping writers learn productive ways of seeking and giving help with writing. It also provides a fair and open method for arriving at grades for the writing class. As your class develops its own methods, suited to the kinds of writing and learning that you have done by the end of the class, try to incorporate features of this sample process. Later chapters will incorporate similar kinds of activity into the projects through which you'll learn about using computers in writing.

LOOKING AHEAD

We began this chapter with the observation that unless you learn to assess your own work, this course—any writing course—will have failed you. As we close this chapter, we want to reemphasize that assertion. And we want to stress, as well, that the best way to gain the ability to self-assess is by working within a community of writers and readers who will help each other learn what works and what doesn't, what is effective and what is ineffective, what communicates and what puzzles. Computers facilitate this kind of learning in several ways: they expose us to new kinds of text, so that we all—teachers and students alike—have to figure out how to read and understand them, and we all have to work together to negotiate the criteria for evaluating these texts.

In the coming chapters, you will participate in just such a community of readers and writers. As you help each other understand the most effective ways to use this new technology, you will also help each other understand the best ways to communicate to readers. The exchanges you have will help each of you develop that all-important sense of community standards. Those exchanges will also help you learn to anticipate your readers' needs and address them. As you learn to accommodate your audience, you will find that grades are no longer a concern. You will be meeting your community's standards for effective writing, according to the shared criteria developed within your community of writers and readers. The key to developing those abilities is self-assessment, and as your ability to self-assess emerges, you will write with more and more confidence. And this course (and this book) will not have failed you.

7

BUILDING COMMUNITY ON-LINE

Human beings are social by nature, so we organize ourselves into a variety of groups: families, teams, clubs, communities, classes, corporations, boards, and so on. Groups offer their members a number of benefits such as emotional security or support, social bonding, and shared intellectual, physical, or economic resources. The members usually need to have something in common—a bloodline, special interests, goals, or geographic location. Well-functioning communities depend on more than these shared characteristics, however. They depend on a variety of conditions, common assumptions, and rules, all of which lead members and prospective members to see the benefits of belonging to the group. Communities to which people want to belong have rather complex rules of membership, sometimes written, most times not. In many cases, members need to infer the rules by observing how others behave and how others react to their own actions and behaviors.

Members need to maintain the harmony of the group by respecting the rights of the individuals in the group, by not making themselves a burden to the group, and by contributing to the group as much or more than they receive. Such "rules" can be heard in the "golden rule" of "Do unto others as you would have others do unto you" and President John F. Kennedy's call to a new generation in the 1960s: "Ask not what your country can do for you but what you can do for your country." Well-functioning communities are characterized by the kinds of emotional bonds among people that foster cooperation, respect, and loyalty.

Any writing course, therefore, that strives to benefit from the potentials of both real and virtual writing communities will benefit from engaging in community-building activities. In the computer-based writing course, we have found the best community-building activities are those that employ both writing and technology and that involve the group in activities that provide real benefits for the members of the learning community.

PROJECT 1: BUILDING COMMUNITY THROUGH COMPUTER-MEDIATED COMMUNICATIONS

Objectives

- To introduce E-mail
- To build community through sharing experience

Technological Requirements

- Access to a computer-mediated communication system is necessary, such as a local area or wide-area network E-mail system or electronic conferencing system.
- This activity works best if the teacher is able to set up a listserv or mail group to which all students are subscribed or to use an electronic bulletin board that facilitates broadcasting of messages in addition to individual messaging.

Participant Prerequisites

- An E-mail account
- If the computer literacy assessment in Part I indicates that most community members don't know the basics of E-mail (launching the E-mail program, composing a message, sending a message, reading a message, and replying to a message), the teacher will need to provide a brief demonstration. Chapters 2 and 3 also offer advice on the effective use of E-mail.

Overview

Most people who facilitate learning communities employ various community-building techniques. Such activities include having the group members introduce themselves to the group by name and tell something about themselves: hometown, favorite color, favorite food, and so on. Depending on the community's incoming computer literacy, similar activities can be conducted on-line.

ACTIVITY 7.1: Assigning Keypals

- Each student writes on a sheet of paper his or her name and E-mail address.
- The teacher collects these and places them into a "hat."
- The hat is passed around the room, and each community member pulls a name (other than their own, of course).

ACTIVITY 7.2: Composing Mail

Each member launches the E-mail program and addresses a message to the person whose name was drawn in Activity 7.1. The message should contain the following information:

- Your name
- Your class year
- Your major
- An explanation of your hometown's claim to fame
- A description of a special talent, your greatest achievement, or whatever you believe makes you unique. If you were to win a major award, what three things would you like the press release to include about you, your accomplishments, or your experiences?
- Your reason for attending this college
- Your reason for taking this class
- A description of your personal learning goals for this class—what you hope to work on, what you hope to learn, the area in which you want to grow
- Your "worst" writing experience, which could be about a particular assignment, teacher, class, letter, whatever. Be sure to describe what made it so.
- Your "best" writing experience, which could be about a particular assignment, teacher, class, letter, whatever. Be sure to describe what made it so.

Once you have composed your message, send it to your E-mail partner.

ACTIVITY 7.3: Responding to E-Mail

Within a few minutes you should receive from the person who pulled your name a message about him or her. Read that person's message and compose a reply in which you comment on the similarities and differences between your experiences, goals, best and worst writing experiences, and so forth.

ACTIVITY 7.4: On-Line Keypal Introductions

If the CMC system you are using allows for broadcasting of messages to everyone in your class (if your teacher has set up a listserv, mail group, or a class electronic bulletin board), send another message to everyone in your class in which you "introduce" your virtual partner. In such a message, you would include the person's name, hometown, and a synthesis of everything else he or she said in the original message.

ACTIVITY 7.5: Face-to-Face Introductions

Finally, go face to face. If your CMC system is not yet set up for broadcasting messages, take some time at the end of the session to have everyone get off the computers, gather in a big group circle, and introduce to the class the person from whom each member received biographical information. Of course, the person being introduced should raise his or her hand so everyone knows who is who.

PROJECT 2: DOCUMENTING THE LOCAL LANDSCAPE

Objectives

- To work collaboratively to learn the technological landscape of your school
- To use writing to learn and describe the technological landscape of your school

Technological Requirements

- Text producers such as word processors or desktop publishing tools
- An electronic conferencing system (optional)

Participants Prerequisites

- Intermediate research skills

Overview

As you probably have learned from listening to the news, your first attempts to use technology, and the computer literacy inventory activity in Part I, the information superhighway has a language and a virtual landscape all its own. One of the problems with the information superhighway as it stands now is that all the "towns" on the highway (the different schools, offices, etc.) all seem to have different hardware, software, and Internet access. And, every "town" has set up different allocation and support systems. So, just as drivers in real life learn how to operate a car first in their own neighborhood and then around town before getting on the interstate, so your electronic learning community must learn the steets, lanes, and boulevards of your local environment, "map" them, and make them accessible to each other and to newcomers.

Of course, if your school has been on-line for a while already, some of these "maps" may already exist. The computing services people and your teacher, for example, may already have written quicknotes for the most popular applications in your classroom, department, or campus. General guides to computing on campus might already exist, and somewhere around your department or campus you will find documentation written by the publishers of the software you will be using. It would seem easy, then, merely to go around campus and collect documents that have already been written and point others to them. As you seek out and analyze these sources of information, however, you may find shortcomings with them, including these:

- *Inaccessibility.* You may find that the quicknotes or software documentation are difficult to track down or are located in a place where members of your community may not be able to get to them easily.

- *Different purposes.* The available documentation may focus, for example, on how to operate the software but offer no information on how you might use the software to accomplish the specific goals of a writing class.
- *Different audiences.* Software documentation is written for a general audience of all potential users of the application and will include information on all features of the software. Thus, it will probably offer more information than your community members need. Even the handouts written by your campus computing services will probably be targeted toward all potential users on campus. The writers of such documents can't accurately focus on the needs of those who want to use the software for novice, intermediate, and advanced users or specifically for writers.

The purpose of this project, then, is to work collaboratively to learn as much as you can about "getting around" in your "town"—the virtual learning environment you and your classmates will occupy during this course. During this project you will collaborate to develop a list of what "newcomers" to your town would need to know, gather into research teams, discover and analyze what documents already exist, and collaboratively write short handouts, crib sheets, or quicknotes that will serve as a starting point for the community's knowledge about the technological features of your neighborhood on the Internet. Along the way, you will need to analyze the needs of your community, determine how well currently available documents address your community's needs, and create documents that draw on what's already available to develop audience-specific handouts. If you have the time and ability, and if the class's objectives support the activity, you may create fancy four-color, four-fold professional "brochures," but that won't be necessary for this assignment. A two-page quicknote, printed on both sides of one sheet of paper, will suffice. Although overall appearance is a positive feature, for the purpose of this activity more emphasis should be placed on content and writing quality than the physical beauty of the handout itself. You may want to consult Chapter 1, "Manipulating Text," for advice on effective layouts and formatting. By the end of the project, various teams within the class will have produced handouts that will be distributed among all the community members.

The Assignment

Work collaboratively with a teammate to produce a brochure or handout to serve as a quicknote or "quickstart" document on some aspect of the technological landscape of your school. The handout should use one sheet of paper, printed front and back. If you have access to desktop publishing software and the expertise to use it, you might consider making a graphically enhanced trifold brochure. Ultimately, your goal is to educate novice users in your learning community on how they, as computer users and writers, can access and use the computer technology available through your school.

ACTIVITY 7.6: What Every Person Needs to Know about Our Town

This activity could be conducted in a couple of ways. Which option your community chooses depends on the type of setting you meet in, (i.e., a computer classroom or a traditional classroom), what kind of computer-mediated communication (CMC) system you have access to, and how much computer experience community members bring with them to class. If your class meets in a traditional classroom, of course, we recommend option 1. You should also consider option 1 even if you meet in a computer classroom with access to CMC applications but the bulk of the community members are novices who have never before used CMC. If, however, most members of your class have some CMC experience, or if the system is simple enough for novices to use within a few minutes after a short demonstration or following simple documentation, you might consider using option 2.

Option 1: Oral Brainstorming

If your community has not yet had an opportunity to learn about and use CMC, you may want to start with a more traditional oral brainstorming activity.

- First, gather together as a large group.
- Have a volunteer write all the suggestions on the chalkboard or overhead projector. Don't take time now to discuss, discard, or classify responses—just get down as many as you can. See step 1 for further details.

Option 2: Brainstorming On-Line

To use this option, your community needs access to a "real-time" or synchronous groupware application, that is, Internet relay chat (IRC), MUD/MOO/MUSH, or other commercially available programs that offer "chat" modes and permit electronic conferencing or "written discussions." An E-mail or Usenet newsgroup could serve the same purpose, but the lag time in asynchronous systems may not permit a rapid exchange of ideas. To use this option, your teacher will need to tell you what software to use, explain or demonstrate how to access and launch it, and direct you to any specific channels (IRC), rooms (MOOS/MUDS), or conferences to join.

Step 1: Brainstorming the Possibilities

Spend as much time as you need until you exhaust the possible answers to the following question: "If you used the metaphor of a 'town' to think about the technological environment of your school, and you were charged by that town's Welcome Wagon Committee to figure out the most important things newcomers would need to know and do to feel comfortable in the new town, what would they need to know?" Examples might include "How do I get an E-Mail account?" "How do I access the World Wide Web?" and "How do I get help when I need it?"

Step 2: Classifying and Dividing

By now you might have dozens of possibilities, including but not limited to how to get an E-mail account, how to use E-mail, how to use the on-line library catalog, how to get help, how to buy software, how to hook up to the Internet from a dorm room, where students can use computers at night, how to do on-line research, and so on. Now you need to classify and divide these. As a group, ask yourselves, "Which items are related?" For instance, if several of the items are something like "What is E-mail?" "What is the best E-mail reader to use?" "How do I use E-mail?" "How do I get an E-mail account?" and "How can I use E-mail from my dorm room?" you might group those together.

After you have classified all the ideas that arose out of brainstorming, you need to divide them into one classification per two-member research team. That is, if you have twenty people in class, you will break out into ten research teams, so you have to end up with ten classifications. It is quite possible, of course, that your community will come up with more classifications than potential research teams. If this is the case, as a group you will need to determine which are the most important. So, if you have fifteen categories but only ten research teams, you will need to arrive at a consensus as to which are the most crucial ten. Or you may decide that some categories will require a lot more work than others. Then you could assign some teams one category and other teams two.

Step 3: Creating Research Teams

Once you've determined how many teams you can make and determined the classifications, you need to create your teams.

Option 1: Random Assignment. You could create teams randomly. Have half the class put their names into a hat. Then, pass the hat along to those community members who did not put in their names and have them pick a name.

Option 2: Computer Literacy Matching. Although random assignment is an excellent way to provide opportunities for community members to work together, you can also create groups by computer literacy levels as identified on the computer literacy inventory. Doing so makes sense because a team of two "passengers" might find the project more challenging than would a team of two "drivers." First, your community has to determine how many of each category exist in your class. Typically, more community members will fall into the "navigator" category than the other two. If, therefore, your community has ten of its twenty members as navigators, put the names of those navigators into a hat and allow the passengers and drivers to pick their teammates from the pool of navigators. In any case, however the distribution of passengers, navigators, and drivers falls out in your community, devise a matching technique that will give all the teams a good balance.

Step 4: Assigning Missions
Now you have your categories and your teams. To match teams with categories,

- write the name of each category on a separate sheet of paper,
- fold the sheets and place them in the hat, and
- have one representative of each team pull a category.

ACTIVITY 7.7: The Scavenger Hunt

To this point your community has decided what categories of information will be most useful to newcomers, and you have divided yourselves into research teams. Now comes the amusing (and the hard) part. Your mission is to work together to conduct a scavenger hunt around your libraries, computer sites, and campus to learn as much as you can about your category. Here you'll find some tips and hints on doing your research collaboratively.

Step 1: Working Out Collaboration Logistics
- Develop an infrastructure for working together. You will need to exchange phone numbers, addresses, E-mail addresses (if you have them yet), and class and work schedules so you can figure out how you can get in contact with your teammate and determine when you can get together for planning, research, and writing sessions.
- Develop a plan. Remind yourself of the deadline your teacher set and map out times when you will meet. Break down the task into its component parts. Divide responsibilities, conduct your scavenger hunt, meet to write up your handout, and so on.

Step 2: Team Knowledge Inventory
Next, you will need to get together to determine what each team member already knows about the category. For instance, perhaps your team has been assigned the "How can I get help?" category. Perhaps one of you happened to see in the campus computing site a sign advertising minicourses on computer literacy. Perhaps one of you remembered from campus orientation someone mentioning that there was a phone number people could call when they needed help with a program. Maybe one of you remembers the last time your computer crashed in the computing center and how a friendly computing site consultant showed you how to recover your crashed file. Whatever your topic and whatever your current knowledge, you and your teammate need to sit down and determine what you already know, what you need to learn, and how you might go about learning it. Each of you might complete the following heuristic by entering the following questions into a word processor and replying to the items *in as*

much detail as possible. After completing the inventory individually, you might then exchange them with your teammate to determine as a team what you already know and what areas you need to research:

- *What do I already know about the topic?* If you pulled "How do I do on-line research?" and even if you have never done it yourself, you at least know some of the basic concepts of research. You could answer this question by replying, "I know that research is looking up information. I usually go to the library and use the card catalog to look up books. Once I used something called the *Readers Guide to Periodical Literature* to look up magazine articles when I did that research paper on the Vietnam War in high school. Sometimes when I get lost in the library, I ask one of the librarians to help me."
- *What don't I know about this topic that I feel I should?* For example, if your team was assigned the World Wide Web, you might know generally what it is and what you can do on it. You may know how to browse the Web using a program like Netscape, but you may not know how to construct your own homepage. You would, therefore, need to learn the language of homepage construction, including terms like http and URL, as well as techniques for creating a home page.
- *How do I normally go about learning something on my own?* You have done a lot of self-education in life. Just think: you got into college, and you never knew how to do that before you did it. So, what did you do? You might have asked people you thought might have some knowledge about your topic like your parents, teachers, guidance counselors, or friends who were already in college. You might have gone to the library or a bookstore to find a book about universities and colleges. You might have visited some colleges. You might have attended a workshop in your school on getting into college.
- *How might I use my normal strategies for self-education to learn about this topic?* As the previous example implies, in the past you've asked people, you've looked things up in books, you've made visits, and so forth. Which of your own strategies might you use in this situation?
- *Whom might I ask for advice?*
- *What materials might I look at for help?*

Tips on Scavenging

A scavenger hunt can be great fun and force you to think creatively about your options. Here are some tips and hints on what kinds of resources may help you in your search:

1. *Print materials.* Most books about the Internet, this one included, offer glossaries of technical terms associated with cruising the information superhighway. Also, colleges with well-developed and well-supported computing facilities probably offer "quick tip" sheets, newsletters, and

other documents to help computer users. Almost all software programs come with manuals and documentation, and the better ones
offer on-line help. Once you gather as much material as you can about
your topic, you need to consider several questions about the materials
you have found:

- What can you infer about the audience of the currently available
  documents? Do they assume, as evidenced by the amounts of technical language and detailed information, a novice or advanced user?
- How long are they? Do they offer quick, clear, and easy access to getting started with the application or topic, or are they too long for a
  user looking for a "getting started" guide?
- What can you infer about the purpose of the currently available
  documents? From the depth of detail, level of technical jargon, and
  tone, are the currently available documents intended as brief over-
  views and "getting started" documents, or are they intended to offer
  deep knowledge to advanced users?

2. *People.* Depending on the size of your school, technology consultants
    might be available to help you. In some schools, you might find these
    resource people in the libraries and in the public computing sites.
    Some schools might have help hotlines that you can call with your
    questions. If you are working in a department-run computer lab, it
    probably has a director and lab assistants who will prove helpful.
3. *On-line help.* You will find that most commercial software applications
    offer on-line help, that is, documentation that is built right into the
    software. The better E-mail discussion groups and newsgroups post fre-
    quently asked question (FAQ) files that you will find useful. Also, your
    local campus technology consultants may have created digital versions
    of printed "help" documents. You will need, however, to ask the same
    questions about these on-line sources as you do of the print documents.

ACTIVITY 7.8: Writing the Handout

To this point you and your teammate have worked together to plan your
research and explore the various resources of your school and computing
facilities to gather information, knowledge, and materials concerning your
topic. Now you need to write up what you've learned so you can share your
knowledge with the other members of the electronic learning community.

First, let's consider what makes a good handout. Indeed, you have read
scores of them in your life, and it would probably be useful to gather a couple you will undoubtedly find scattered across your campus, doctor's
office, college's admissions office, or any public office. Think carefully
about what a typical handout is and does. The typical features of a short
handout include these:

- *Brevity.* Some may be printed on 11" × 17" paper and folded into four panels, some are 8 ½" x 11" paper folded into three panels, and others are merely printed traditionally on both sides of one sheet of paper. This brevity allows us to infer the audience for and purpose of such handouts. We can infer, for example, that brochures are intended for readers who probably know little about the topic and want a quick introduction.
- *Readability.* Because brochures are intended for nonexperts who need general information quickly, the brochure is set up to be as readable as possible. We know, for example, that narrow columns of text are easier to read than page-wide columns. Also, most brochures will rely heavily on "chunking," that is, breaking up the text into topical sections. And, brochures often rely on numerous bold, italicized, or capitalized section headings.
- *Attractiveness.* Although many brochures employ graphics and color printing, not all need to be flashy to be effective. They do have to be laid out attractively and clearly, however. That means the reader need not squint to read very tiny print, that the text moves smoothly from one column to another, and the whole movement of the text helps the reader move through the information easily.

Step 1: Structural Analysis Handout

The features of brochures and other sort of quicknote handouts described earlier are by necessity very general. To get a more specific idea of how brochures and the like work, it will be useful to conduct an analysis of the actual type of document you are actually trying to produce. To learn more about such documents, consider these suggestions:

- Gather as many brochures and handouts as you can. If your school already has some technology-related ones, collect several of those. Your teacher may already have samples for you to review, too.
- Gather as a large group or within your teams and "study" the documents, focusing on the following:
  - How long are the documents?
  - What do the documents look like? Do they include graphics? Do they leave a lot of "white space," or does information, graphic or textual, cover most of the page(s)?
  - How is the information "chunked"? Are there headings and subheadings? Are there blank lines between paragraphs?
  - Is the document written in a "friendly" tone employing personal pronouns or impersonal pronouns (i.e., *you* as opposed to one) or a more formal tone? Are the sentences long, complex, and "academic sounding" or short and simple, perhaps employing sentence fragments for effect?

— What can you infer about the intended audience(s) of the document(s) based on the language, tone, and level of detail?

- If you have collected a number of documents, which are most "attractive," which are easiest to read and understand, which one has a layout and structure you prefer, and why?
- Which do you deem most effective, and why?
- Which one(s) would you consider as model(s) for what you are trying to create?

Step 2: Audience Analysis for Handout

First, the whole class might hold a discussion, either face to face or on-line, depending on the community's comfort level with CMC, with the goal of analyzing the audience for the community's handouts. The following questions will help your group consider the needs of the audience:

- Who might be interested in reading these handouts?
- What can you assume about their prior knowledge of the topic? Will they know more, less, or the same as you about the topic?
- Why would they read the handout?
- What might they expect to get from the handout?
- What do you want them to know after they read the handout? What do you expect them to do after reading the handout?

Such audience issues become especially important when you realize that you and your teammate are not the first ones writing about the topics you have chosen. In most cases, your task won't involve writing something from scratch but rather synthesizing all the available information and presenting the appropriate details in appropriate language and format for your particular audience. After the whole class has considered the audience issues for the handouts generally, you and your teammate should get together to consider the audience needs specific to your handout.

Step 3: Drafting the Handout

Now that you and your teammate have (1) gathered all the information you believe you need, (2) determined your purpose, and (3) defined your audience, you can begin to write the document. First, you have to figure out an equitable work plan. By the end of the project, you will have to compose the document; revise it; format it; edit, proofread, and correct it; test the procedures in it; print it; and make enough copies for everyone in your class. You should sit down together as you begin step two to determine who will take responsibility for doing which parts, when you will do them, and where you will do them.

After you have worked out a production plan, you and your partner need to sit at a word processor, either separately or collaboratively, and begin drafting your handout. Undoubtedly, during your research you learned much more about your topic than you can possibly fit into a two-page document. You probably uncovered a bit of technical jargon, leads to other sources of information about your topic, in-depth explanations and definitions, and so on. Now the challenge is to gather all the information about your topic and organize it in a way that fulfills the purpose of the document and meets the needs of your audience. As you gather, filter, categorize, and synthesize information, it is crucial you avoid plagiarism—a rather serious, sometimes criminal, and at least academically unethical, transgression. To do so:

- Keep careful notes about what information you glean from what documents. First, you may find you will need to offer some information in your document that you will need to cite. Second, you may want to include a section on your handout such as "Sources for Further Information" that will read your leaders to more detailed documents.
- Use your own words as much as possible. It will be quite tempting merely to copy what has been said already, but a number of problems arise in doing so. First, using someone else's work without properly giving credit to that person or those persons constitutes plagiarism. Second, as noted earlier, the documents from which you are drawing information probably were written with a different audience and purpose in mind. So, not only will unauthorized and undocumented use of someone else's words be illegal, it will also not necessarily lead to an effective document.

Now, gather all the information you've collected. Then, look for similarities and differences among the documents and come up with some working categories. For instance, if your team is writing a brochure on using the World Wide Web, you have probably come across technical terms and acronyms including but not limited to *browser, HTML, http,* and *URL.* All such terms might be lumped, therefore, into a "Technical Terms" category. During your research you might also have come across historical information about the World Wide Web, descriptions of different uses of the Web, or instructions for creating a homepage. Such information might be arranged into categories such as "Historical Background," "What the Web Is Used For," and "How to Use the Web." The more categories you can come up with the better.

Once you've categorized and classified the various types of information you've found, prepare with your partner a working outline using the category titles you devised. Your categories, for example, might include "Resources for Further Information," "Technical Terms," "Overview of Typical Uses," "How to Navigate the Web," "How to Research on the Web," "How to Create Your Own Homepage," and "History of the Web," to name a few.

Given your audience—typically novices working in a particular setting (your school)—and your purpose—a getting started guide—think of a logical sequence for your categories. For instance, you might consider starting with a general overview of the World Wide Web, including a brief history and what it is used for. A brief section on technical terms might follow to introduce readers to jargon they will need to know to understand later sections. The next section might be something like "How to Access the Web," in which you explain different software options and how to use those applications most widely available, used, and supported at your school. Subsequent sections might include tips on using the Web for research, creating a homepage at your site, and a brief listing of where to get more detailed help.

After creating a working order for your categories, begin filling in as much information as you have in each category. You will probably find that you will have much more than you can fit on two pages, but that is the way it should be. Remember, you are drafting here. Also, you will probably discover gaps in your information and thus discover areas in which you will need to do some more research.

ACTIVITY 7.9: Revising the Handout

Now that you have a working draft of your handout, you will need to go through a series of steps to revise. These steps include intra- and interteam evaluations of the content, structure, and style and format of the document.

Step 1: Revising for Content

At this point you should have a several-page document with a plethora of information about your topic. Some categories may be chock-full of detailed information; some may be relatively skimpy. Some information may not fit easily into any of the categories you've created. And, not all of the information your research turned up will fit into the final two-page format or meet the needs of your audience. Here are a number of considerations you and your peer can think about when deciding what to include and what to cut out during revision.

- Revisit your planning work and fine-tune your understanding of your purpose. What is it?
- Revisit your planning work and fine tune your audience's needs. What are they?
- How long is your current document? How many pages will you have to cut?
- How many categories do you have? In terms of your audience and purpose, which three, four, or five categories do you consider crucial and why? You might rank all your categories from most important to least.
- Look at your ranking. If you cut out the last half of them, what would your document lose in terms of fulfilling the audience's needs? What would your document gain?

Because you've been doing the invention and composing activities on a word processor, you can now reshape your document based on your revision analysis. Because you are still revising, however, you don't want to lose any of the original information you found. During subsequent revisions, you may find you need some information or language you had in the first draft. To make a new working version of your draft, simply create a new file and copy and paste out of the first draft only those sections and information you need into the new file. *Give the new file a different file name.* By doing so you will still have a copy of the first draft and the more recent revised version.

Step 2: Revising for Clarity and Style

At this point your draft should be around two pages long and include the most important information about your topic arranged in the most logical order given the parameters of your purpose and audience. Now you will want to check the content for accuracy and revise the language of the document for clarity and correctness.

First, depending on how you and your partner divided the workload, both partners should check independently any procedural sections you might have included. If, for example, your document offers a procedure for sending an E-mail message, make sure you and your partner follow the procedure precisely to make sure it works. If either one of you gets lost in your own directions, revise accordingly.

Next, have one partner read the document aloud to the other. Does the prose sound telegraphic, that is, short and choppy? Or, do long-winded sentences cause the reader to gasp for breath? Are all the sentences so similar in length the prose sounds monotonous? Is the tone friendly and inviting, using common and informal language, or does the document read like an impersonal technical document burdened with undefined jargon? Of course, how you want to your document to sound depends on the purpose and audience goals you've defined, but given the purpose of introducing a relatively novice audience to a seemingly complex topic, you will probably want a "friendly" document that speaks to users as people and uses language that's as simple as possible.

If, therefore, this draft suffers from inaccurate procedures, inappropriate tone, or uninspiring style, revise the language and content accordingly. Finally, print out several copies for "field-testing" the document in the next step of the process.

Step 3: Testing the Handout

So far your work has been shared only among teammates, and during that sharing your document has been fashioned from an unstructured compendium of unrelated ideas to roughly a two-page document. Now it is time to field-test the document by sharing your draft with another team.

First, gather with another team and exchange drafts of your documents. The teams might be matched randomly, or they can be matched based on the similarity of their topics. If, for instance, one team is working on "An Introduction to the World Wide Web" and another team is working on "Building Your Own Homepage on the World Wide Web," those two teams might field-test one another's documents. By doing so the two teams might dovetail their documents to minimize redundant information between them.

Read over the drafts and consider the following items:

1. Comment on the organization and structure of the handout.

   - Write a brief outline of the handout. Do the various categories of information flow logically? For instance, does the handout start out with a "how to operate X" and then go into background information, such as what one might use a particular application for? If so, you might consider whether the background information on why someone would use the World Wide Web, for example, should go before procedures for using the World Wide Web.
   - Are there technological terms that need definition or clarification? The World Wide Web, for example, has a language all its own. Someone writing a handout about using the World Wide Web would need to use acronyms and terms such as *http, URL, link,* and so on. If readers don't know what those terms mean, and if those terms were crucial for understanding how to browse the Web, readers might find the handout confusing. A future revision, therefore, might require defining such terms.
   - What information do you as a user need that is not presented? For instance, perhaps the handout talks about the World Wide Web but neglects to inform you what applications, such as Lynx, Mosaic, or Netscape, you would need to browse the Web.
   - Is there any information or sections that don't seem necessary? Does the handout launch into a lengthy history of the application or procedure, one that may be interesting but doesn't necessarily lead to your understanding how to use the application?

2. Read the other team's draft aloud and listen carefully. Comment, either in writing or in a face-to-face conference, on the readability by addressing the following:

   - Is there a telegraphic or monotonal sound to the prose? Identify groups of sentences that might be combined to vary the rhythm.
   - Were there any words or phrases that made you stumble, forcing you to read them a second or third time? Underline those words or passages over which you stumbled.
   - Were there any sentences or passages that left you gasping for breath? Underline those sentences.

3. Does the handout include procedures on how to operate a certain piece of software such as Netscape for the World Wide Web? Go to a computer, follow the procedures, and evaluate them.
   - Are they written clearly?
   - Did you come across any technical terms that were not defined?
   - Did you understand why you were doing what you were doing?
   - Did the procedures work perfectly or did you have to ask the authors additional questions or advice? Take notes on where and how you got "lost," and share with the writers suggestions on how the procedure could be clearer.

4. Comment on the clarity, attractiveness, and layout of the document.
   - Is the handout written as if it were an essay with text running from margin to margin? If so, and given the constraints of audience, purpose, and space, is this the most effective layout? You might suggest alternative formats with a rationale for how the alternatives might create a more readable document.
   - Is the handout broken up into discernible chunks? If so, are subject headings formatted (bold, italics, all caps, a different font) in such a way to make them stand out from the text itself?
   - Have the writers used fonts (the style of the print) and point (the size of the print) that aid or challenge the reader? Remember, the smaller the print, the more difficult it is for readers' eyes.

Step 4: Reflecting on and Revising the Handout

At this point you and your teammate have analyzed your draft yourselves and have field-tested the document by sharing it with another team. Your teacher may even have created opportunities to repeat step 3 with other teams and offered some feedback. Before you begin your final revisions, take a few minutes to reflect on the feedback you've received:

- As a group, what categories of revision has your draft received? For instance, some reviewers might have focused on technical issues, some on formatting issues, and others on stylistic issues.
- What is the range of positive feedback? Some reviewers, for example, might have approved of the tone; others might have found the procedures particularly clear; others might have lauded the overall attractiveness of the draft.
- What are the common areas of positive feedback? In other words, what positive comments did all the reviewers offer?
- What is the range of suggestions for revision? Each of your reviewers might have focused on different areas of improvement, and it is important for you to consider all of them.
- Is there a consensus among your reviewers about areas of improvement? If so, what is that consensus?

- As you and your teammate reflect on the feedback, you'll need to decide among yourselves which are most important. Then you'll need to come up with a revision plan.

Next, revise your document accordingly. When you are confident you have the content, structure, and format in the most appropriate fashion you can build, given your audience and purpose, revise the document for "correctness." Proofread for punctuation and appropriate grammar and usage. Use your word processor's spelling checker to check for typos, misspellings, and duplicated words.

ACTIVITY 7.10: Sharing the Handouts

The final step of the project includes distributing the documents with other members of the community. A number of options exist depending on both how much time is allotted for this project and the sophistication of technology available to your learning community.

Option 1: Sharing Hard Copies

Print out your handout, make enough copies for everyone in your class (including your teacher), and distribute them during class time. Everyone in class can then keep the handouts in their notebooks or files and use them as reference guides when they want to use E-mail, Gopher, the World Wide Web, and so on.

Option 2: Class Presentations

If your computer classroom has overhead display capabilities, each team can also take about twenty minutes (or however much time your teacher makes available) to offer a class presentation in which they demonstrate for classmates how to access and operate the application about which they wrote their handout.

Option 3: Electronic Publishing

Depending on the class's level of technological expertise, you can also distribute the handouts electronically.

- If your class uses an E-mail group or listserv, each team can broadcast text-only versions of their handouts.
- If your class uses a Usenet newsgroup, the teams can post their handouts there.
- If your class uses an FTP space, the handouts can be made available there.
- If your class uses Gopherspace, copy the handouts there.
- If your class is constructing a World Wide Web site, you can make the handouts available there.

8

TALES OF CYBERSPACE

Telling stories remains one of the basic things humans do with language. Pre-literate humans told stories to share news and history in the form of oral epic narrative poetry. As a youngster, your first experience with the written word was probably in the form of stories. We tell stories to entertain, illustrate points we are trying to make, and teach. Narratives can be composed about almost anything and told at anytime, but a particular kind of narrative, the travel narrative, is often told about journeys people have taken. Such tales, on one hand, entertain with adventurous and suspenseful tales of challenges addressed and overcome and, on the other hand, educate by describing foreign or new lands, points of interest, and the people who inhabit these places.

If we think of cyberspace as a place, albeit a virtual one, and our learning about it and its resources as a journey, we can use narrative as a way to explore it. Tales of cyberspace, then, would be akin to the stories of the new land sent home to Europe during the sixteenth century by colonizers of America or the stories of the American West sent back east by nineteenth-century pioneers. You are among the first explorers of cyberspace, a fact that offers ample opportunities for you to use narrative to entertain, make cyberspace less intimidating for those who will follow you there, and show those who follow you the way, so to speak. What follows in this chapter, therefore, are a number of activities that will lead you through telling the tales of cyberspace.

FEATURES OF NARRATIVE

In its most fundamental form, a narrative is a story. The basic structure of a narrative essay involves characters, usually a primary and then one or more secondary characters; a setting; a conflict the characters must address; and a plot, which arises based on how the characters deal with the conflict and how that conflict affects them. The trick as a writer is to create a relationship among all these variables and put the story into a style and language that will engage your readers for the sake of both entertaining and educating them. Below find brief discussions of each of the elements you might need to consider when writing a narrative.

Characters

One basic element of any narrative is its characters. To develop characters, you need to know as much about them as you can, and probably much more than you will reveal to your readers. You need to know their physical characteristics (gender, race, appearance) and their personality traits (bold, shy, talkative, quiet, etc.). You need to know their belief systems (politically liberal or conservative, religious or not, materialistic or idealistic, etc.), their educational background (high school, college, professional degree, etc.), and the way they speak (formal or informal, brash or reserved, etc.).

Setting

In many stories, the setting serves as a backdrop to set time, place, and mood; in other stories, the setting itself nearly becomes a character. Stories that take place indoors have a different mood and feel than those that take place outdoors. Those that take place in basements of abandoned buildings have a different feel than those that take place in grocery stores. Those that take place on the beach on a hot sunny day create a different mood than those set in a blizzard on a mountain. Daytime stories are different from nightime stories, and so on.

Conflict

Robert Penn Warren, an American novelist, when offering advice on writing fiction, stated, "No conflict, no story." If you had richly developed characters sitting around talking in a vividly described parlor but no problems arose among them or during their conversation, you would have, perhaps, an interestingly described vignette, but you would not have a story. There is perhaps no more crucial element to a narrative than the conflict that drives the characters. Typical conflicts include these:

- Person versus person
- Person versus society
- Person versus self
- Person versus nature
- Person versus the unknown

It is important to understand that a good narrative may include more than one conflict, just as it might include more than one character. So, for instance, a narrative that begins with a person-versus-person conflict in which two characters disagree on basic beliefs over a controversial issue might also lead to person-versus-self conflict as one of the characters struggles to come to terms with her own belief system. Or, a person-versus-nature conflict in which a hiker gets lost in the forest develops into a person-versus-the unknown as night falls and he deals with his fears of the things that go bump in the night. In fact, the most interesting narratives will be those that weave together various conflicts into a complex examination of the human condition.

Plot

Once you have characters in a setting confronting some sort of conflict, you are on your way to developing a plot. The plot is basically the series of events and actions characters undertake as they interact with one another and deal in some form with the conflict. The events in the plot are linked by causation, so that event A caused event B, which in turn caused event C, and so forth. Not all the events in a narrative are part of this chain of causation, but event A must be linked to event X by that string of causation. Otherwise, readers won't understand how the ending came about.

Narrative Technique

A common expression narrative writers live by is "show, don't tell." In other words, strong narratives develop characters, describe settings, introduce conflicts, and unfold plots in such a way as to make readers feel as if they are experiencing what the characters are experiencing. Various techniques exist to bring characters and settings to life. For example, when creating characters, you want to relay to readers the characters' voices through using dialogue. You will need to describe physical appearances, nonverbal gestures, show their attitudes toward other characters, and so on. Painting pictures with words is a more effective way to describe setting than mechanically, if accurately, describing the surroundings. Rely on details rather than adjectives. If your story is set on a hot day at the beach, don't *tell:* "It was hot." Rather: "As I walked the twenty yards from my beach blanket to the water, the sand scorched the tender arches of my feet." The latter phrasing lets your reader know "it was hot" in a fashion that makes the experience sensory.

PROJECT 3: TALES OF CYBERSPACE

The Assignment

Write a four- to seven-page or 1,000- to 1,500-word (or of a length determined by your community or teacher) narrative essay about an experience you've had with computer technology. This experience could be a "real" one you've had with some aspect of computer technology culture or a "virtual" one during your travels in cyberspace. Minimally, the document should be word processed and printed, but, depending on your current level of technological expertise, the essay could also be "published" and made available to readers electronically. Later in the course you may decide to use the skills you will learn in Chapter 12, "Writing for the World Wide Web," to publish your narrative as a World Wide Web page.

Objectives

- To write a narrative essay about your experiences with technology or about one of your voyages in cyberspace

Technological Requirements

- A word processor
- Access to one of the following virtual communities:

  — A Usenet newsgroup
  — An IRC channel
  — An E-mail discussion group (listserv, listproc, majordomo)
  — A MOO, MUD, or MUSH site
  — The World Wide Web

Participant Prerequisites

- Basic Internet literacy
- Enough experience w/ computers to have a story to tell

ACTIVITY 8.1: Finding Places to Begin

Starting on a journey can often be the hardest part. Here we offer three options for exploring your experiences or identifying experiences you'd like to have. In the first one, we suggest how as an individual you can use a prewriting technique called *freewriting;* in the second one, we describe how to collaborate with peers in a face-to-face setting; and in the third, we offer suggestions on using computer-mediated communication for social brainstorming.

Option 1: Individual Freewriting

Freewriting is a prewriting activity that can help you discover and explore your experiences and thus come up with a topic for your narrative. Your goal is to write as much as you can for as long as you can. In freewriting, you are not interested in writing well for an audience. Don't be concerned with spelling, grammar, complete thoughts or sentences. Your main purpose is to generate as much text as you can. (See Chapter 1 for more details on freewriting and invention.)

Step 1: Freewriting

Launch your word processor and start a new file. Consider the following items and write as much as you can about each. When your responses evoke other ideas, feel free to go off on tangents and sidetracks. See whether you can keep your hands on your keyboard for at least ten minutes—longer, if possible.

- Describe the first time you ever used a computer.
- What are your greatest fears about computers?
- What has been your best experience with computers?
- What has been your worst experience with computers?
- How did you learn to become a computer user?
- If you own a computer, how did you go about buying it?
- When was the last time you were lost in a computer program, and how did you find your way out?
- Have you ever used your school's public computing sites? What is the space like? Did you ever have computer or program problems? How did you fix the problems? Who have you met in such sites?
- Have you ever participated in a newsgroup, a discussion list, an electronic conference, an IRC session, a MOO? If so, how did you get there? Who did you meet there? What did you learn there? Did you ever get flamed? Did anyone ever intimidate you? What was the best part of the experience? The worst?
- Have you ever entered Gopherspace or browsed the World Wide Web? If so, how did you get around? What were the best parts of the journey? What were the worst parts? What are the most informative, interesting, or entertaining Web pages you have found? What made them so? How did you find them?
- Who has had the most influence on your growth as a computer user? Have you met any "gurus" who seem to know everything about technology?

Don't forget to save your file.

Step 2: Reflecting on Your Freewriting

If you think about your freewriting as mining—that is, digging up all your thoughts, ideas, and feelings regarding your experiences with technology, cyberspace, and the information superhighway—it is now time to separate the precious metals from the ore. Reread your freewritten text, asking the following questions of what you wrote:

- How many of the previously listed items were you able to answer?
- Which ones were easiest to write about?
- Which ones did you write the most about?

Those experiences that you found easiest to write about or about which you found you had much to say will probably serve as the richest ore in which you'll find the most valuable metals.

Step 3: Finding a Focus

Isolate two or three responses that you think are most promising, and start a new file with your word processor for each one. So, if you found yourself uncovering many memories about the night you sat up in the computer lab until 3:00 A.M. because you accidentally erased a file you were working on, you might start a new file called "Lost in Lab." And, if you remember getting into an especially heated discussion on an IRC channel one night, you might start another file called "IRC."

After identifying these two or three possibilities, conduct focused freewriting for each. To get started, consider the following:

- Who were the people involved? Were you alone, with friends, or with a group of strangers?
- What do you remember of your emotions and psychological state at the time and afterward?
- Was there any conversation during the event? Who said what to whom? How did they say it?
- What happened first, second, third, and so on, until the experience was over?
- Why were you there in the first place?
- Describe the "place." Was it physical like in a computer lab, or was it virtual like a Web site or a MOO room?

Option 2: Oral Collaborative Brainstorming

Collaborative brainstorming can be conducted either before the individual freewriting or after individuals have had an opportunity to explore their own experiences. The benefit of the "before" approach is that hearing what kinds of experiences others have had might remind you of experiences you have forgotten. Thus, when you embark on individual freewriting, you might have more areas to explore. On the other hand, freewriting first allows you to think through your own experiences as a way of warming you up for the group brainstorming.

Step 1: Sharing Experiences

Gather as a large group or in several smaller groups of three to five members each. Appoint someone to write all the suggestions the group offers on the chalkboard, whiteboard, or overhead display such as an LCD panel connected to a computer running a word-processing program. Have each member of the group complete the following phrases:

- The worst experience I ever had with computers was when . . .
- The best experience I ever had with computers was when . . .

- The angriest I ever became when using a computer was when...
- The most interesting computer user I know is...
- The latest night I ever had in the computer lab was when...
- The most interesting computer-mediated discussion I ever had was...
- The best piece of information I ever found on the Internet was...
- The best Web site I ever visited was...

Step 2: Reflecting on What You Heard
As soon as possible after the group brainstorming session, take a look at the ideas your group generated and freewrite again for a while by considering the following:

- What was the most interesting or unique experience you heard from your peers?
- Were there any common experiences among your peers?
- How do your own experiences compare to those of your peers?
- Which of your peers' experiences would you like to have?

Option 3: Computer-Mediated Collaborative Brainstorming
On-line collaborative brainstorming offers several advantages over oral brainstorming. For example, in oral group discussions everyone needs to take turns offering contributions to the conversation. The amount of time available limits the number of turns certain people might take. On-line conferencing, though, allows for more participation by more people. Also, much of what is said in an oral conversation is often forgotten. On-line conferences result in permanent written records of people's contributions, which can be read long after the conversation has ceased. Consult Chapters 2 and 3 for advice about using E-mail for collaborative invention. Once your community decides which kind of computer-mediated communication you will use, use the questions in option 2, *"Oral Collaborative Brainstorming,"* to guide and structure your on-line discussions.

ACTIVITY 8.2: Embarking on Your Journey in Cyberspace

Activity 8.1 might have helped you explore some experiences you've already had, but if at this point your computer technology experiences are limited, the following options could help you gather some new experiences. If you are new to cyberspace, your first thought upon receiving this assignment might be "How can I write a tale of cyberspace? I've never even been there." Well, you might begin with where you have been so far. Even if you haven't yet participated in any virtual communities or explored the World Wide Web, you have probably already entered the sometimes strange world of technological culture. For example, you may have already, in attempting to complete assignments for another course or out of simple curiosity, found yourself trying to use a certain type of computer or software application for the first time. And, the effort perhaps led you on a journey or an "adventure" of sorts—you had to find the computer lab, teach yourself the hardware or software, or seek out the counsel of a computer lab consultant. If you have, perhaps a narrative can grow out of such experiences. If you have not yet experienced a virtual community or explored the World Wide Web, a great way to get started would be to seek out and join one or several virtual communities. Chapters 3 and 4 will help you find ways into virtual communities in the forms of newsgroups, electronic discussion lists, IRCs and MOOs, and the World Wide Web. What follows are some ideas for developing some cyber experiences. Before you embark on any journey, take some time to think about all the options.

Option 1: Real-Life Experiences in an Unreal World

As already noted, even if you have not yet explored virtual spaces, you have probably had real-life experiences with technology. You might have, for example, had any one of the following experiences with computer technology:

The first time I ever touched a computer. Even if this class entails your first extensive experience with computer technology, it is most likely you have at least "touched" a computer before. By doing so, you crossed, even if it was for a fleeting moment, the border between the technological and non-technological world. When did you have the experience? Why did you have the experience? Whom were you with? What was your reaction? What were your thoughts? What were your emotions? What makes the experience significant in your life?

Buying a computer. If you currently own a computer or have at least gone through the process of buying one, you started one place—not knowing what to buy or where to buy it—went through a series of events, and ended up another place—owning a computer. As you went from not owning to owning a computer, you perhaps explored different options, spoke to various experts and nonexperts, visited stores and read catalogs, went through a series of decisions and recisions, and finally bought your computer. The journey you went on to enter tech culture could provide a topic for a narrative.

Exploring the world(s) of software. Similar tales could be told about getting and learning a new piece of software, particularly if you've used the sort of fantasy and simulation programs in which you literally go on virtual journeys.

Computer lab experiences. If you find yourself frequenting a public computing site in your dorm, the library, or a computer lab to do your work, your experiences there could serve as a topic for a narrative. In some schools, for example, the computing sites are open twenty-four hours a day, 360 days or so a year. We have been amazed to learn that even at 3 A.M. the computing sites are filled with bleary-eyed students attempting to find an empty workstation. Such sites often have their "regulars" whose peculiar habits or dress make for interesting people watching. The community of these night people might make an interesting narrative—what goes on in the computer lab when most people are sleeping.

Negative experiences with computers. No matter how much experience you gain with computers, eventually you will suffer some sort of accident or problem. Floppy diskettes will crater in that few minutes between the time you finish that paper you've been working on for weeks and the time you print it out, thus destroying all your efforts and leaving you stranded moments before you are to turn in your assignment. Printers will jam, most often at the most crucial moments when you are pressed for time. Programs will crash and freeze up the computer between "saves" and thus destroy hours of unsaved work. Those who spend too much time in front of a computer monitor sometimes suffer eye strain, those who sit too long and with poor posture at keyboards sometimes develop stiff necks and bad backs, and more and more cases of carpal tunnel syndrome, a sometimes debilitating affliction of the hands and wrists that results from excessive repetitive motion, like typing, are being reported as more and more people spend significant chunks of time working at computer keyboards. If you have suffered some personal experiences with computer technology, you might write a narrative about those.

Option 2: Seeking Out a Virtual Community to Explore

A virtual community is composed of people around the world with shared interests who use computer-mediated communication as a way of doing what members of real communities do—that is, exchange information, socialize, argue, gossip, and almost anything else groups of people might do with language. As noted in Chapter 3, you will find virtual communities on almost every topic imaginable, and that chapter will show you how to find and join these communities. Such virtual communities exist in a number of forms:

- A Usenet newsgroup
- A listserv, listproc, or majordomo
- A local electronic bulletin board
- An IRC channel
- A MOO, MUD, MUSH, or chat room

Do note that even though you have an interest in a particular area and you may find a virtual community built around your interest area, not all virtual communities are very active, at least not active enough to generate the kinds of events you might write a narrative about. So, you would do well to take a few days to join and lurk in several types of communities (e.g., Usenet, listservs) and in a couple of topic areas (e.g., your favorite hobby, intellectual pursuit, musical group) until one emerges that both interests you and is active enough to write about.

If you have identified a real or virtual community or landscape you would like to check out, you need to follow it for an extended period of time, perhaps as long as two weeks or so, to get a sense of the place. When you first join a virtual community, see if there are any related frequently asked questions (FAQ) files available. Log on at least once a day, more if you have time and access, and lurk for a while. To lurk is to spend some time reading what others have to say without saying anything yourself. By doing so you give yourself a chance to learn about the topics and the acceptable rules of behavior within a particular community. Save everything you can electronically—newsgroup threads, E-mail discussions, IRC and MUD/MOO transcripts. Take careful notes of who visits, who "speaks," and what they say. Note any conflicts that arise and how they are resolved or otherwise dealt with. Think of your time with the virtual community as a drama. Instead of the actors performing on an actual stage, however, they are writing their own lines on a virtual stage.

Option 3: Seeking Out a Place to Explore

Whereas a computer-mediated community can be thought of as a place inhabited by people, exploring other parts of the Internet, particularly Gopherspace and the World Wide Web, can be thought of as a virtual treasure hunt. Again, using the techniques described in Chapters 4 and 5, spend several days browsing the Web freely by merely jumping from link to link to see where they take you, or take a more systematic approach by conducting World Wide Web searches on a topic of interest. If, for example, you have a particular fascination for a country such as Costa Rica, use the various World Wide Web search engines to find as many Costa Rica–related sites as you can. Take careful notes of where you started and where you went. If working with your own version of a browser such as Netscape, use the "add bookmarks" feature to customize your own bookmarks. Keep track of the most interesting and boring sites you visited and describe what made them so. Keep track, also, of those sites that had links that didn't work or led you down dead ends. By doing so, you will be developing knowledge and experiences to write a travelogue that can lead your readers to the treasures you discovered.

ACTIVITY 8.3: Drafting Your Narrative

To this point you have explored some real or virtual communities, focused on one, hung around for a given period of time, taken extensive notes and/or saved messages and transcripts from the computer-mediated community, and freewritten and brainstormed. You are ready to begin drafting your narrative.

Step 1: Reporting Events

Begin your narrative by telling the story in the exact chronological order in which you experienced it. As you write each event or episode of your narrative, consider the following items:

- Where did you go?
- How did you get there?
- Describe the "places" in as much descriptive detail as possible.
- Who did you "meet" on your journey?
- What were their names? Were they using true identities or pseudonyms?
- What did they say to you? What did they say to others?
- How did they "speak"? That is, were they serious all the time? Were they humorous? Sarcastic? Did they use emoticons? Did they type in conventional ways, or did they use all lowercase or all capital letters? Did their writing conform to conventions of standard written English, or was their writing sprinkled with grammatical and spelling errors?
- Did any conflicts arise between members of the virtual community? What or who caused them? How were they resolved? Did the conflict result in a "flame war"? Did one of the participants retreat altogether and leave the community? Did one participant convince the others? Did a third party intercede and settle the dispute? Did you play a role in the dispute?
- What did you learn while participating in the virtual community?
- What thoughts did you have while participating?

If you have decided to write about a virtual place, like the World Wide Web, you will have to address a different set of questions:

- Where did you go and how did you get there? In this case, you will need to keep track of all the pages you visited, as well as the URLs for those sites. Did you browse informally or use search engines to seek out particular sites?
- What did you learn that you didn't know before?
- What were your greatest surprises?

Step 2: Show, Don't Tell

As you write your narrative, remember to "show, not tell" as much as possible (see the "Features of Narrative" section at the beginning of this chapter for more details). Pretend, if you will, that you have a video or movie camera in your hand instead of a keyboard under your fingertips. Paint visual pictures with your words whenever possible. Let your readers learn about the characters by letting the readers "hear" the characters' own words in the form of dialogue.

ACTIVITY 8.4: Getting/Giving Feedback

In Activity 8.3 you drafted your narrative. It is now time to get some feed-back from other members of your classroom learning community. Getting and giving feedback can be conducted both face to face or on-line, depending on your technological setup.

Option 1: Face-to-Face Oral and Written Feedback

This option includes both oral and written feedback. To prepare for this activity, you will need to organize yourselves into groups of about three members each, and make enough copies of your draft to share with your group and possibly with your instructor, too.

Step 1: Sharing Drafts
Take turns reading your drafts aloud to one another in the group. Read as slowly, clearly, and dramatically as you can to make the listening experi-ence enjoyable for your peers. In step 2, each group member will be receiv-ing oral feedback, so as each writer is listening to the oral feedback, he or she should take notes.

Step 2: Offering Feedback
Listeners need not offer critical feedback immediately but rather address the following in an oral fashion:

- According to your hearing, what would you say the essay was about?
- What worked the best in the draft? In other words, were characters developed in an interesting fashion? Did the plot move along at an interesting pace? Was there a particularly well-written or memorable passage?
- What did you learn about cyberspace you didn't know before?
- What did you learn about writing narratives you didn't know before?
- What questions do you have about the draft? Do you feel like part of the story was missing? Did you want to know more about a particular character? Did you get a sense not only of what happened in the story but also what point the writer was trying to make by telling the story?
- If you were telling this story, what would you do differently?

Step 3: Preparing Your Draft for Written Peer Critiques
The oral feedback session(s) have now served as a prewriting activity, if you will, for written peer evaluations. Before you share your draft with peers, write and append to the end of your draft a reflective statement in which you address the following items:

- What were your goals for this draft? In other words, what was your purpose? What effect were you trying to have on your readers?
- What is your favorite part of the draft?

- What are your greatest concerns about the draft?
- If you had had more time to prepare this draft, what would you have done?

Step 4: Writing Peer Critiques

Each member of your peer response group should use the following criteria to develop written feedback for each of the other group members. Because you probably won't have time to write these critiques in a regular class period, you will need to determine, based on how many members are in your peer group and how often your class meets, when you will return the critiques to the authors of the drafts you're reviewing. Before addressing the following items, read the draft in its entirety, including the reflective statement. Then go back and read the draft again with an eye toward addressing the following items. When you complete your critiques, save them, print them, and give them to the writers.

- What was the most interesting event in the narrative? What made it so? The way it was written? The way the event was "set up"? The way the event ended up or affected the characters or outcome of the essay?
- Who was the most interesting character in the narrative? What made it so? The way the character was portrayed? The personality of the character? The way the character behaved?
- What was the most interestingly written passage in the narrative? What made it so? The language used? The way the passage made you feel? The way the passage let you visualize what was happening?
- What did you learn from the narrative? Did you learn something about virtual communities you didn't know before? Did you learn something about developing characters, creating tension, or rendering setting that you didn't know how to do before?
- What is this narrative about? You are not so interested here in a summary of the essay or the topic of the essay but rather what point the author is trying to make. In other words, what is the "moral" of the story? What point about cyberspace is the author trying to make? What point about the human emotions and/or relationships is the author trying to make?
- What effect did the narrative have on you? Did the essay have any emotional impact on you? Did it make you laugh? Did it make you think of things you hadn't thought of before?
- Evaluate the content of the narrative. Can you find any information gaps in the essay? In other words, what more do you want to know about the characters? What more do you want to know about the setting? What more do you want to know about the events?
- Evaluate the conflict(s) in the narrative. Can you identify a central conflict, such as person versus person, person versus society, person versus the unknown, and so forth? Does the conflict come through

clearly? If not, suggest what possible conflicts you see within the story that might be clarified in future drafts.

- Evaluate the structure of the narrative. How does the writer handle time? Is the story told in chronological order? Does the writer use flashbacks? Would the narrative be more interesting or dramatic if the events were told in a different order? If the story were told "backward"?
- Evaluate the character(s) in the narrative. Do you get the sense you "know" these characters? Do you know enough about their physical, intellectual, and psychological characteristics to make them come alive? Do you get to "hear" them speak?
- Evaluate the language used to construct the narrative. Does the author tell or show? Are certain words repeated often, are sentences mostly of the same type and length, or has the writer used a rich variety of words, sentence styles, and sentence lengths?
- What might be cut from the narrative? Do all the events, scenes, or episodes seem necessary? Are all the characters necessary? Is there too much dialogue? Are some settings described in such extreme detail that they serve to slow down rather than advance the narrative?
- Final comments: Consider all the comments you offered in response to the preceding items. Think of them as a group, and generate revision ideas and strategies for your peers.

Option 2: On-Line Feedback

Most of what is suggested in option 1 can be done on-line. In fact, in some cases, on-line collaboration can be more efficient than face-to-face or paper-based critiques because face-to-face discussions and paper exchanges require that peers meet at the same time in the same place to interact. Exchanging drafts and feedback via computer-mediated communication can make the process more convenient. Here you'll find some procedures for getting and receiving feedback on-line. Also, consult Chapter 2 for more ideas about collaborating on-line.

To conduct peer review on-line, of course, you and your peers need to have E-mail accounts, belong to a common electronic bulletin board, or have access to a common Usenet newsgroup. What follows are procedures and tips for conducting peer reviews on-line.

Step 1: Sharing Drafts Electronically

Send your draft to your peers. As noted in Chapter 2, you have a number of options depending on the CMC system you are using. In some systems you can copy and paste your draft into an E-mail message and mail it to your peers at their E-mail addresses. Using other types of E-mail programs, you can attach your draft to an E-mail message. If your teacher has set up an E-mail group or listserv list, you can send your draft as an E-mail message or an attachment to the whole list, and your peers, who will also need to be subscribers to the list, can pick up your draft there. Remember, however, that on mail lists, the message, in this case your draft, is broadcast to all members of the list. If your class has twenty or so members, all of them might receive much more E-mail than they have to, so other options may be preferable.

Step 2: Writing Feedback On-Line

After receiving your peers' drafts via E-mail, use the feedback items in option 1, step 4, to fashion a reply to your peers. Your response can take one of several forms.

In one scenario, you can reply to the draft *without* quoting the original message, in this case the draft. By doing so, you will only send back to your peer a document similar to the feedback document you created in option 1, step 4.

In another scenario, and depending on your E-mail program and system, you can *quote* the original message, again in this case the draft, as part of your reply. Doing so permits you several options. Many E-mail programs that allow you to quote messages in replies also allow you to edit and enter text right into the message you are quoting. You can, therefore, insert your comments right into your peers' drafts. In using this technique, you must make sure that your peer can clearly see the difference between your comments and his or her text. Here again you have a number of options, but not all are equal. For instance, you could use all caps for your inserted comments, but some writers interpret such type as SHOUTING and therefore infer a less than collegial or friendly tone. So, if you do wish to insert comments, it is best to insert your cursor where you want to make the comment, hit Return a few times to create several line breaks, then type in your comment.

The best approach for on-line commentary combines both approaches. Indeed, when writing an essay-type response to a draft, it is difficult to refer to particular passages, for instance, without quoting them. On the other hand, inserted comments are useful for focusing on particular details within the draft, but such focused insertions don't lend themselves to talking about more general concerns. It is best, therefore, that in your reply you insert a general critique at the beginning of the draft essay. If you have comments about particular passages, you could then insert them into those passages.

ACTIVITY 8.5: Revising Your Narrative

You have now received feedback on the first draft of your narrative from one or more peer reviewers. Now you need to analyze the feedback you've received, perhaps engage in a computer-mediated dialogue with your peers to solicit more feedback, and revise your narrative based on the feedback.

Step 1: Reflecting on Your Own Draft

If you had more than one peer read and critique your draft, chances are you received some varied responses. The critiques might focus on different issues, and where they do intersect, it is possible the advice is contradictory. First, think back to your original goals and purposes for writing the narrative by considering the following:

- What effects were you hoping to have on your readers? Were you trying to entertain? Were you trying to be humorous? Were you trying to inform?
- What point were you trying to get across?
- What were your favorite parts of the narrative?
- What were your greatest concerns about this draft?

Step 2: Making Sense of Feedback You've Received

Once you have reminded yourself of what you were trying to accomplish, read your peers' responses carefully and consider the following items:

- Were all the comments clear? Which did you not understand? Did reading the comments make you wonder about other aspects of your draft?
- Reply to the E-mail feedback you received from your peers by asking for clarification of their comments. If one reader pointed out one problem with your draft and the others didn't, you might ask the latter group to look at the same section again to see what they think. Having now read the feedback from your peers, do other questions occur to you? E-mail your peers with those questions.
- How were your peers' comments similar to those you made about your draft in the reflective statement?
- How are the critiques similar? In other words, are there certain features of your draft all your readers liked or disliked? Did they have similar comments about the content, structure, or style of your draft? Make a list of all the common comments.
- How are the critiques different? Did they comment on different aspects of your draft? Did one applaud you for a section while another reader identified that same section as an area needing improvement? If you do get contradictory comments on the same aspects of your draft, what might that mean? List all the areas of improvement or contradictory comments.
- What did you learn about writing effective narratives from the critiques of your writing partners' drafts? Was there anything you said about their drafts that might equally apply to your own?
- Reflect on the lists you've made, as well as on what you noticed in your peers' drafts, and develop a revision strategy for yourself. You might begin this strategy by completing the following phrases:
  — What my readers most appreciated in my draft was . . .
  — According to my readers, the areas of improvement for my next draft include . . .
  — In my next draft I plan on doing . . . because . . .

Step 3: Revising Your Draft

Revise your draft based on the feedback you've received. Here are a few techniques you might use to "play" with your draft to see what different kinds of effects you may be able to create. Remember, you can manipulate your draft using the cut-and-paste techniques described in Chapters 1 and 6, so feel free to play. Because your playing with text may not yield favorable results, do keep a copy of your original draft. You can do so by saving your experiments using the Save As command of your word processor. So, if you named your first draft file "Narrative," save your revised versions as "Narrative2," "Narrative3," and so on for each successive draft. By doing so you will leave the original draft intact.

- Imagine telling the story in the reverse order from the one you used. How would that change the overall effect of the narrative?
- Try rewriting the narrative as if you were writing a play in which you have to rely mostly on dialogue. How might that change the overall effect of the narrative?
- Start the narrative in a different place or at a different point in time. For example, if your narrative begins with your walk to the computer lab and then focuses on how you discovered the World Wide Web and a cool site for spring break vacation ideas, try starting the story with when you first laid eyes on the dazzling graphic depicting a palm tree–lined beach. Then fill in the previous details with flashbacks.
- Tell the story from another character's point of view. If, for example, you told from your point of view the story of how the helpful computer lab aide assisted you in saving your diskette that gave the message "Fatal Disk Error," try telling the story from the computer lab aide's point of view.
- Imagine your narrative was submitted to an exciting new magazine on cyberspace. The editor tells you, unfortunately, she would really like to use your piece, but she only has space in the next issue for a document two thirds the size the one you submitted. If your current draft is around 1,500 words, for example, try cutting it down to 1,000. What effect would such a cutting job have on the narrative? What parts would you cut, and which would you keep while maintaining the gist of the story?

ACTIVITY 8.6: Second Draft Critiques

Now that you have had a chance to revise your draft, and if time permits, arrange another round of peer reviews.

Step 1: Reflecting on Your Revisions

First, write a new reflective statement about the most recent draft by considering the following. Be sure to append your reflective statement to the draft before sharing it with your peers.

- What did you change to create this most recent draft, and why did you do so?
- What is your favorite part of this draft?
- What other revisions are you planning on making?
- Are there particular sections you want particular type of help on? Are there some particular issues you want your readers to focus on?
- If you had had more time to prepare this draft, what would you have done differently?

Step 2: Sharing Second Drafts

Exchange your draft with the same or new peer critics in hard copy or electronic file or as E-mail or an E-mail attachment. Peer critics should use the criteria described in Activity 8.3 to generate feedback on this most recent draft.

ACTIVITY 8.7: Revising for Style

After two or more rounds of peer review and revisions, your narrative should be taking shape in terms of its content and structure. And, as you've been revising, it's very likely you have paid some attention to language, style, and correctness. Complete the following steps to fine-tune your narrative.

Step 1: Reading Aloud to "Hear" Your Draft

Read the draft aloud slowly, to yourself, a classmate, a friend, or family member (or have one of them read it to you), and listen for the following:

- Do you hear any "echoes," that is, certain words that are used over and over in close approximation to one another?
- Do you or your reader stumble over any words or phrases? Stumbling may indicate missing words or awkward constructions.
- Do certain sections sound telegraphic? Mark those passages and see whether you can revise them to eliminate choppy phrases and incomplete sentences that may be fragments.
- Do certain sections leave you or your reader breathless? Mark those passages and see whether you can revise them to be less wordy.
- Do some sections sound droning and monotonal? Check those passages to see whether you can vary the styles and lengths of a group of sentences so the rhythm is more varied.

Step 2: Spellcheck and Proofread

Remember to use your word processor's spelling checker to seek out and correct typos, misspellings, and repeated words.

ACTIVITY 8.8: Sharing Your Narrative

Remember, the goals of writing Tales of Cyberspace include practicing the narrative writing genre and, more important, affecting a particular audience of readers, that is, to reveal to them something about your experiences with technology and your explorations of cyberspace in both an entertaining and informative fashion. The final activity of this chapter, then, is sharing your narrative with real readers. Once again, depending on the technological setup of your institution, you have a number of options.

Option 1: Sharing Hard Copies

This is the option to which you are most accustomed, probably. Print several copies of your final version and distribute them to the peers who read the various drafts of your narrative. If your peers share their drafts with you, be sure to send them an E-mail message with your thoughts on the final result of all your hard, collaborative efforts. When replying to your peers' drafts, you need not offer more critical feedback. Just tell them your favorite parts, what you learned that you didn't know before, and so on. By praising their work and offering them a virtual pat on the back, you increase your chances of receiving favorable reviews of your narrative.

Option 2: Sharing Electronic Texts

By now you have plenty of experience sharing texts electronically. As when you shared your drafts, you can take these steps:

- Send your final version to your draft reviewers as E-mail or E-mail attachments. When you receive final versions from others, be sure to reply with sincere words of praise and encouragement.
- Post your final version as an article on a newsgroup if your teacher has set one up for your class.
- If you have the technological access and ability at this point to construct your own site on the World Wide Web, "publish" your narrative there. Chapter 5 offers a brief introduction to constructing Web pages. In Chapter 12, you will find more suggestions for constructing a Web site of your work.

9

WRITING TO ANALYZE

ACADEMIC WRITING: OVERVIEW

Writing in the academy is a context-rich kind of writing. That is, what one person writes contributes to an ongoing, extended written "conversation" about a topic. Someone, somewhere, raises an issue. Someone else reads that first statement and responds with a new idea, agreeing, disagreeing, complementing, or supplementing what the first writer said. A third person, reading what each of the other two have written, pitches in with a heretofore unexamined problem or issue. And so it goes. In this way, Aristotle began a conversation about rhetoric that continues today, even in this textbook and this class. Similarly, Freud began a conversation about the human mind, and that conversation produced the field of psychology. And when Jung responded to Freud, he did so in a way that showed his awareness of the context Freud had provided. And when B. F. Skinner joined the conversation, he did so in a way that showed he was aware of Freud's and Jung's writings. Then the cognitive psychologists joined in and, well, you get the picture.

As you can guess from the last paragraph, academic writing involves more than just writing. Reading supplies the context for a piece of writing, so reading is almost as important in academic writing as writing is. Academic writing is done in the spirit of inquiry and with the recognition that no one person can have the whole answer, even to a narrow question. So the writer in the academy must read and evaluate what others have said before she can contribute to the conversation. (In a similar fashion and for similar reasons, you lurked in a computer-based community in earlier chapters before you jumped in with your own comments.) To write effectively—to join this extended, context-rich, written conversation—you first use the tools of inquiry and analysis.

Inquiry

First, you have to find out what others have said. Kenneth Burke likened this to entering a parlor where a group of people are carrying on a conversation. Before you enter that conversation, you have to listen for a while. You have to find out what the topics are, where the conversation has been, where it is headed. You want to know who is advancing what ideas and who is agreeing and disagreeing on what issues. You want to know whose statements are most influential. In short, you want to know enough about the conversation to feel safe entering it, secure that you won't be saying something that's already been said, that the others are taking for granted, or that the others think is silly, stupid, or just plain obvious. In Burke's parlor, you gain the knowledge you need by listening; in classes, you gain that knowledge by reading.

Analysis

After you've inquired in this way, you have to analyze. Once you know where the conversation is and where it is headed, you have to weigh what is being said to find out what, if anything, you can contribute about the topics under discussion. You'll read what the major writers, researchers, or scholars have written, and you'll weigh what they've said against each other and against your own experience. You'll decide what issues interest you, and you'll follow those threads of the conversation, reading what major and minor figures have contributed. Maybe you'll begin by finding statements you agree or disagree with. That's a good start. Eventually, you'll learn to weigh all that writing and find issues the others have missed, or you'll be able to apply recently developed knowledge to verify, critique, or elaborate upon earlier statements. In short, your skills of analysis will bring you to the point at which you realize that you have something to say, something to add to the conversation. You may have written during this process—taking notes, writing summaries or abstracts of your readings, writing reports for your professor or your classmates—but for the most part, you will come this far by reading. This kind of reading is itself pretty specialized, but you'll have a lot of practice as you do the reading and writing in preparation for writing in all your classes. In most academic settings, however, inquiry is rarely enough; it is usually a step in the process toward a higher goal—analysis. To analyze means to sift through a set of events, circumstances, or readings to make sense of them, to bring coherence to them, to make them meaningful.

This chapter will lead you through two analytical writing projects. The first one, "Analyzing Virtual Communities," will have some similarities to one of the projects in Chapter 8, "Tales of Cyberspace," if you chose to tell a story about a virtual community you joined. Whereas your goal with that project was to write a narrative essay, one that might have offered some analysis, in this project you will be asked to analyze some feature of a virtual community such as the language participants use, the types of relationships members create, and so on.

The second project, "Writing to Read Critically," will lead you through a procedure of using writing to read critically sources you may find on the Internet as you conduct research for papers and argumentative essays. As will be explained in more detail in that project, although doing research on the Internet can save you much of the time associated with doing research, such as getting to a library, learning its systems and looking up resource materials, and tracking down those materials, in some ways Internet research requires more intellectual work. This is the case because much of what you might find for research in a traditional library has in one way or another already received a "seal of approval." In most cases, what you would find in a library has gone through a series of "filters" by publishers who judge the quality of a piece before agreeing to publish it; by editors who, often with the help reviews by other experts on the topic, certify that the essay, article, or book makes a reasonable contribution to the ongoing conversation in that field; and by librarians who deem the work valuable enough to include it in their library's collection. By contrast, much of what is "published" on the Internet has not gone through such filtering processes, and although such filtering agencies are emerging daily, the fact remains that much of what you might find on the Internet lacks the levels of validity and reliability often deemed necessary by an academic community to make a serious contribution to the field. As a result, if you do use the Internet for research, you have a greater responsibility than ever to read potential sources very critically.

PROJECT 4: ANALYZING VIRTUAL COMMUNITIES

Objectives

- To study a virtual, on-line community
- To learn how virtual communities conduct themselves with the goal of becoming a more knowledgeable and effective member of virtual communities
- To learn and practice a major tool of academic life—analytical writing

Technological Requirements

- A word processor
- Access to virtual communities such as
  — Usenet newsgroups;
  — listservs, listprocs, majordomos;
  — electronic bulletin boards;

— Internet relay chat (IRC); and
— MUDs/MOOs/MUSHes

Participant Prerequisites

- Intermediate Internet literacy skills, including knowledge of
  — how to find virtual communities;
  — how to join virtual communities;
  — how to participate in virtual communities; and
  — how to capture threads (Usenet), E-mail messages, and synchronous conference transcripts

Overview

As noted earlier, you will be required to write analytical papers for most of the different subjects you will study at the college level and beyond. In an English literature class, you may write a "literary analysis" in which you had to interpret a poem, short story, or novel. In a science class, you may write an analysis of the chemical reactions during a lab experiment. In a history class, you may write an analysis of the causes of the Vietnam War. In a business class, you may write an analysis of a marketing campaign.

Although each of these assignments asks you to analyze something different and perhaps use different analytical techniques, they all have several features in common. First, in each case you would have an object of analysis. That object might be an actual or tangible "thing" (e.g., a clump of soil or a type of leaf), a visual stimulus (e.g., a painting or a photograph), a language construct (e.g. a poem or a novel), or a phenomenon (e.g., a historical event or a dispute between or among authoritative people or publications). Such analyses would also have common analytical goals of close observation or reading, a breaking of the whole into parts, evaluating similarities and differences among the parts, and analyzing how they work together to make the whole, all with the intent of making sense of the object or phenomena. Finally, these types of analyses also result in some sort of writing. More important, they don't just *result* in writing, but writing is the vehicle through which the analysis develops.

This project leads you through an analysis of a virtual community. In some ways, the object of analysis, an on-line community bound together through computer-mediated communication, is similar to one of the "Tales of Cyberspace" options in Chapter 8. Once again you will be asked to join a virtual community, but this time instead of telling a story about it, you will be asked to analyze it. Indeed, you may find yourself using some narrative techniques to describe the community, but this time you will be required to break down the whole into parts in an attempt to teach your readers what makes your community unique and how it works. If we can think of description based on your observation as "what" you are studying, an effective analysis will go beyond description to answer the "so what?" question.

The Assignment

Write a four- to seven-page or 1,000- to 1,500-word analysis of a virtual community of your choosing. Your goal is to describe the community as deeply as possible, break the components of that community into definable parts (membership, purpose, language, behaviors, interaction patterns, etc.), and analyze how the community works. Your audience is other members of higher education like yourself. You might assume they have the same or less technological knowledge than you do, that they have the same or less knowledge of cyberspace than you, and you can expect they will know less about your particular virtual community than you do. As an academic audience, however, they expect an academic style including formal language, discipline-appropriate documentation, and evidence of analytical thinking. In short, they expect you to sound and act like others in the community of higher education. At the same time, however, they expect sophisticated but clear writing that conforms to the rules of grammar, usage, and punctuation of standard written English.

ACTIVITY 9.1: Finding a Community to Join

At this point in the course, you may already have been a member of several virtual communities. If you wrote a tale of cyberspace about a CMC community, you've already gotten some insight into how these communities work. If you have now become comfortable with E-mail, IRC, Usenet newsgroups, or other CMC applications, you may have joined other communities, even if only to exchange E-mail regularly with friends across campus and across the country. And if your class has enjoyed the technological ability to create a virtual community of its own through CMC and the World Wide Web, you are now a member not only of a learning community that meets face to face a couple of hours a week but also one that includes a virtual element. So you already have places to begin. Also, you will probably want to revisit Activity 8.2, option 2, in Chapter 8 and Chapters 2, 3, and 5 for reminders on how to find potential virtual communities for this project. The following options and steps might also help you discover virtual communities to join.

Option 1: Oral Collaboration

Whether or not your whole class is on-line during class meetings, most of you at this point in the course have visited and joined various communities. Some might have been busy, highly interesting places; others might have been so quiet that there wasn't much to observe; and others, though the members contributed lots of messages, might have been deadly boring. With this option, you might gather as a large group and have a face-to-face discussion built around the questions in step 1. If your community does choose this option, you might consider writing up in advance your responses to the questions in step 1 and making enough copies for everyone in class. If you decide not to share written responses, everyone else in class will need to remember to take notes during the conversation that results from step 2.

Option 2: On-Line Collaboration

If at this point in the semester your class has gone on-line by way of a special newsgroup, listserv, MOO room, or some other sort of CMC application, you may want to exchange ideas on potential communities to join. Again, if you choose this option, structure your on-line conversation on the issues in step 2.

Step 1: Reflecting on Virtual Communities You've Visited

Regardless of what option your class uses to share previous experiences with virtual communities, you can still explore those experiences through writing. Doing so will help you think more deeply about where you've been and also help you prepare your contributions to the sharing discussion in step 2. Launch your word processor, start a new file, and respond to the following items:

- What CMC-based communities have you already visited? Don't forget, if your class uses CMC among yourselves, your class would qualify as a virtual community.
- What memorable experiences did you have?
- What were the worst aspects of joining that community?
- What do you remember about your reactions to joining the community? Was it exciting? Scary and intimidating? Boring? Intensive and time-consuming?
- What do you remember learning about the people, the way they communicated, how you learned about CMC, what you learned about the topics discussed on-line?
- The virtual community you visited was supported by one type of CMC system such as E-mail. Are there any other types of CMC communities you've heard about but haven't yet tried out? For example, while you explored an E-mail list, perhaps one of your classmates visited an Internet Relay Chat channel. Have you become curious enough to try out one of the other types of communities you've read or heard about from your peers in this class?
- Have you kept up with the community? If so, you must know much more about it now than you did when you first joined. Do you think the same community would serve as a good site to study for this project? If you haven't kept up with it, would you consider joining it again to learn more about it?

Step 2: Sharing Previous Experiences with Virtual Communities

While writing "Tales of Cyberspace" many of you explored different virtual communities supported by different types of CMC systems and concerning different topics. Share with your classmates, orally or on-line depending on which of the options your community chose, the following information:

- What virtual communities have you visited in the past? Be sure you include:
  - the CMC system (i.e., Usenet newsgroup, IRC, MOO, listserv, listproc, majordomo) and
  - the access information for the community (i.e. the newsgroup name, the exact IRC channel, the Telnet address for the MOO, the listserv address, etc.).
- How would you describe the ones you've visited? What was (were) the major topic(s) of discussion? What was the theme of the virtual community? Were there a lot or only a few messages? Were the threads, strands, and conversations lively, interesting, boring?
- How did you find out about the(se) community(ies)? Were they recommended to you by a friend? Did you stumble on them randomly? Did you "search" for them using techniques described in this book or other on-line sources?
- Would you recommend any to a friend? Why?
- Knowing what you know about this project at this point, can you think of any communities you've joined that you think would lend themselves to a fruitful discourse analysis?

Step 3: Making Sense of Sharing Experiences about Virtual Communities
OK, now you've heard or read about other's experiences with on-line communities. Consider the following items as a guide to help you think about communities you might join:

- Which of the virtual communities you heard about from your classmates did you find most interesting? Are they ones you would consider joining and studying?
- What questions do you still have about the communities that interest you most? For example, you might have questions about the amount of traffic, how to find and join the communities, what software to use to gain access to them, and so on. If your sharing was conducted face to face, ask the person who shared the community with you. If your class's sharing was conducted on-line, send an E-mail message with your questions.

Step 4: Deciding on a Community to Join
By following the previous steps, you have made a thorough investigation of communities you might join to analyze. Now you need to decide on one. Here are criteria for choosing a virtual community:

- *Choose one in which you have an interest.* Your interest could be in the topic or theme of the group, the kinds of people who participate there, or the type of CMC used. Because you will be studying this group, you want to make sure you follow your interests and curiosity.
- *Choose one you've visited before (if possible).* If you wrote about a CMC community in "Tales of Cyberspace" and that community was an active and interesting one, you might consider continuing your participation in that one. If you've been hanging around there for a while, you probably have a better idea of how it works than you would if you had to join one cold. You might, too, already have saved E-mail messages and transcripts from your earlier visits, so you'd have a good start on the data collection. Of course, if you were never really interested or if you lost interest in that community, there is no need to join it again.
- *Choose one with a considerable amount of traffic.* If you choose a community with relatively low volume of messages or participants (e.g., a listserv on which only three participants send messages every other day or a MOO room where only a couple of people meet during the times you can join), you probably won't be able to collect enough data to write an in-depth analysis. On the other hand, if you join an extremely busy community, you may find yourself flooded with data. Erring on the side of too much data is preferable, however.
- *Choose one with collectable data.* Some types of CMC communities better lend themselves to data capture. If you belong to a listserv, for example, you can create a folder in your E-mail program to store all the messages you receive as a member of that community. IRC discussions, however, can be more difficult to capture, depending on the client software you are using to participate in the channel. Before you commit to a particular community, you will want to determine what kind of software you'll be able to use and how well that software allows you to save transcripts of discussions.

ACTIVITY 9.2: Investigating the Community

Now that you have decided on a virtual community to study, you need to join it, lurk in it, and to participate in it for a given period of time. Your teacher and your class will be able to determine how much time you will have to investigate your community. Remember, the more data you collect, the better your chances are of conducting an in-depth analysis. You should plan on logging on to your community at least once a day—more, if possible.

Step 1: Collecting Data

Start keeping a log of your visits and observations. Each time you log onto your virtual community, you should note the date, day of the week, and time. Whenever possible, capture a transcript, save the newsgroup thread, or save in a folder E-mail messages you receive from your community's list-serv. During and at the end of each on-line session, write a reflection on what you observed or learned about the community during that session. The following items will help you structure your observations. Note that these are suggestive rather than exhaustive. The type and nature of the community you actually study might lead you to create your own questions and categories. Also note that the following are investigative categories. Although they will help you observe, evaluate, and categorize your data, you should realize that you may or may not use all your observations, and the items below do not constitute an outline for your paper.

- Information about the community
  - Is there a frequently asked questions (FAQ) file or message available for the group? If so, seek it out and read it carefully. Such documents often give crucial background information such as the purpose of the group, the owner of the list, and the rules of participation.
- Quantitative data
  - For a synchronous environment, how many messages are sent during a given session? For an asynchronous community, how many messages are sent over a give time period—a day or a week?
  - How long are the messages (in number of words)? How long are the longest ones? How long are the shortest ones? What is the average message length?
  - How many people contribute messages in a given session or over a given period of time?
- Demographic data
  - How many females contribute to your community? How many males?
  - What can you tell about the race, class, education levels, and ages of the members of your community? In following a listserv or a Usenet newsgroup, you can often infer much about participants' ages, genders, and affiliations if they use a signature file with their messages. Such "sig files" might offer professional titles, places of work, and so on. Also, you can often tell people's affiliations from their E-mail messages. For example, wbutler@umich.edu indicates that my E-mail account is through an educational institution (edu) and, more specifically, the University of Michigan (umich). By contrast, some participants might have name@aol.com addresses, which indicates they are America Online members.
  - How many people are subscribed to the listserv? You can get a directory of a list's subscribers by sending a REVIEW message to the listserv that hosts the list. For example, if we wanted to get a list of subcribers to the list acw-l (The Alliance for Computers and Writing), we would send the following message to listproc@listserv.ttu.edu:

REVIEW acw-1

— Looking at the list of subscribers, can you tell where most of them are from? Do their E-mail addresses connect them with educational institutions (edu), businesses (com), the military (mil)? Do country extensions identify some members as international (ca = Canada, au = Australia, uk = United Kingdom, etc.)? How many names are clearly masculine? How many clearly feminine? How many are ambiguous (Leslie, Jan, Dene, Kim, etc.)? How does the overall list compare with the list of active contributors? What's the overall gender balance in this community?

- Social dynamics
  — Describe any "incidents" within the community such as flame wars, poignant moments of community building, and so forth.
  — Do any "personalities" emerge? Who are the more frequent participants? Who seems to ask questions? Who seems most often to answer questions?
  — How much do participants interact?
  — Any evidence that participants "listen" to one another or not?
  — Which participants seem to be "friends" and which seem to be "adversaries"?
  — Who seems to lead and who seems to follow?

- Linguistic/content data
  — What kind of language is used? Is most of the language informal, characterized by slang, profanity, and speechlike writing? Is most of the language formal, characterized by essaylike writing with objective language, technical jargon, complex sentences, and other markers of formal language? Or, does the formality or informality of language vary from participant to participant, topic to topic, time to time?
  — What kinds of information are shared? How much of the content of the contributions is factual, information giving, question asking, playing/socializing, and so on?
  — What can you infer about the community's standards of netiquette? Do longtime members greet newbies graciously, or are naive questions by newbies met with insults and derision? Do members chide those who use profanity or contribute off-topic messages?

ACTIVITY 9.3: Making Sense of Your Observations

After you have visited your virtual community for a given period of time, collected data, and taken extensive notes about your observations, you need to start making sense of what you've observed. That is, you need to analyze it. Remember, your goal is not merely to describe the community, that is, the "what," but rather to analyze some aspect of the community— the "so what?"

Step 1: Reflecting on Your Data and Observations

Launch your word processor and open a new file. Freewrite for as long as you can and address the following:

- What are your initial impressions about your community? Is it friendly, social, intimidating, serious?
- What are your initial impressions about the language the community uses? Do participants tend to use informal, speechlike language? Do they tend to use formal, "written-type" language? Is there a wide range of language styles?
- To the best of your memory, what is the purpose of the community? Do members pretty much stick to the purpose, or do they stray often? What is the range of topics?
- Are there any particular messages that you remember as being insightful, poignant, or which in some way or another had an effect on you?
- Do any particular "characters" stick out in your mind?
- Do any particular "events"—a flame war, the death or illness of a member, a blossoming on-line romance—stick out in your mind?
- What impressions do you have about the social relations among the members of the group? Is there a wide range of participants, or do most of the participants have much in common in terms of gender, interests, occupation, and so on? Does one group seem to dominate another, such as males over females, technological experts over technological novices, content experts over content novices?

Step 2: Looking for Patterns

To this point you have hung around your virtual community, collected and categorized data, and reflected on your observations. Now you need to start looking in a more detailed fashion for patterns or themes that arise out of your data and observations. The most dominant of these patterns or themes may well become the focus of your analysis. Look back on your freewrite reflections and ask yourself the following:

- Of all the observations you made, which two or three stick out most in your mind?
- Were there any memorable flame wars?
- Were there any examples of sexism, racism, ageism, classism?
- Who were the "best" writers in the community?
- Who among the membership seemed difficult to understand?

ACTIVITY 9.4: Social Invention

Unless you happened to be studying the same virtual community as one of your classmates, you haven't had an opportunity to "bounce" your ideas and observations off your classroom learning community. At this point you may be sailing along smoothly and already have discovered some patterns and determined a focus. On the other hand, you and many of your classmates may be finding yourselves wallowing in a churning sea of data and unconnected observations and ideas. If this is the case, you may want to share some of your work in progress—share what you've discovered so far and find out what others have learned. As with earlier activities, you have two options: sharing in large- or small-group face-to-face discussion or sharing ideas on-line.

Option 1: Face-to-Face Oral Discussion

Gather into small groups of three-to-five people or a large group, and use the suggestions in step 1 to guide your sharing of works in progress.

Option 2: On-Line Sharing

Use your class's CMC capabilities to share your works in progress, and use the suggestions in step 1 to guide your discussion.

Step 1: Sharing Works in Progress

- Use the freewriting document you created in Activity 8.3, step 1, as a basis for sharing with your peers:
    — A brief description of your group (name, kind of CMC technology that supports it)
    — Your general impressions of the community
    — What patterns you see emerging
- If possible, share with your peers your current thoughts on what focus or angle you might take in your analysis and why you're considering those options.
- Listen to (or read if on-line) your peers' impressions about their works in progress. Have you learned about patterns you hadn't thought of yourself but that may in fact be relevant to your community?
- Do you have any questions about your own progress that you would like to get advice on from your peers?

ACTIVITY 9.5: Writing the First Draft

By now you should have all you need to begin your first draft. You have read, observed, reflected on, and shared with others your impressions and progress. Your thoughts may still be in an unfocused state, but the very act of composing the first draft should help you narrow and focus.

Step 1: Finding a Focus

You have probably collected enough data and have thought of enough random observations to write a twenty- or thirty-page paper, but your goal, you will remember, is only four to seven pages. So you need to find a focus. In fact, all the prior activities were designed to help you start narrowing in on two or three features of your virtual community that might serve as a focus for your paper. Here are some suggestions for determining a focus:

- *Focus on one member.* You might select a person because he was outrageous and stirred up lots of trouble, because she was thoughtful and wrote well enough to emerge as a leader, or because he somehow served as a model for the membership of the community. What characteristics (nature of contributions, writing style, interactions with other) did that person display that made him or her stand out from the crowd?
- *Focus on a small group of people who either formed a clique or who engaged in virtual tugs of war on certain topics.* What bound these people together? What effect did their clique have on the rest of the community.
- *Focus on a dramatic event like a flame war.* What caused the event? Profane language, clashing beliefs, misunderstandings, miscommunications? What effect did the flame war have on the community? Did others join in? Did the event cause others to sit back and wait it out? How did it end? Did "calmer voices" prevail? Did it just sputter out from lack of interest on the part of the combatants? Did one side or other offer a white flag? Other on-line "events" might include romances, deaths, births, and so on.
- *Focus on gender, race, or class issues.* Did males tend to dominate in one way or another? Did there appear to be an equal number of males and females on-line? If so, how did the number of contributions from each group compare to their numbers? How did the males treat the females? Was one group taken more seriously than another group?
- *Focus on a particular topic, strand, or thread.* Which topic seemed to dominate while you were on-line? What were the range of contributions? What made it a dominant strand? Were there lots of differences of opinions on a controversial topic that led to debate? Was it a complex topic that required lots of people to contribute different bits of information and knowledge? How did the strand contribute to or otherwise affect the community's knowledge or harmony?
- *Focus on language.* Did a particular style of language dominate? If so, how? Did the language, style, and content of some subgroups' messages (i.e., males, females, experts, nonexperts) demonstrate or reveal anything about that subgroup?
- *Focus on how the virtual community you studied was like or unlike more traditional communities to which you've belonged.* For instance, was your community like (or unlike) an educational community (a classroom), a religious community (a parish or congregation), a social community (a fraternity/sorority, a club), a family?

Step 2: Developing a Tentative Thesis

Once you have zeroed in on a focus, try writing a tentative thesis that will serve as your controlling idea for the essay. By tentative we mean to imply that as you actually develop the paper, you may need to further narrow and revise the thesis itself, but articulating one now will give you something concrete to work with. Some samples are described here. Yours, of course, will be different based on the realities of your virtual community.

- Focus on a person:
  "Of the thirty members of the rec.autos.crashes newsgroup, one stands out. Mario Andretti, even though he didn't send as many articles as some others in the community, was the most influential member of the group and thus controlled the directions that topics and the community took. His influence can be seen through the number of topics he initiated, the number of responses his articles received, and the number of times his words or comments were quoted by others. He was able to play such a leadership role because he was among the most knowledgeable about the topic threads and he wrote well."
- Focus on a clique:
  "The IRC Channel 'tv' was dominated by three males, Tom, Dick, and Harry. These three, bound by their shared interest in flirtatious behavior and ribald humor, effectively shut out others by sending a rapid succession of messages that 'drowned out' other's contributions, by frequently making laudatory references to one another's contributions, and by engaging in gender baiting which made 'tv' an uncomfortable environment for women."
- Focus on how the virtual community compares to more traditional communities:
  "The listserv discussion list Novels-l@upu.edu, a virtual community dedicated to the discussion of 'serious novels,' is like the most intimidating and boring class I was ever in. Its membership is divided into three basic categories: those who ask questions, like students in a classroom; those who participate but have little of substance to say, like class pets; and those who pontificate, like the worst of overbearing teachers in traditional classrooms. For a relative novice and fan of 'trash' novels like myself, I felt unwelcomed and at times humiliated."

Step 3: Describing Your Community

As noted at the beginning of this chapter, much analytical writing involves breaking the whole into its component parts. In most cases, you have some sort of "object" of analysis, be it a molecule, a painting, or an event. Because your readers, most of whom we can assume have not visited your virtual community, need to understand the "object" you are analyzing, you could help them better understand your analysis by describing in some detail your community.

- What was the name of your virtual community, and where is it located (listserv address, IRC channel, newsgroup name, etc.)?
- What was the stated or implied purpose of the community?
- What kind of data did you collect, and how did you collect it?
- During what time period did you make your observations? For an asynchronous community (listserv, newsgroup, bulletin board service), when did you begin and end your data collection? For a synchronous community (IRC, MUD/MOO/MUSH), exactly when (what days and dates, what times, for how long) did you visit?
- What is the demographic makeup? (number, gender, race, class, educational level of participants) of the community?
- What was the traffic volume (total number of messages, average number of messages per participant, etc.)?

Step 4: Building Your Analysis

After you have offered a detailed description of your virtual community and drafted your thesis statement or controlling idea, you need to begin building your analysis. In general, you are trying to construct logical support and clarification for your controlling idea. Let us take the example thesis offered earlier about Mario Andretti and his dominance in the rec.auto.crashes newsgroup as an illustration of the kinds of information a reader might expect to find:

> Of the thirty members of the rec.autos.crashes newsgroup, one stands out. Mario Andretti, even though he didn't send as many articles as did some others in the community, was the most influential member of the group and thus controlled the directions that topics and the community took. His influence can be seen through the number of topics he initiated, the number of responses his articles received, and the number of times his words or comments were quoted by others. He was able to play such a leadership role because he was among the most knowledgeable about the topic threads and he wrote well.

To support the assertions in this statement, you would have to do these things:

- Offer evidence about how many messages Mario sent as compared to others in the group.
- Offer evidence of his "influence" by showing:
  — how many and which of his messages initiated topics,
  — how many of his messages received responses and/or were quoted by others,
  — what in his messages illustrate his superior knowledge, and
  — what in his messages illustrate how well he wrote.

What counts as evidence? The best, of course, would be direct quotations from the articles Andretti posted. You do, however, want to select your examples judiciously. It will not suffice to string together lengthy quotations just for the sake of doing so. You want to select only those messages or, better yet, the portions of those messages, that directly support the assertions you are making.

ACTIVITY 9.6: Sharing Drafts

Now that you have completed a draft, this would be a good time to share that draft with peers to get some feedback. As has been the case at this stage on previous projects, you have the option of giving and receiving feedback in small or large face-to-face or on-line groups, depending on how much class time you have to dedicate to this stage of the project or what kind of CMC system is available.

Consult Activity 3.4 in Chapter 3, Activity 8.4 in Chapter 8, and Activity 9.4 in Chapter 9 for an array of guidelines for organizing the feedback process.

No matter what type of feedback process you choose, it is still important that you reflect on your own draft, to help you make sense of both what you've accomplished thus far and what you want to accomplish on future drafts. Reflecting on your progress to date also helps you prepare the draft to share with your peer reviewers.

Step 1: Reflections on the First Draft

Open a file in your word processor and address the following:

- What parts of the process involved in writing this paper, from collecting data to writing this draft, went best for you? Describe those parts of the process in some detail and offer reasons why they went well.
- What parts of the process thus far have proved most challenging? Why did those parts cause problems?
- Remind yourself of your purpose. In twenty-five words or less, summarize what point you are trying to make about your virtual community.
- Remind yourself of your audience. Have you provided them enough information about your virtual community so they will understand what you are analyzing? Have you used language appropriate for the audience and purpose? Have you provided appropriate amounts and types of details to support your assertions?
- What are the successful aspects of your draft thus far? Describe in some detail what works and why.
- What are some of the areas needing improvement in the current draft? Describe in some detail what areas you want to improve and why you want to improve them.

- If you were to share this draft with readers, what questions might you ask them? What kind of feedback would you like?
- Articulate for yourself a revision strategy that includes what you feel the draft still needs and what you plan to do to make the essay more effective.

Step 2: Preparing Your Draft for Peer Reviews

Your reflection process will help you prepare your draft for the peer review process. Append to your current draft an assessment of what you think works in the draft and a list of questions you would like your reviewers to address as they review your draft.

ACTIVITY 9.7: Giving/Receiving Feedback

Read your peers' drafts (depending on how your peer review process has been organized) twice: once silently and again aloud. Then, use the following items to guide your written feedback.

- Initial responses
  — What are the best parts of the draft?
  — What did you find most interesting?
  — What was the best passage or detail of the draft?
  — What was the best-written passage?
  — What did you learn about the virtual community?
- Describing the draft
  — Write a fifty-word abstract of the draft.
  — Construct an outline of the draft, using a Roman numeral for each part of the essay (i.e., introduction, body, conclusion), a capital letter for each paragraph, and an Arabic numeral for each supporting detail.
- Evaluating the draft
  — Is the draft "analytical" or more descriptive or narrative?
  — Were there any points where you got "lost" in the draft? What might have caused your confusion?
  — Look at the outline you wrote. Does it flow logically from point to point, or do you think that some parts might be rearranged?
  — Evaluate the content. What else do you think you need to know to understand the draft? Did you find any generalizations or assertions that could use more support? Any generalizations or assertions that could use better support? Are the details used judiciously?
  — Evaluate the language and style. When you read the draft aloud, did you stumble over any phrases? Did you notice any drawn-out sentences that left you nearly breathless? Did you notice any short, choppy sentences that might have created a staccato, telegraphic rhythm? Is the level of formality and sophistication appropriate for the audience?

- Revision ideas
  - What are the good parts of the draft the writer might build on?
  - In general, what are the areas needing improvement?
  - In detail, what do you believe the writer needs to do improve the draft? For example, does the writer need to add more information? Where? What kind? Cut out some details? Which ones? Why?

ACTIVITY 9.8: Revising Your Analysis

You have now received feedback on the first draft of your analysis from one or more peer reviewers. Now your task is to analyze the feedback you've received, perhaps engage in a computer-mediated dialogue with your peers to solicit more feedback, and revise your analysis based on the feedback.

Step 1: Making Sense of Feedback You've Received

Read your peers' responses carefully and consider the following items:

- Were all the comments clear? Which did you not understand? Did reading the comments make you wonder about other aspects of your draft?
- Reply to the E-mail feedback you received from your peers by asking for clarification of their comments. If one reader pointed out one problem with your draft and the others didn't, you might ask the latter to look at the same section again to see what they think.
- Having now read the feedback from your peers, do other questions occur to you? E-mail your peers with those questions.
- How were your peers' comments similar to those you made about the draft in your reflective statement?
- How are the critiques similar? In other words, are there certain features of your draft all your readers liked? Did they have similar comments about the content, structure, or style of your draft? Make a list of all the common comments, both the praise and the constructive criticism.
- How do the critiques differ? Did they comment on different aspects of your draft? Did one applaud you for a section while another reader identified that same section as an area of improvement? If you do get contradictory comments on the same aspects of your draft, what might that mean? Make a list of all the areas of improvement or contradictory comments.
- What did you learn about writing an effective analysis from critiquing your writing partners' drafts? Was there anything you said about their drafts that might equally apply to your own?
- Reflect on the lists you made and what you noticed in your peers' drafts, and develop a revision strategy for yourself. You might begin this strategy by completing the following phrases:

— What my readers most appreciated in my draft was . . .

— According to my readers, the areas of improvement for my next draft include . . .

— In my next draft I plan on doing . . . because . . .

Step 2: Revise Your Draft

Revise your draft based on the feedback you've received.

ACTIVITY 9.9: Second Draft Critiques

Now that you have had a chance to revise your draft, and if time permits, arrange another round of peer reviews.

Step 1: Reflecting on Your Revisions

First, write a new reflective statement about the most recent draft by considering the following. Be sure to append your reflective statement to the draft before sharing it with your peers.

- What did you change to create this most recent draft, and why did you do so?
- What is your favorite part of this draft?
- What other revisions are you planning on making?
- Are there particular sections you want particular types of help on? Are there some particular issues you want your readers to focus on?
- If you had had more time to prepare this draft, what would you have done differently?

Step 2: Sharing Second Drafts

Exchange your draft with the same or new peer critics either in hard copy or electronic file or as E-mail or an E-mail attachment. Peer critics should use the criteria described in Activity 9.6 to generate feedback on this most recent draft.

ACTIVITY 9.10: Revising for Style

After two or more rounds of peer review and revisions, your analysis should be taking shape in terms of its content and structure. And as you've been revising, you have very likely paid some attention to language, style, and correctness. Complete the following steps to fine-tune your analysis.

Step 1: Reading Aloud to "Hear" Your Draft

Read the draft aloud slowly, either to yourself, a classmate, friend, or family member (or have one of them read it to you), and listen for the following:

- Do you hear any "echoes," that is, certain words that are used over and over in close approximation to one another?

- Do you or your reader stumble over any words or phrases? Stumbling may indicate missing words or awkward constructions.
- Do certain sections sound telegraphic? Mark those passages and see whether you can revise them to eliminate choppy phrases and incomplete sentences that may be fragments.
- Do certain sections leave you or your reader breathless? Mark those passages and see whether you can revise them to be less wordy.
- Do some sections sound droning and monotonal? Check those passages to see whether you can vary the styles and lengths of a group of sentences so the rhythm is more varied.

Step 2: Spellcheck and Proofread

Remember to use your word processor's spelling checker to seek out and correct typos, misspellings, and repeated words.

ACTIVITY 9.11: Sharing Your Analysis

The final activity of this project is sharing your narrative with real readers. Once again, depending on the technological setup of your institution, you have a number of options.

Option 1: Sharing Hard Copies

This is the option to which you are probably most accustomed. Print several copies of your final version and distribute them to the peers who read the various drafts of your analysis. If your peers shared their drafts with you, be sure to send them an E-mail message with your thoughts on the final result of all your hard, collaborative efforts. When replying to your peers' final versions, you need not offer more critical feedback. Just tell them your favorite parts, what you learned that you didn't know before, and so on. By praising their work and offering them a virtual pat on the back, you increase your chances of receiving favorable reviews of your analysis.

Option 2: Sharing Electronic Texts

By now you have plenty of experience sharing texts electronically. As when you shared your drafts, you can do a few things:

- Send your final version to your draft reviewers as E-mail or an E-mail attachment. When you receive final versions from others, be sure to reply with sincere words of praise and encouragement.
- Post your final version as an article on a newsgroup if your teacher has set one up for your class.
- If you have the technological access and ability at this point to construct your own site on the World Wide Web, "publish" your analysis there. Chapter 5 offers a brief introduction to constructing Web pages. In Chapter 12 you will find more suggestions for constructing a Web site of your work.

PROJECT 5: WRITING TO READ CRITICALLY

Objectives

- To use writing as a way to read critically
- To provide a tool for collaborative research

Technological Requirements

- A word processor
- Access to on-line research sources including on-line library catalogs, Gopherspace, and the World Wide Web
- Access to a computer-mediated communication system such as a local area network or wide area network E-mail system or electronic conferencing system

Participants' Prerequisites

- Basic knowledge of conducting research on-line, including (see Chapter 4 for information about these techniques):
  — searching on-line library catalogs using Boolean search techniques,
  — searching Gopherspace using Archie and Veronica,
  — searching the World Wide Web using search engines, and
- Basic knowledge of using asynchronous CMC (newsgroups, E-mail groups) to share information

Overview

You have heard time and time again two sayings pertaining to reading critically: "You can't tell a book by its cover," and "Don't believe everything you read." The first one is a way of saying don't be fooled by appearances, and the second one implies that just because something is in print doesn't automatically mean the information is valid and reliable. If these phrases kept you on your toes as a navigator and consumer of print text, they will serve you even better as you explore the world of digital text or what is often referred to as electronic or E-text. Indeed, because much of the print text you find in newspapers, magazine articles, or books got there as a result of a sometimes lengthy "filtering" process of reviewing, editing, and revising, you could, for the most part, believe that at least somebody besides the author evaluated the piece for validity, reliability, and writing quality.

As you begin reading and using digital text for research, you will have an even greater responsibility as a reader to evaluate critically what you find there before and as you consider using the information in your own quest for knowledge. Because World Wide Web texts can be so much easier to access than print ones in the library, uncritical readers could be seduced into using whatever they find. Also, since hypermedia documents combine text, colorful graphics, and even sometimes audio and video, the appearance—the presentation—could easily lead uncritical readers into believing the content too is valid and reliable.

This project is designed to help you use writing as a way of filtering, understanding, and evaluating electronic texts. The activities will lead you through processes of writing what we call a "critical annotation" to help you understand, evaluate, and critique what you read. A critical annotation is a hybrid between an annotation (traditionally a 50- to 250-word abstract or summary of an article or book) and a critique (usually a text of several pages with the goal of not merely summarizing the text under analysis but also evaluating and judging it). Both kinds of writing are used often in school, but we've created this special category because both lack necessary features to be effective and efficient critical reading tools. The brevity of an annotation rarely requires evaluation; the critique is often so long and in-depth that you couldn't get through enough resources to get to actually writing a research paper. The project will also suggest ways you can use your computer-mediated learning community as the sort of filtering agent that you can often take for granted in the world of print text.

First, of course, you will need to conduct on-line research to find texts you may want to use in a paper you may be writing in this or other courses. You will find techniques for gathering digital information and texts in Chapter 4. Also, in many ways this project serves as a prerequisite for the kinds of writing projects you might undertake in Project 7, "Arguing Controversial Issues about the Information Superhighway" in Chapter 10, and Chapter 11, "Writing in the Disciplines." Because in those chapters you will be doing the kinds of context-rich academic writing that require research, you will need not only to understand what you read but to evaluate it as well.

Your class will also need to determine how you will use the critical annotations as a way of thinking about how many you may need to write. For example, if your group is completing this project as an exercise to learn to read more critically, doing one or two critical annotations might suffice. If, however, you are completing this project as part of your research process for one of the projects in Chapters 10 or 11, you will have to seek out and evaluate a number of sources—perhaps anywhere from five to ten or more, depending on what you find and how much evidence and support you will need to write your researched documents. If you are going to be doing a researched document, we suggest you write a minimum of five critical annotations. Yes, doing so will be time-consuming, but learning to read critically is a crucial skill. The more you practice critical reading using the processes we recommend here, the better you will become at it. You can expect that the first several critical annotations will be difficult to do well, but as you follow the procedures more and more, you will begin to incorporate the processes into your reading habits. You will find that after a while asking the kinds of questions offered here will become an automatic and transparent part of your research and reading process. When that happens, the critical annotation process will become easier.

ACTIVITY 9.12: Gathering Information

Information-gathering techniques are described in detail in Chapter 4. But before you begin looking for something, you have to have some general idea of what you are looking for. You have a couple of options here.

Option 1

If you are completing this project as an isolated excercise, then the topic that guides your search could be wide open. You might want to choose one of your hobbies or follow your curiosity to focus on a topic. If horseback riding is your hobby, you could conduct on-line research on that. If you have a vacation coming up and you can't decide whether you want to go to the Grand Canyon or Mexico, you can use on-line research to gather information on those. If you are a sports fan and want to learn more about your favorite sport or team, you might use that interest to help focus your on-line research.

Option 2

There is also a good chance you are completing this project as a prerequisite to doing the projects in Chapters 10 and 11. If this is the case, you might already have your topic in hand. For instance, perhaps you have chosen to write an argumentative essay on censorship in cyberspace. If so, then it would serve you well to use this project as a way of evaluating the on-line sources you might use in developing that project.

Whatever option you pursue, your first step is to track down an on-line text which could be a Gopher document, a World Wide Web document, or even an E-text made available through CMC (a lengthy E-mail message or Usenet posting). If you are evaluating E-texts as part of your research for an analysis or argument, you probably want to find a group of potential readings based on your topic.

ACTIVITY 9.13: Setting the Stage for Reading Critically

Step 1: Choosing a Format for Your Reading

Once you have found an E-text to critique, you could, of course, read it on-line. A number of drawbacks to doing so exist. Some people find extended reading on a computer monitor difficult and stressful on the eyes. If you are gathering E-texts on a system that charges for on-line time, or if you're hooked up via a modem and you're paying the phone bill, you may not want to spend valuable hook-up time reading. Also, you may be using a public access machine in the library or computer lab, and reading on-line might deny others use of the machine. Finally, you might have time constraints yourself: if you only have an hour or so to spare now, your time might be better used finding rather than reading and critiquing the sources. Before you decide in what format you want to read, scan the E-text quickly to see whether it fits your needs. Scanning is especially important if your search leads you to numerous E-texts on the same topic. Once you have determined that you actually want to read the E-text more carefully, consider the following:

- Many E-texts can be copied electronically as text files onto your hard or floppy disk, and that text can later be opened with a word processor. If the E-text you have found is copyable, make an electronic copy, which you can print out at a later time or read on your computer monitor.
- Some computing facilities allow you to print E-texts immediately. Before you do so, however, you want to make sure you really need and can use the document. Printing documents you don't need wastes paper and computing resources, and paying for copies out of your own pocket wastes your own money.
- Some complex E-texts, such as World Wide Web sites that have multiple links to other documents, may be too difficult to print, unless you have time to pursue all the links and print those pages individually, too. Because complex WWW documents are best read on-line, be sure to keep a list of the URLs you come across so you can revisit those sites as time permits.

Step 2: Preparing a Reading Log

Once you have chosen an E-text and determined in what format you want to read it, you will want to take notes as you read. We recommend you create a file in your word processor. Of course, you could accomplish much of the same with pen and paper, but doing so on the word processor will allow you to more easily revise your notes into a critical annotation. And you may end up writing some ideas and text you may eventually use in your essays. To prepare your reading notes file, you should read through Activities 9.14–9.17 so that you can better anticipate what kind of information you will be looking for. Also, you might consider typing in the items in the box entitled "Critical Reading Template" to create such a template. Detailed explanations of what to look for in each of the categories is provided in Activities 9.14–9.17.

Step 3: Logging Bibliographical Information

Begin your reading file with the following:

- Record full bibliographical information. Depending on what discipline you're writing in or what directions your teacher has given you, you may want to use Modern Language Association (MLA), American Psychological Association (APA), Chicago style, or whatever style is preferred in your discipline. In addition to basic information like author's name, title of document, place and date of "publication," and page numbers (if applicable), you may also need to include the URL if you're reading a Web page, the Gopher address if you're reading a Gopher document, and so on.

Critical Reading Template

1. Bibliographical information:
2. Initial impressions:
3. Genre:
4. Main idea:
5. Audience analysis:
6. Author reliability:
7. Evaluation of structure:
8. Evaluation of content:
9. Evaluation of writing quality:
10. Evaluate usability for your purposes:

- Note how you found the E-text. Did you use a WWW search engine? Were you browsing around some professional or government organization's Web Site and happen upon the source? Remember, there are many ways of getting to an E-text; keeping track of how you found it will help you find it again a later, if you need to.

ACTIVITY 9.14: Reading for Comprehension

Step 1: Initial Pass-Through

- Read through the steps and criteria in Activities 9.15–9.17. Keeping these in mind will help focus your reading.
- Read through the document once as you normally would. Don't worry about taking notes now.
- Jot down your first impressions about the text. Did you enjoy reading it? Was it easy or difficult to read? What sticks out in your mind as the most important idea?

Step 2: A Focused Reading

Read the following items as a way of focusing your examination of the text, and then read the text a second time with the goal of addressing these points in writing:

- What kind of E-text is this? An E-mail message? A Usenet posting? A Gopher document? A World Wide Web page?
- In your own words, what do you understand to be the main idea of the text?
- Can you find a controlling idea or thesis? You might want to write that down. If you do, make sure you put it in quotation marks in your notes and write down the page number, URL, and so forth. This information will be crucial if you decide to use this text in an essay.
- What kind of text is this? Is it a factual report in which the writer merely explains something? Is it an argument in which the author

takes a position on an issue? Is it a narrative in which the author is tell-ing a story about a person or event?

- What can you infer about the intended audience? Is the language for-mal or informal in tone? Is the bulk of the vocabulary specialized and familiar only to other experts in the field or geared more to a general audience of nonexperts? Is the content general or in-depth?

ACTIVITY 9.15: Evaluating Ethos

Ethos is a term often used in rhetoric to refer to the character or authority of the writer or speaker. Unlike in the world of print text in which docu-ments are typically published by some entity that takes some steps to cer-tify the quality of the writing, anyone with CMC, FTP, Gopher, or World Wide Web access can "publish" their ideas, views, and opinions. As a result, you have to work more diligently and critically to determine the intellectual value of E-texts you may find. In general, the greater ethos the writer has, the higher the level of validity and reliability. Here are some items to consider when evaluating the writer's *ethos:*

- What can you learn about the writer's level of expertise on the subject? There are a number of ways to learn about the author in various E-texts. For example, CMC writers often include signature lines on their messages. Let's say you are researching a subject in biology and you join an appropriate listserv. The participants on that list may sign their messages with information that tells you about their level of education (Ph.D.), their academic title (Professor of molecular biology) and their professional affiliation (Harvard University). If that person were talk-ing about some research in his field of expertise, you can infer the writer has a high ethos. Remember, too, that such information doesn't automatically give that writer authority. The opinion of a Ph.D. in molecular biology has weight in a discussion about molecules but not necessarily about censorship. If such information is not supplied, your evaluation of the author's ethos becomes more difficult. If your E-text is a World Wide Web site, you may have to search a little to learn more about the author's ethos. If the page itself doesn't offer information about the writer, poke around to see whether you can find a link to the author's home page. If she has one, it will probably offer crucial infor-mation about the writer's expertise and authority on the topic.
- What can you infer about the author's ethos from the place where the E-text exists? Did you find the E-text, a WWW page, for instance, through a professional organization? The National Science Founda-tion, for instance, has its own Web site that includes links to thou-sands of documents. You can probably infer that such an organization has conducted at least a rudimentary evaluation of the document before offering to link to it.

- What can you infer about the author's perspective or biases? If you were doing research on automobile safety, for example, and you found E-text on the safety of Chevrolets, you would have to evaluate the objectivity of the E-text. If you found it on General Motors' commercial Web site, which would have a .com suffix, you would have to consider the information in light of the fact that GM has a commercial interest in Chevrolets. You could expect a higher level of objectivity from a site that had no financial interest in the product. Also, numerous interest groups sponsor WWW sites. So, if you were doing research on gun control, you'd have to make sure you understood whether the writer or E-text was somehow affiliated with the National Rifle Association, which would not support gun control, or with some group that endorses gun control.
- What can you infer about the author's point of view, perspective, or beliefs from the tone of the E-text? Does she reveal any biases in the kind of language she uses? Inflammatory or slanted language can indicate the writer's biases even if she doesn't articulate a bias.
- What can you infer about the author's point of view, perspective, or beliefs from the content of the E-text? Does he reveal any biases in the kinds of evidence used to support his position? If the writer, for example, is arguing for a particular Presidential candidate, does he draw examples and support from nationally prominent conservatives, moderates, or liberals? Whom the writer chooses to quote can reveal much about the writer's own background and biases.
- What kind of evidence does the writer use to support his assertions? If quantitative, statistical data are used, does the author show where those data come from? How reliable is that source? How close to the data is the writer? Has she conducted the research herself, is she citing someone else's research which she has read, or is she citing someone else's reading of the original research?
- What does the writer *not* say? As you are reading, especially if you have some prior knowledge about the topic, it might have occurred to you that the writer didn't bring up an idea you believe to be crucial. Often what a writer doesn't say can also reveal much about his point of view, beliefs, or biases.

ACTIVITY 9.16: Evaluating Structure, Content, and Quality

Once you have a general idea of the main ideas in the E-text and once you have evaluated the author's ethos, you need to conduct a closer reading of the structure and content of the text.

Step 1: Outlining the Text

Construct a rudimentary outline of the document by considering the following:

- If the text offers subheadings, write those down in the order they appear. They can serve as headings in your outline. If the document doesn't offer subheadings, you will have to create your own.
- Summarize or quote the sentence or group of sentences you consider to be the thesis statement.
- Summarize or quote the topic sentences of paragraphs that develop or offer support for the thesis.

Step 2: Evaluating the Content

- Are all the author's assertions or generalizations supported with evidence and examples? How many unexamined opinions, unsupported assertions, or unsubstantiated claims can you uncover?
- What kind(s) of evidence does the writer offer? Types of evidence include personal experience, examples from other's experiences, expert testimony or opinion, research, and statistics (either original or reported).
- Of these kind(s) of evidence, which kind does the author tend to rely on most heavily to develop the document?
- How valid and reliable is the evidence? Personal experience, for example, is very valid—what people experience first hand is, if they are telling the truth, very true to them. But their personal experience may not be true for all people in all circumstances. Citing experts, those who are either commonly known to the general reader or those who hold titles and other signs of expertise, can be effective, but the technique also can be used deceptively. Just because a writer quotes someone else doesn't mean that person has high validity and reliability. And even research statistics can be misleading.

Step 3: Evaluating Writing Quality

The written quality of an E-text can tell you much about the validity and reliability of it. Of course, an established expert in vascular disease need not write like a novelist, nor does a beautifully crafted essay necessarily include valid and reliable information. However, a sloppy, awkward, clearly ill-constructed document does indicate something about the quality of the information the document contains. As you are learning in your own writing experiences, a well-written document indicates to the reader that the writer has taken the topic and the audience seriously enough to present the best document possible.

- Evaluate the coherence, cohesion, and unity of the document. Do all the ideas hang together well? Does the evidence clearly and logically support the writer's generalizations? Are the ideas connected to one another logically and smoothly, or do you get lost as the text jumps from one point to another one or veers off on a tangent?

- Evaluate the style of the document. Is the text dominated by short, choppy, simple sentences or long, ponderous, sophisticated, complex sentences? Or, is there an appropriate balance among sentence style and lengths that keeps your interest through variety?
- Evaluate the "correctness" of the text. Is the text free of grammatical, punctuation, or spelling errors, or is it littered with mistakes in grammar, punctuation, and spelling? If the E-text is a World Wide Web hypermedia document, test the links. Were any "dead"? Was it easy to navigate, or did links take you places without any way of getting back?

ACTIVITY 9.17: Evaluating Usability for Your Purposes

Now that you have evaluated the E-text, you need to reflect on how you might use it for your own research and in your own writing.

- How did the E-text affect your knowledge of the topic? Did it offer statistics, examples, or expert testimony that you didn't know about before?
- How did what you learned affect your position on the topic? For instance, perhaps you are conducting research in preparation to write an argumentative essay for or against censorship in cyberspace. Did some statistic, example, or argument confirm your belief? Did some statistic, example, or argument counter your belief? (Even if the text contradicts your position, you will still be able to use the E-text in your argument, because you will address counterarguments to your position.) Did something in the E-text lead you to consider an angle on the topic you hadn't thought of before?
- What specifically might you glean from the E-text for your own essay? By "specifically," we mean information you will want to write down, including the pertinent bibliographical information like page numbers, the exact statistics, references to research, and so on.
- Did the E-text bring up any related topics or issues that you want to know more about? Make notes for yourself on topics you might want to do follow-up research on.
- It is quite possible you found several E-texts on the same subject. If that is the case, rank all those you've read and analyzed from most useful to least useful for your purposes.

ACTIVITY 9.18: Writing Critical Annotations

To this point you have gathered a number of E-texts related to a topic of your choice. You have read them closely and taken extensive notes while evaluating the documents. Now you can use those notes to write a critical annotation of the E-text. If and how well you write the critical annotation depends much on what you will eventually do with the annotation. If you are doing this project for your own benefit only, the notes you have taken

already may suffice. Notes, nonetheless, tend to be scattered and discon-
nected, and the process of writing the critical annotation will help you
make sense of what you have read. It will also provide you with a central
source to work with if and when you return to the E-text as you write your
essays. You will find that the more E-texts you read as potential sources for
your essays, the more difficult it will be to keep them all straight in your
mind. Writing the critical annotation will serve you well, even if it is for
your eyes only. The critical annotation could serve other audiences, too,
and if it will be read by others, then you will have to consider the needs of
those readers, too.

Minimally, your teacher may want you to submit a series of critical
annotations with the essays in which you use the sources. Sharing the critical annotations with other members of your learning community can
help them with their research and critical reading, too. We'll talk more
about that process in Activity 9.19. In any case, your goal is to write an
approximately 500-word (or whatever length your community and your
teacher deem appropriate) critical annotation. Regardless of the length,
you need to give your readers enough information to know what the
E-text is about and enough analysis and evaluation to help your readers
consider whether they too want to read the original E-text.

Step 1: Rereading Your Notes

Reread your notes on the E-text. If anything else about the E-text, the
topic, or your feelings toward the issue occurs to you, add those thoughts
to your notes. Even if you have taken your notes on a word processor, you
might want to start a new file to write the critical annotation itself.

Step 2: Getting the Bibliographical Information Straight

The purpose for the bibliographical information is to give those who might
read your work a lead to the original source you are using. It's important,
therefore, for you to have it down correctly on your critical annotation.

- Consult your teacher as to which discipline-specific style you are to use.
  The humanities often use Modern Language Association style or Chicago style, whereas the social sciences often use the American Psychological Association style. You can learn more about these styles
  generally and the specifics of documenting E-texts at these addresses:

      http://www.utexas.edu/depts/uwc/.html/citation.html

      http://www.lib.lehigh.edu/footnote/chicelec.html

- Type out the bibliographical information at the top of your document.

Step 3: Writing about the E-Text

In seventy-five words or so, respond to the following:

- Where did the E-text appear, and how would one find it?

- What genre is the E-text? Is it argumentative, narrative, expository?
- What is the general subject?

Step 4: Summarizing the E-Text

In 150 words or so, summarize the E-text by addressing the following:

- What is the purpose of the E-text—to persuade, argue, analyze, inform?
- What is the thesis or controlling idea of the E-text?
- Summarize the line of development. What is point A, point B, and so forth?
- What kinds of evidence, examples, and so on, does the author use?

Step 5: Evaluating the E-Text

In about 150 words evaluate the E-text by addressing the following:

- What are the strengths of the E-text? Informative? Appropriate language, content, and structure for the implied audience and purpose? Well developed with concrete, valid, and reliable support? Well written?
- What are the drawbacks of the E-text? Does it do anything so poorly as to undermine your faith in its validity and reliability? Do you notice any underlying biases based on the writer's tone, the kinds of evidence used, the implied point of view of the site where you found the E-text? Do you suspect any flaws in the writer's thinking based on evidence of poor reasoning or poor writing?

Step 6: Putting It All into Perspective

Depending on your audience and purpose for writing the critical annotation, you might want to handle this part differently. What you include in this section might vary if you're writing it for yourself or for an audience of your peers.

- How did reading the E-text affect your knowledge, beliefs, or point of view on the topic?
- What parts might you use in your own thinking and writing about the topic?
- How does this E-text compare with other texts, digital or print, you've read on the same topic?
- Would you recommend this E-text to others conducting research on a similar topic? Why?

Step 7: Polishing the Critical Annotation

This step is less important if you will not be sharing your critical annotation with others. But if you intend to share the critical annotations with your teacher or peers, don't forget to do the following:

- Read your draft aloud. Listen for long rambling clauses, phrases, and sentences and short, choppy constructions.

- Does your annotation read like an essay or series of short answers to questions? If you are going to share the annotation with others, it needs to read like an essay. If you merely answered the items in the preceding steps, your critical annotation may not make sense to a reader who may not know what the questions were. If that is the case, you'll probably have to go back and create transitions between ideas and paragraphs that will help make the document more reader friendly.
- Proofread the critical annotation for grammar, usage, and punctuation.
- Spellcheck the document for typos, misspellings, and repeated words.

ACTIVITY 9.19: Sharing Critical Annotations

Why share critical annotations? If your previous research experiences have been good ones, you have probably learned much about the topics you've researched, and that kind of independent learning can often be more fulfilling and satisfying than learning from lectures. You have also learned that research is sometimes grueling work, fraught with dead ends, unretrievable sources, and sheer information overload. Although on-line research can offer you easier and better access to more information sources that you don't have to trudge off to the library to track down, a simple, if unfocused, search on a World Wide Web search engine can lead you to hundreds of sources. As you get better at conducting focused searches and better at reading and evaluating on-line sources, your research will become more streamlined and efficient.

One individual, however, can only go so far. By pooling your efforts, each member of the community can get leads to more and different kinds of sources than any individual can find alone. If five people are interested in researching and writing about the use of computer technology in education, for example, each individual would do well to come up with a dozen or so sources. If those five, each of whom might have found a dozen unique sources of information, pooled what they have found and share that with everyone else interested in the topic, each member would then have leads to forty-eight additional sources—far more, of course, than any individual might need to write a well-researched and -documented paper on the topic. Well-written critical annotations, however, will help individuals sort through and evaluate the various sources and help them determine whether a particular source is worth seeking out. This activity, then, offers suggestions for sharing critical annotations.

Step 1: Determining the Number of Critical Annotations to Share

Your learning community, that is, your teacher and your classmates, will first need to determine how many critical annotations each person in the class will share. How many each person will write and how many each will share depend much on your class's purposes for writing the annotations. Your learning community might have engaged in this project merely to learn a tool for evaluating and critiquing E-texts—an exercise that in itself has merit as a critical reading activity. If this is the case, your class might decide to have each person share just one critical annotation as a way of exploring the various approaches people can take to complete the activity.

On the other hand, maybe you wrote the critical annotations as the preliminary step toward your research to write other documents, such as those discussed in Chapters 10 and 11. If this is the case, these annotations could serve collaborative research purposes. Thus, your group needs to decide how many critical annotations each person will write. In the introduction to this chapter, we recommended writing at least five critical annotations as you conduct background research. How many each person will write and how many each person will share depends on the class's goals for this activity. If, ultimately, your community will create a database of critical annotations for everyone in the community to draw upon to find leads for their own research, each member of the class might want to share five or more critical annotations.

Your class, then, will need to engage in an on-line or face-to-face discussion about the learning community's goals. The discussion should lead to concrete decisions about how many critical annotations each person will write and how many they will share.

Step 2: Determining with Whom to Share the Annotations

Your community also needs to determine how widely to share the annotations. If, for example, your community has subdivided itself into peer groups of three to five members each, you might decide to share your annotations just with the members of those groups. Or, you might have divided yourselves by topic interests so that all those working on censorship issues, for example, will work together in one group, those interested in economic issues will work together in another group, and so on. The critical annotations, therefore, might be shared just among members of those groups. A case could be made, also, for everyone to share all their critical annotations with everyone else, especially if the activity is being used to help community members think about topics they might write about. The biggest determining factor hinges on how much information community members are able to handle. For example, if you have twenty-five class members and each writes five critical annotations that are to be shared with everyone in the class, everyone will receive 120 critical annotations!

Step 3: Determining How to Share Critical Annotations

How your community will share the critical annotations depends much on the kinds of technology your community has available to it and how comfortable with the various forms of technology each member has become. Here you will find some options to consider.

Option 1: Sharing Critical Annotations through CMC

You could use various forms of computer-mediated communication, including E-mail, Usenet newsgroups, or electronic bulletin boards, to share your annotations.

- If your class has decided to have everyone share all their annotations with the whole group, send your annotations as E-mail messages or newsgroup articles to your class E-mail group or newsgroup.
- If your class has decided to work in smaller groups—preformed writing groups or topic-centered groups—you will want to develop a way to share the critical annotations with those people only. You can accomplish this in a number of ways:

  — Your teacher (or whoever has the expertise, access, and authorization to do so) can set up a separate E-mail list, newsgroup, or bulletin board conference for each of the subgroups. Members of those groups can share the annotations with fellow group members by sending the annotations as E-mail messages, newsgroup articles, or bulletin board postings to that group only.
  — Many E-mail programs allow individuals to set up groups as part of the application's address book function. Each individual in the group could create address book groups that would include only the other members of the group.

- Whatever method you use, remember to offer your readers as much descriptive information as possible in the header of your CMC message. A real possibility exists that people could be receiving scores of critical annotations; therefore, you need to provide them ways of determining whether the contents of the message are something they should consider reading. Be sure, then, to put the most focused, accurate description you can on the subject line of your message header. For example, if you were sharing a critical annotation on an E-text you read about freedom of speech, you could write in the subject line one of the following: "Annotation," "Freedom of Speech," "Free Speech Annotation," or "Pro–Free Speech Annotation." The first example wouldn't give your potential readers much to go on, other than the fact that the contents of the message includes a critical annotation rather than an invitation to a party. The second one would offer more information—the message is about free speech—but the reader wouldn't know whether you were sharing a critical annotation about an E-text on free speech or your personal opinions on the topic. The third one would at least cue in your readers that the message contained an annotation about a free-speech E-text. The last one would tell your reader that the message was a critical annotation about a pro–free speech E-text. Your busy classmates will much appreciate the more detailed, descriptive subject line.

Option 2: Sharing Critical Annotations through the World Wide Web
If the members of your community have access to and have developed World Wide Web authoring skills, you may decide to share your critical annotations on the Web. Doing so has the advantage that those who are interested in your annotations only can seek them out without having to trudge through scores of E-mail messages, newsgroup articles, or bulletin board postings to find what they are looking for. On the other hand, other members of the learning community may not know where to look for your annotations. Again, a number of possibilities exist:

- Class members could place their annotations on their individual Web Sites. If you choose this option, you will need to send a CMC message to all your classmates or at least to the subgroup with which you're working, informing them of your URL and the general contents of what critical annotations they will find there. Such information will permit those classmates interested in the same topic to seek out your annotations.
- By this point in the semester, your class might have begun a collaborative Web site authored by one Webspinner, a delegated group of classmates, or everyone in the community. The benefit of placing all the community's annotations on the same Web Site is that the community creates a central repository that makes finding the annotations easier. The logistics of creating a collaborative site include these:
  — Individuals place annotations on their individual Web Sites, and the designated Web spinner(s) makes links to the individuals' sites. In such a scenario, the Webspinner(s) might categorize the annotations by topic area or student. If organized by topic, all the links to annotations dealing with censorship in cyberspace, for example, would be listed together.
  — All members of the class are given access privileges to the server, directory, and html document where the course Web Site resides. As individuals write their critical annotations, they can tag them in html code and add their contributions to the critical annotation site. Be forewarned, however, that such collaboration requires much agreement on formats and styles. And the more access the more people have to a collaborative document, the more confusion can arise.

SOME CONSIDERATIONS ON USING THE SHARED ANNOTATIONS EFFECTIVELY

Your community has now created a rich database of sorts about a wide range of E-texts on a wide range of subjects. What you have done for one another is provide multiple access points into the vast universe of information on the

Internet. As a group you have not uncovered everything, of course, but you have created leads—places to start—on your individual quests to learn more about a particular subject so you can write about it. How each individual uses these leads is crucial.

When you first started looking for E-texts, your search was necessarily broad. Some of what you found individually might have provided general background information about the topic or very specific statistics dealing with one specific aspect of your topic. Undoubtedly, some of the E-texts you found contributed very little to your knowledge about the topic, and some might not have contributed to the focus of your research. If you are using the critical annotation project as part of the research process, you will find that as you start to write your researched document, you will need specific kinds of information to support various parts of your document. For instance, if you were writing an argument about freedom of speech on the Internet, you might realize that having a copy of the First Amendment or various legal rulings and interpretations of it would be useful. You have a couple of options to find such specific information. Of course, you could conduct a whole new search on the First Amendment. Although doing so would be worthwhile, the fact is you might come across hundreds of E-texts on the subject and you would have to read and evaluate many of them to determine which might best serve your purposes. Another, perhaps more efficient method is to see whether any of your classmates interested in the same topic wrote a critical annotation about some aspect of the First Amendment. If the annotation was well written, you will be able to evaluate rather quickly whether the original source is worth tracking down and reading on your own.

You must also keep in mind the purpose of the critical annotations so you can make effective and ethical use of them. The annotations serve only as an *evaluation* of an E-text and should not be used in place of the E-text itself. No matter how well written and documented one of your peers' annotations might be, you cannot use that annotation as a source. You can only use the annotation to determine whether the source looks like something worth looking up yourself. Remember, a peer's annotation is only one reading and one perspective on the source. If your peer did a poor reading of the source and you used that source in your paper without reading it yourself, you could end up using the source in a misleading fashion.

In short, do not cite a source you know about only through a peer's critical annotation. Use an annotation only as a lead to a potential source. Decide from the annotation whether the source is worth tracking down yourself, and read and evaluate the source on your own before using it in your paper.

10

WRITING ABOUT ISSUES: ANALYSIS AND ARGUMENT

Of all the kinds of writing you might do in college, and later in your professional life, the most prominent may be one of the various forms of argumentative writing. When you are asked in a literature class to interpret a short story, for example, you are writing a type of argument in which you take a position about a theme, symbol, or character, and then conduct an analysis of the appropriate aspects of the short story to support your position. You could be asked in a history course to take a position on a controversial issue such as the long-term effects of a Supreme Court case and support that position by analyzing how the Supreme Court's ruling affects some aspect of society today. In a science course, you may be required to propose how introducing some chemical into a stream might affect the aquatic life living in that stream. When you graduate and enter your field, you will very probably be asked by supervisors and clients to write reports in which you advocate one business, sales, legal, or medical strategy over another. Although the structures you might use and the types of evidence and methods of development available to you will vary from academic discipline to academic discipline and from professional field to professional field, in all these cases you are engaged in some form of argumentative writing.

As we've established throughout this book, as a college student you will use various forms of writing to engage in processes of the context-rich kind of activity we called "academic writing." You may remember that we described a cycle of inquiry, analysis, and argument. During the inquiry stage, you might use writing-to-learn activities to explore your interests. Once you've identified those interests, you might learn what others who are interested in the same topics have thought and said about the topics. In a traditional educational setting, you might seek out and read what others have already written about the topic. On the information superhighway, of course, you can get crucial background information and learn how others think and write about your topic by joining and participating in various CMC venues like listservs and listprocs, Usenet newsgroups, and electronic bulletin boards. And you can conduct research in Gopherspace and on the World Wide Web to discover what others think about a particular topic.

As suggested in the critical annotation project in Chapter 9, you can use writing to think critically about what you have read. Although the critical annotation tool takes you through the process of analyzing individual contributions to the ongoing conversation about a topic, we made the point also that you have to analyze the issue as a whole. That is, you have to look at the history of the issue, examine the various ways people have defined the topic, discover the range of possible positions on the topic, and study how those arguments have been made. By doing so, you will be able to determine what you can contribute to the ongoing conversation surrounding the issue. So, whereas in Chapter 9 you learned how to analyze an individual E-text, your next step is to analyze an issue you might write about—whether you use electronic sources or not.

Once you've used your tools of inquiry to find out about the conversation and analysis to discover how you might contribute to the conversation, you will turn to argumentation to make a point, an assertion. Arguing in this way does not involve anger, though a certain passion for the subject can come in handy. Academic arguments employ reason more than emotion, logic more than intuition. This kind of argument provides a survey of the context from which it emerges, a weighing of the conclusions one might draw from that context, and, finally, a reasoned choice—the final one in the succession of reasoned choices that comprise the writing process. This final choice is your conclusion, the point you have argued toward during the whole essay. It is the fullest, most definite statement of the major assertion your argument contains: your controlling idea.

Establishing that controlling idea—explaining, supporting, and clarifying it—is the goal of the argument. In the process, you will turn that idea over and over, figuratively speaking. You will examine it, test it against others' ideas and the evidence for and against it. You'll weigh your controlling idea against the other possibilities, the other major assertions one might make—or that others have made. You'll consider the issues you've raised in their full complexity. The goal here is not to simplify but to complicate—in a positive sense, of course. You want to convince by being thorough, by revealing what you know, by developing a kind of presence, a persona, whom readers will recognize as an authority. And you want to pursue the major positions openly and objectively, so that readers will feel that the persona you have developed is also honest and trustworthy. If you can do all this well—bring a wide range of resources to bear on your topic, weigh the evidence and the alternatives carefully, make effective choices, and reason your way to a fully developed conclusion—then your voice will be heard. More important, you will find that your voice is one people respect.

The first project in this chapter, "Analyzing Controversial Issues about the Information Superhighway," leads you through procedures for entering the "ongoing conversation" among those who have examined topics and issues before you. As noted earlier, knowledge in a given field of inquiry is constructed through the interaction among people who observe a phenomenon, analyze it, and offer hypotheses and theories about it. They then share their ideas with others through conversation and, in the academy, through writing. Those ideas are then critiqued, confirmed or refuted, and then elaborated, which results in even more contributions to the ongoing conversation. You must remember that nearly every topic you might write about analytically will have been researched, studied, and argued before you decided to pursue the topic—you are always joining a conversation in progress. Hence, you are obligated to learn what has been said before you join the conversation and analyze it before you join in.

The lessons learned from "Analyzing Controversial Issues about the Information Superhighway" project will prepare you for writing arguments that you will take up in this chapter's second project, "Arguing Controversial Issues about the Information Superhighway." The "Arguing Issues" project is designed to work in conjunction with the "Analyzing Issues" project because, as we've noted previously, you need to analyze an issue to learn more about the ongoing conversation that you seek to join with your argumentative essay about that issue.

PROJECT 6: ANALYZING CONTROVERSIAL ISSUES ABOUT THE INFORMATION SUPERHIGHWAY

Objective

- To analyze an issue as a way of entering the ongoing conversation about that issue

Technological Requirements

- A word processor
- Access to on-line research sources including on-line library catalogs, Gopherspace, and the World Wide Web
- Access to a computer-mediated communication system such as a local area network or wide area network E-mail system or electronic conferencing system

Participant Prerequisites

- Basic knowledge of conducting research on-line, including (see Chapter 4 for information about these techniques):

— Searching on-line library catalogs using Boolean search techniques,
— Searching Gopherspace using Archie and Veronica,
— Searching the World Wide Web using search engines , and

- Basic knowledge of using asynchronous CMC (newsgroups, E-mail groups) to share information

Overview

As we noted in Chapter 9, to analyze "means to sift through a set of events, circumstances, or readings to make sense of them, to bring coherence to them, to make them meaningful." In that chapter, we led you through two projects that asked you to analyze a virtual community and to analyze E-texts you might come across during your on-line research. This project will lead you through an analysis of an issue. As such, the project serves as a prerequisite to the argument you might write in the next project in this chapter. Analyzing an issue is similar to analyzing anything in the sense that you still want to examine something, break it down into its constituent parts, and analyze the relationships among the parts as a way of better understanding the whole. So, when you wrote about a virtual community, for example, you examined the characteristics of various community members, what they "spoke" about, what kind of language they used to interact with one another, and so on. As a result of this analysis of the constituent parts of the community, you were able to offer some generalizations about the community as a whole. The specifics of analyzing an issue include the following considerations, at least:

- What are the various definitions of the issue?
- What is the history of the issue?
- Whom or what does the issue affect?
- What are the various positions surrounding the issue?
- Who has these positions and why do they take them?
- What are the perceived effects of the various issues?
- What are the critical differences and similarities among the positions?

The Assignment

Write a 1,000- to 1,500-word academic analysis of an issue for a college-educated audience. Your community, including your instructor, can negotiate the length. You should remember that "depth" is more important than word count or length in pages. The issue can focus on some aspect of cyberculture (e.g., intellectual property rights, censorship on the Internet, the appropriate roles of technology in education, etc.) or some topic relating to our larger, general culture (e.g., equal rights, gun control, economic inequities, etc.). Your college-educated readers will expect the following qualities:

- A comprehensive description of the context of the issue (i.e., what is it? What is the history of it? What is the cause of the controversy?)
- A focused and clearly written statement of the problem—your controlling idea
- A description, classification, and logical analysis of the various positions and perspectives surrounding the issue
- Evidence that you have researched the issue, of effective use of sources, and of appropriate documentation of the sources you do use
- Conventions of standard written English and a formal writing style appropriate for an academic audience

Because your goal with this project is to analyze an issue rather than argue a position on the issue (something you will do for the next project), you need not take a position. Instead, your thesis or controlling idea will offer a synthesis of the various positions on the issue.

What Is an Issue?

You are probably most used to calling what you write about a "topic," and though you will choose a topic for this project, you need to keep in mind that an "issue" is a "topic" that generates differences of opinions, differences that could lead to debates among reasonable people. So, for example, a topic might be "computers and writing." Various issues arise out of that topic. For example, there might be debate surrounding questions such as "Do computers help writers write better?" "Do style checkers help students learn grammar?" or "Is writing on-line better than traditional forms of writing?" As you can see, then, issues are capable of being posed in the form of a question.

You need to remember, too, that not all topics turned into questions—issues—are equal. Some questions generate yes/no answers. For example, if we were to ask, "Should all schools use computers to teach writing?" most reasonable people would say yes, because most people recognize that computer literacy is a crucial educational and professional skill. An issue phrased thus will not generate much debate. But if you were to rewrite the issue to ask, "Who should pay to put computers into every English classroom?" you would create a more fertile site for debate. Some people, for example, might argue that individual school districts should pay; others might argue that state governments should pay; still others might argue that the federal government should pay. You might even come across those who advocate corporate sponsorship of schools in which private industry picks up the tab or those who believe that parents should provide the computers their children use in school.

Other issues that don't lend themselves to effective analysis are those that are easily answerable. For example, a question such as "Are there more women on the Internet than men?" would make a great inquiry question (it is something worth knowing for many reasons), but it would not lead to much debate. After just a little research about Internet demographics, you would quickly discover that males outnumber females on the Internet. A more controversial issue on a related topic might read, "Given that the Internet is dominated by males, what are the effects on females?" Again, some might argue the effects are minimal, and others would argue the effects are debilitating.

Finally, many issues are difficult to argue because the differences of opinion don't lend themselves to reasoned, logical debate. Most points of view about our culture's most hotly debated and pressing social issues such as capital punishment, abortion, and creationism versus evolution grow out of people's belief systems. Those whose opinions about abortion, for example, grow out of their religious convictions will never be persuaded by those whose opinions on the issue are shaped by legal or medical principles, because the two groups don't share the same belief system. The activities that follow will help you find a topic, explore the possible issues that grow out of it, and help you shape those issues into the kinds that lend themselves to analysis.

ACTIVITY 10.1: Finding Something to Write About

Your first—and perhaps most crucial—task is to find something to write about. Analyzing an issue effectively requires a significant investment of your time and intellectual energy. It is imperative, therefore, that you select a topic that piques your curiosity, that you have a sincere interest in learning more about, and that you have a passion about. Because you will be working with this issue for an extended period of time, you will want to make every effort to start off on a path you can pursue doggedly. Of course, if your original topic takes you down a dead-end avenue or you grow bored with it, you can always change it, but doing so will put you in a situation where you will be making up for lost time and energy.

You should understand from the outset that finding a suitable topic—one that you'll turn into an issue—is an exploratory and recursive process. You will need to mine your interests and experiences. You will need to conduct research to find general and broad background information to learn what others have reported about the topic, how they have analyzed various components of the issue you are exploring, and how they have argued various perspectives on the issue. Once you have developed adequate background information on the issue, you will need to focus the issue more narrowly and then conduct further research to learn more details. As you develop your analysis, you will need to identify gaps in your knowledge and information and seek out even more detailed and focused information to close those gaps. And, as you delve deeper and deeper into your issue, you will find, in many cases, that you will need to revise the focus of your analysis, and such revisions to your focus will then require you to conduct more research to pursue information your revised focus demands.

A number of considerations arise when seeking a writing topic, and a number of ways of testing the feasibility of that topic and exploring it as you turn it into an issue are possible. Potential topics can grow out of your direct experiences, reading, interactions with others, and, of course, outside agencies such as your teacher. Here are some considerations:

- Most important, choose something in which you are interested, if at all possible.
- Although this book has focused on the information superhighway, you need not limit yourself to that subject. Part of the goal of this book and its writing assignments is to help you learn about the infohighway and the information age through writing; thus, you might consider focusing on topics and issues that rise out of the information age.
- Choose something in which readers would be interested. Try to avoid topics that your potential readers might have come across time and time again. For example, your first impulse might be to take on an issue that comes out of our national debates such as abortion, gun control, euthanasia, and so on. These are important topics, but chances are your readers, and particularly your teacher, have read about these before. A good way of thinking about this consideration is to think for a moment about how some diving competitions are judged. In such competitions, divers are judged not just on the execution of the dive but also on the difficulty of the dive. A diver who attempts a very difficult dive and executes it adequately might earn an equal score as the diver who attempts a relatively simple dive and executes it perfectly. On the other hand, the diver who adequately performs a difficult dive could outscore the one who performs adequately on an easy one. In any case, if you do decide on a commonplace topic, you will need to find a unique angle on it to make it fresh to the reader.

Step 1: Exploring Your Own Experiences

Take thirty minutes or so to think about what you've read in books, magazines, newspapers, and the Internet and the conversations, debates, and arguments you've had during the last several months, and ask yourself the following. We suggest you write up your responses and ideas as a word-processed document so you have a record of your thoughts.

- When was the last time you became really angry or sad over something that happened to you, that you read in the newspaper or heard on the radio or television news, or that someone said to you? Experiences that evoked some sort of strong emotional response in you can generate excellent topics because the emotional reaction can provide you with a passion for the topic.
- When was the last time you heard or read something that taught you something so significant that it altered your view of yourself, society, reality? As you have grown intellectually, you have, undoubtedly, experienced "A-ha!" moments, when the proverbial "light" has gone on. As you develop intellectually, you often experience epiphanies—moments of recognition when you understand or realize something

for the first time—that often serve to alter not only your knowledge but also your perspective and belief system. Such moments, and the events or ideas that sparked them, can often serve as good topics because they tap into your intellectual curiosity.

- When was the last time you heard or read something that confused you? Recognizing what you don't know or understand is often the most crucial place to begin your quest for knowledge. Our desire to clarify confusion—to get to know what we don't know—is also an excellent way to develop topics for writing. Confusion can often serve as an excellent catalyst for intellectual curiosity.

Step 2: Collaborative Invention

After you have given some thought to your own experiences, you will find it useful to share your ideas with others in your class. By sharing your ideas, you will offer classmates ideas they hadn't thought of and vice versa. You have a couple of options here depending on the technological context of your class.

Option 1: Oral Brainstorming

Gather into a large group or small groups of three to five students, and have one person take notes on an overhead, chalkboard, or whiteboard (if working in a small group, appoint one person to take notes for the whole group).

- Have all the members of the class or group read aloud what they wrote about in step 1. The group or class recorder should make a list of the ideas each individual shares.
- After each individual has contributed a set of possible topics, allow the whole group to look over the list. For each of the listed topics, generate another list of related topics and ideas.
- By now you should have a long list of possible topics. Be sure each individual copies the list of ideas, or have the group note taker make enough copies for everyone in the group.

Option 2: CMC Brainstorming

The goal of brainstorming on-line is the same as those for oral brainstorming: to generate a list of possible topics. Depending on your class's technological context, you could use E-mail, Usenet newsgroups, or a synchronous conference to share the ideas individuals generated in step 1. The benefit of such electronic brainstorming, of course, is that in most cases your group can capture a transcript of the possible topics generated by the group. Your goal at this point is not to "discuss" the topics at any great length but rather to spend your time generating as many ideas as you can as a group.

Other Suggested Topics

Listed here are possible topics you might consider for this project:

Intellectual property rights. Our current copyright system is bolstered by a system in which writers and publishers "own" what they produce and receive royalties on their intellectual property. Our culture has a large body of laws protecting the rights of those who own intellectual property, but many of those laws and principles are based on print technology. Given the new means of distribution and access of intellectual property made possible by the Internet, who "owns" information distributed on the Internet? How should they be compensated for the use of their intellectual property? What new laws need to be considered?

Censorship. The Internet has the potential of allowing more people to share more information than is possible in traditional media such as print and television broadcasting. Much debate has arisen, however, about how much control should be placed on types of information, such as pornography and hate speech. Should the Internet be censored? If so, by whom and how? If so, what should be censored? If so, what are the consequences for "free speech"?

Economics. The Internet is not free. Much of the start-up costs of what is known today as the Internet were underwritten initially by the federal government and educational institutions. But as demand for Internet access and better Internet computers and software increases, debate centers around who should pay for the Internet. Should the government pay for the technological infrastructure? If the government "controls" the Internet, will the huge bureaucracy of government slow the Internet's growth? Should private industry? If private industry foots the bill, will the Internet be shaped in the interests of big business? How much of the cost should be passed along to individual consumers? If individuals are expected to pay, will there be a greater gulf between the wealthy, who would have the money to pay, and those on the economic margins, who won't be able to pay?

Education. Some educators and politicians have represented the Internet as the next major revolution in education. Can the Internet and other computer technologies really improve education? A wide range of more focused questions grow out of that question. Are some technologies, such as computer-mediated communication or the World Wide Web, more or less effective than stand-alone applications, such as interactive individual programs and CD-ROM simulations? What effects do computer technology have on achievement and attitudes toward learning in various subject areas (e.g., math, science, reading and writing, history, etc.) and for different populations (e.g., elementary, high school, and college students; non-native speakers of English, learning disabled and gifted students)? Will the effects on teachers and our current educational structures be positive or negative?

Politics. Some political pundits and Internet advocates envision the Internet as a way of providing citizens more access, through more information, to our political system and politicians. Ideas like virtual town meetings, real-time polling and on-line voting, candidate Web Sites, and so on, are hailed as the cornerstones of a computer-mediated participatory democracy. Will the Internet really give the populace more access to and influence over the political process? Will that access, and the power that comes with it, be distributed equally?

Society. Society as we know it is a conglomeration of small communities, and these communities provide emotional, social, and economic support to their members. Some critics have argued that the suburbanization of the United States and the population shifts caused by job transfers and the like have pulled at the social fabric of American culture. Some have considered the Internet a means by which "virtual communities" can help tie people together and provide the kinds of social support traditional communities have provided. Can computer-mediated social interactions effectively replace face-to-face interactions? What positive or negative effects might the Internet have on social interaction? Will the world be a better place in which to live because of technology, or will technology further alienate us from one another?

Culture. The arts—literature, dance, film, painting, photography— have always played a significant role in shaping our culture's belief system. Throughout history we have identified a canon of works of literature, paintings, and other creative forms that represent our beliefs about truth, beauty, good and evil, right and wrong, and so on. The Internet has the potential of undermining the canon by permitting those voices and visions that traditionally have been underrepresented to contribute to the ongoing conversations about the "big" questions. Will the information superhighway diffuse our culture, and, if so, will that be a positive or negative phenomenon?

Individual rights. In his novel *1984*, George Orwell told a futuristic tale in which a totalitarian government became a "Big Brother" that controlled citizens' lives through thought control. Some technology critics believe the information superhighway can and will become a tool of government for surveillance of citizens and thus threaten our right to privacy. Might this happen? Will the benefits of the Internet outweigh the loss of individual privacy?

Step 3: Settling on a Broad Topic

Completing steps 1 and 2 should have created for you and your classmates a broad and deep pool of possible topics to write about. Now you will need to pick one to explore more deeply. Remember, the topic you select now can be a tentative one, and, by nature, it will be very broad at this point, probably too broad to write about effectively. As noted earlier, however, once you have a tentative topic, you will go through a series of activities to help you explore the topic and learn more about it, turn the topic into an issue, and focus the issue.

- Look through all the topics you and your classmates generated during individual freewriting and social brainstorming sessions.
- Select three to five topics that you might be interested in.
- Evaluate each of the topics by asking the following:
  — What do I already know about this topic? Do I have enough background knowledge through personal experience, a course of study, or previous reading or viewing to pursue the topic?
  — What do I already believe about the topic?
  — How much "passion" do I have toward this topic and why?
  — How much "intellectual curiosity" do I have toward this topic and why?
  — Why would my readers be interested in reading an analysis of this topic?
- After you have evaluated all the topics, rank them in order of preference from the one in which you have the most knowledge, passion, and/or curiosity to the least.

Step 4: Sharing Your Tentative Topic with Peers

After you have gone through an individual process of selecting a topic, you may find it useful to share your thinking with peers. Such sharing will allow you and your classmates to learn more about one another's thinking processes and thus help each of you think about your topics both more broadly and deeply. Also, completing this step will let you and your fellow learning community members know who shares an interest in common topics. Such information about one another's interests will help your group organize itself into writing groups and research teams, as will be suggested later in this project.

- Write up—as a CMC message or as word-processed document you can import as a CMC message to the entire class—a 150- to 250-word statement about your topic in which you
  — name your topic;
  — describe why you've chosen it in terms of your prior knowledge, your passion for it, and your intellectual curiosity;
  — describe why you think readers will be interested in reading an analysis of the topic;
  — summarize everything you know about the topic already; and
  — offer a list of tentative questions you think you'll need to ask about the topic.
- Once your classmates have posted their topic statements, read as many of them as you can, and then take these steps:
  — Look for topics similar to your own.
  — Ask yourself how their topic statements compare to your own in terms of how the topic is stated, the underlying motivation for

choosing the topic, prior knowledge about it, and the kinds of questions asked about it.

— Consider the scope and focus of your topic statement in light of what others have written, and look for ideas and questions that can help you think more broadly and deeply about your topic.

— After having read everyone else's topic statements, determine whether you have new ideas or questions about your own topic. Have you read about a topic you realize you have more interest in than the one you've come up with? If so, now is the time to change topics because you're about to begin the long exploration of your topic. Once you get a certain way down the path, turning back and starting over will be difficult.

ACTIVITY 10.2: Exploring the Topic

Once you have completed Activity 10.1, you should have a topic in mind and a number of ideas about the topic. Now you need to explore that topic by evaluating your prior knowledge about it and completing some background research. Once you get a good general understanding of the topic, then you will transform the topic into an issue by asking a series of questions about the issue, exploring those questions, and finally narrowing the topic down to one issue that seems most interesting and promising. The next several steps offer you techniques for the stages of working through the issue.

Step 1: Exploring Your Current Knowledge about the Topic

We assume you chose your current topic because you have some prior knowledge about it. Now is the time to explore that prior knowledge as thoroughly as possible. Start a new word-processing document, consider the following items, and write as much as you can. The items here are suggestive rather than exhaustive, so don't feel you need address every one of them, and feel free to go beyond them. Because this document is a writing-to-learn activity and you are the primary audience of it, you need not concern yourself too much with issues of audience, organization, clarity, and so on. In step 2, however, we recommend you and your classmates share your prior knowledge inventories via CMC. So, although this is not a formal writing task, do write it well enough so that you can communicate your ideas to others.

- Begin by breaking the topic into as many parts as possible and then asking as many questions as you can about those parts. If you have chosen to write an analysis about "Censorship and the Internet," for example, you might come up with the following questions (the following items are suggestive and illustrative, your actual list could be longer):

  What is censorship?
  What are the current laws on censorship?

Why do we have it?

Why does it cause controversy?

How is censorship carried out and enforced?

Whom does censorship affect?

What does censorship affect?

What is the Internet?

What is the history of the Internet?

What technology makes the Internet possible?

What kinds of things can people do on the Internet?

Is it technologically possible to censor the Internet?

Should all or only certain parts of the Internet be censored?

What is the history of censorship on the Internet?

How do current laws on censorship affect the information on the Internet?

Have there been any new laws proposed and passed since the inception of the Internet?

Has there been any censorship of the Internet thus far?

Have certain parts of the Internet (i.e., Usenet groups vs. the World Wide Web) been under more or different scrutiny?

- What do you currently know about the history of the topic? For example, you probably already know that the issue of censorship generally has a long history stemming from our rights under the First Amendment.
- What do you know about the "players" involved with the topic? To use the censorship topic again, you may already know whom censorship affects, who is responsible for censorship policies and regulations, and so on.
- What controversies or debates are you aware of surrounding the topic? You probably already know something about the debates surrounding your topic. In the case of censorship on the 'Net, you already know that some individuals and groups favor certain degrees and kinds of censorship on the grounds that certain types of "free expression," such as hate speech, are harmful to society at large, whereas other individuals and groups are against censorship in all forms because they fear that our larger rights under the First Amendment will be undermined.
- What do you currently know about the kinds of arguments made by the various individuals and groups engaged in the controversies surrounding your topic?
- What *don't* you know about the topic? Yes, it is hard to recognize what you don't know, and the next step will help you learn more about the topic by doing some broad background research. Still, you might know that the First Amendment protects freedom of speech, but you may never have read the First Amendment yourself. Therefore, you might not know what the First Amendment actually says. Or, you might

remember from watching television news that great controversy and debate raged over the Communications Decency Act, but you may not know exactly what it was.

Step 2: Sharing Prior Knowledge

Just as you did when you shared your topic statements with your classmates, you may want to share, via electronic mail or Usenet newsgroups, your knowledge inventories with others who have shown interest in the same general topic or one somehow related to your own. If this is the case, you should consider setting up topical mail groups or electronic conferences consisting of those individuals who share an interest in a particular topic. Doing so will allow those who share interests to share knowledge, too, so everyone thinking about similar topics can learn more about the topics from everyone else's prior knowledge. To do so:

- Decide on a CMC medium (E-mail groups, newsgroups, bulletin board subconferences, etc.) to use.
- Create CMC groups consisting just of those individuals who have related topics.
- Send to all members of the topic group a copy of the document you created to explore your prior knowledge on the topic.
- Read all the prior knowledge explorations everyone else in your group shared.
- Reflect on how your prior knowledge differs from that of your peers, and consider how their prior knowledge enhances your knowledge and understanding of the topic.

Step 3: Conducting Background Research

Step 1 permitted you to explore what you already know about the topic, and, more important, it gave you some ideas about what you don't know. Now you need to conduct some general research to flesh out your knowledge about the topic. As you begin this step in the process of exploring your topic, you will need to consider what kind of information you are looking for and where you might find it. And you will want to determine what you will do with that information. For example, in the previous steps of this project, we have suggested you share your topic statements and explorations of your prior knowledge about your topic with your classmates, particularly those who share your interest in a topic. In step 4, we will suggest you share your research notes with those members of your class who share your interests as a way of streamlining the research process for individuals while simultaneously broadening the knowledge of the community as a whole. If you take notes for yourself, you will only need to jot down enough information to jog your own memory. If you are going to share those notes, you need to write them clearly enough to address the needs of an audience—your research group peers.

Because you are at the beginning of your exploration, your goal is to find general background information. General background information is the kind you might find in mass media information sources available to the general public such as newspapers, popular magazines, and general reference sources such as dictionaries and encyclopedias. So, general information on "Censorship and the Internet" will often be written by newspaper and magazine journalists who report on what others have researched firsthand by identifying the broad issues, selecting details and information appropriate for a general readership, and writing about the topic in a way that appeals to a general readership consisting of nonexperts in the field. Such information will be enough to get you going by teaching you about broadly accepted definitions of the topic, the major components of the topic, the major categories and reasons for differences of opinion about the topic, and what some major figures or representative experts believe to be true about the topic. As you focus your topic and issue more narrowly, develop it more deeply, and therefore ask more specific and probing questions, you will later need to seek out more specific and detailed information—the kinds generated by experts on the topic and often made available in professional journals and other discipline-specific publications and resources.

Information sources include general references such as dictionaries and encyclopedias, newspapers and magazines, and, of course, electronic texts on the Internet. Your school library will probably offer the best access to print texts on your topic. Even though this book focuses on the information superhighway, do remember that at this point in history the infohighway has not replaced the traditional repository of information and knowledge—the library. The electronic texts on the infohighway should not be the beginning and end of your research; you will want to use a wide range of research techniques to find a wide range of information sources. Here are some suggestions to get you started:

- Strive to find as much as you can given the time you have; six sources should be your minimal goal. And remember, these will just serve to fill in background information. Some of these may appear in your final paper; some will not. You will be doing more focused research down the road.
- Keep your eyes open for a wide range of information. You will come across the following types of information: research reports, news reports, histories, statistics, and opinion pieces—editorials, position statements, and arguments.
- Try to maintain a balance among the various types of information you will come across. For example, if you find an argument in favor of government censorship of the Internet, seek out other arguments that represent opposing points of view.

- Keep a journal or notes of your exploration. Write down what you looked for, if you were able to find it, and how and where you found it. Although some of what you find during this stage of the process will not fit your immediate needs, as you develop the project more, you may find you could use a resource you originally rejected. Of course, you could go through the labor of making photocopies of everything you find, but doing so before you make an initial evaluation of the source would be a waste of energy and resources.
- Before you do a careful reading of or take any notes about the sources you come up with, casually read through the documents you find to see whether they will teach you something you didn't already know about the topic or whether they are too narrow and specific to offer you the general background you are looking for.
- Once you have determined which sources will be useful, prepare yourself to take notes about your background reading. If you have decided to share your research with others, we suggest you take a look at Chapter 9, Project 5, to remind yourself of the elements of the critical annotation technique we described as a process for using writing to read critically. Writing critical annotations of the sources you find in this step will help you produce reports and evaluations of your research, ones you may want to share with peers. Even though you are trying to enhance your general knowledge about the topic, and even though not everything you find and read during this stage of your exploration will seem useful now, you may come across ideas, data, details, and other nuggets of information you may want to use eventually. So, consider these tips:

  — Begin a separate note card, page, or electronic file for each document you find and read.
  — Write at the top of each card, page, or file all the bibliographical information available to you (author, title, publisher information, page numbers). Also make some notes about where and how you found the information in case during some later stage in the process you want to return to that source.
  — As you take notes, be sure to write down direct quotations exactly and write down page numbers to accompany all the quotations, summaries, and paraphrases of information you will need to attribute to the sources.

- Visit the reference section or room of your library. With your topic in hand, let's say "Censorship and the Internet," look at several unabridged dictionaries to learn more about the definitions and histories (etymologies) of some of the key terms in your topic. Look up the term *censorship,* for example, and take notes on the various definitions offered.

- While at the reference room, browse through a couple of the most recent and comprehensive encyclopedia sets and look up the various key terms of your topic. Pay close attention to the cross-references and "see also" notations at the end of the encyclopedia articles for further leads. For example, if you were to look up *censorship* in an encyclopedia, you might also be directed to articles about the First Amendment, freedom of speech, the Supreme Court, and so on. Follow those leads as far as you can, taking notes along the way.

- Your library will also have various indexes for tracking down printed information in newspapers, popular magazines, and professional journals by subject, keywords, and author. Many of these indexes, such as the *Readers Guide to Periodical Literature* and the *New York Times Index* you will find in hard copy. It is quite possible, also, that your school has various computer tools (CD-ROM databases of the *Readers Guide to Periodical Literature* or ERIC) and on-line searching tools ("The National Newspaper Index" or "The Wilson Guide") for looking up books and articles in newspapers, magazines, and scholarly journals. If you don't know how to use these tools already, ask the reference librarian for assistance. Once again, use these tools to find leads to newspaper and magazine articles about the keywords of your general topic.

- Use the techniques described in Chapter 4 for searching electronic texts on Gopher and the World Wide Web. To search for Web sites related to your topic, for example, you could use one of the various World Wide Web search engines such as InfoSeek, Lycos, or Alta Vista to search on key terms such as *censorship, First Amendment, hate speech,* and so on. Jot down the titles of the pages and the URLs. If you have your own copy of the World Wide Web browser, make electronic bookmarks of the Web sites you determine have some potential.

- Join a "virtual" conversation in progress about your topic. As we noted in Chapter 3, you will find on the Internet thousands of computer-mediated virtual communities where people gather on mail lists and Usenet newsgroups to discuss issues and share information. Use the techniques described in Chapter 3 to find virtual communities related to your topic, join the community, and keep up with it so you can learn more about your topic from a wide range of individuals who share your interests. You can take advantage of your membership in these virtual communities in a number of ways. After you have lurked or participated for a while, you will be able to recognize how amenable the group may be to helping you with your research. If you feel a spirit of cooperation and helpfulness, you might send a message to the virtual community telling them about your project and asking the membership for leads to research on the topic. Or, if the group discourages such activities, you might identify several members of the group whom you could E-mail individually to ask for their opinions, advice, or leads to helpful information. As we noted in Chapter 9, Project 5

"Writing to Read Critically," you have to read and evaluate the contributions of virtual community members very carefully to separate facts from rumors and unexamined opinions from informed arguments.

Step 4: Sharing Your Background Research

Conducting research can be time-consuming, frustrating when your leads end up as dry wells, and exhilarating when you find an illuminating nugget of information that somehow alters your knowledge, understanding, or point of view. You and your learning community members can share the burden of research and the wealth of knowledge stemming from it by using CMC techniques. If you have set up topical mail groups, Usenet newsgroups, or other types of electronic conferences for sharing the prior knowledge explorations you generated earlier, you can probably use those groups again for sharing your research notes. If you have turned your research notes into critical annotations (see Chapter 9, Project 5), you can send your research notes or full-blown critical annotations as CMC messages to everyone in your interest group. By doing so, you can contribute to everyone else's knowledge, and by reading other's contributions, you can learn more about your topic. As we noted in Chapter 9, Project 5, relying on other people's annotations of what they found does *not* replace your own research, however.

Step 5: Reflecting on What You Know and Have Learned about Your Topic

So far, you have taken an inventory of what you already know about your topic, and you have fleshed out your basic understanding of the topic by doing some background reading and reading your peers' annotations. Now you need to take stock of your current knowledge of the topic. The purpose of this step, then, is to reflect on what you have learned about the topic and what issues others have brought up about the topic as a way of helping you transform your general topic into an issue you can analyze.

- Reread all the documents you have created so far, including the topic statement you created in Activity 10.1, step 4, the prior knowledge inventory you generated in Activity 10.2, step 1, and the background reading notes you generated for Activity 10.2, step 2.
- Create a new document in which you reflect on the new knowledge resulting from your background reading by addressing the following:
  —What did you learn about the definitions for the keywords of your topic?
  —What did you learn about the history of your topic?
  —What did you learn about the people affected by or involved in your topic?
  —What new aspects or branches of your topic did you learn about, especially ones you didn't consider in your initial exploration of your prior knowledge?

— What did you learn about controversies arising out of your topic?

— What did you learn about the causes of those controversies?

— What did you learn about individuals or groups who represent different sides of the controversies? Who are these individuals and groups, why do they believe the ways they do? What arguments do they make, and how do they make them?

— What was the most interesting thing you learned about your topic?

To this point you have undertaken a thorough exploration of your topic. You have gained knowledge that will help you understand enough about the various aspects and diverse variables of your topic to turn it into an issue and narrow that issue down to something you can analyze effectively.

ACTIVITY 10.3: Creating and Narrowing An Issue

Developing a workable issue involves a multistep process of coming up with as many tentative issues that grow out of your topic and then testing and revising each of those variations until you come up with a focused issue you can address effectively in 1,000–1,500 words. The following steps will lead you through these processes.

Step 1: Turning Your Topic into an Issue

Your initial research into your topic should have provided you with not only facts and historical background but also some possible perspectives and points of view various individuals and groups take on the issue. All the various perspectives on an issue, furthermore, may not even revolve around the same understanding or definition of the topic. Your research might have illuminated for you not only differences of opinion but also the numerous ways the general topic has been and can be divided, focused, and narrowed. Your own critical thinking skills, too, can allow you to imagine what various aspects of the topic could exist and what perspectives are possible. Your goal in this step is to reflect on your new knowledge of your topic to turn your topic into as many as issue questions as possible. Let's take as an example the topic "Censorship and the Internet." Take your topic and turn it into as many questions as possible. For example, using the "Censorship and the Internet" topic, we might ask:

- Should the Internet be censored?
- Who should censor the Internet?
- Why should the Internet be censored?
- What on the Internet should be censored?
- How should the Internet be censored?

Step 2: Testing Your Issue

Once you have turned your topic into a series of tentative issues, you need to test each of them. That is, you need to ask three questions of each one to determine which will be best suited for your analysis. Those questions are as follows:

- Is the issue "controversial" enough to generate legitimate and reasoned debate?
- Can the issue stand on its own as a starting place, or does it represent a subcategory of a larger issue?
- Is the issue focused enough to permit a careful and detailed analysis within the constraints of the assignment—a 1,000- to 1,500-word analysis?

By way of example, let's test some of these issues, starting with the first one, "Should the Internet be censored?"

Test 1: Controversy
Yes, a great deal of controversy over this issue exists. Because we have seen some instances of hate speech and pornographic images and ideas being made available and exchanged on the Internet, some people advocate some level of censorship so that the hate speech doesn't violate the rights of the hate-speech targets and the pornography isn't made available to minors. Others are against censorship of the Internet on the grounds that our First Amendment rights guarantee freedom of speech and that hate speech and pornography are protected as free speech. And, as you know if you happened to choose this topic and did some background research on it, the debate has become decidedly complex. So, the issue "Should the Internet be censored?" passes the first test—it is certainly a controversial issue with many subtle nuances and complexities, characteristics that makes it well suited for analysis.

Test 2: Does the issue serve as a starting place, or is it a subissue?
Before we examine the issue "Should the Internet be censored?" it will be useful to look at another of the issues listed earlier, one that clearly fails this test. Let's look at the issue "What should be censored on the Internet?" Such an issue is a very worthy one in one sense—it is extremely controversial. We can imagine very sophisticated arguments for allowing X, Y, and Z and censoring U, V, and W. However, before one can get into a reasoned argument surrounding "what" should be censored, the conversants must agree that the Internet should be censored at all. If the conversants don't or can't agree on the principle that the Internet should be censored, there is no ground for debate over what should be censored. So, this issue "What should be censored on the Internet?" though controversial enough, does not pass the second test. The question "Should the Internet be censored?" however, does pass the second test.

Test 3: Focus
Remember that your goal for this project is to write a 1,000- to 1,500-word analysis of an issue. You could, of course, write 1,000 words on just about any topic, but the broader the topic, the less you can say about the various

components of the topic, and your analysis will suffer from being too general. Your analysis will be much more effective if you can get into great depth and detail about a narrowly focused issue than if you are forced to be fairly general about a broad topic. Let's look, then, at "Should the Internet be censored?" as an example. When we first looked at the topic "censorship and the Internet" we broke down the key terms, *censorship* and *Internet,* into constituent parts.

Censorship:
    What is censorship?
        Official control of community-agreed on objectionable speech, text, and images.
    What are the current laws about censorship?
        First Amendment
        Supreme Court interpretations
        State- and local-level laws
        Telecommunications Act
        Communication Decency Act
    What gets censored?
        Sexually explicit texts and images
        Hate speech
        Politically unpopular ideas
    What are the benefits of censorship?
        Protect children
        Protect rights of targets of hate speech
        Protect community standards of decency
    What are the drawbacks of censorship?
        Infringes First Amendment rights
        Violates intellectual freedom
        Limits new or unpopular ideas
    Who should get censored?
        No one
        Those whose individual tastes, ideas, and morals don't conform to community standards
        Those who produce and distribute sexually explicit materials
        Those who hold and disseminate racist, biased, or prejudiced beliefs toward others
        Those who hold and proclaim antidemocratic beliefs
    Who are or should be the censors?
        Federal government
        State governments
        Local governments
        Self-censoring of information providers (TV stations, movie producers, newspaper editors, Internet access providers, etc.)

Internet
  A network of networks
  Hardware
    Personal computers
    Network servers
    Network cables
  Software
    PC operating systems
    Network operation systems
    Communications software
    E-mail software
    Synchronous conferencing software
    Gopher
    WWW browsers

Things you do with the Internet
  Computer-mediated communication
    Synchronous
      MUDs/MOOs
      Internet relay chat
    Asynchronous
      Electronic mail
      Usenet newsgroups
      Electronic bulletin boards
  Information Sharing
    Ways to share information
      File transfer protocol
      Gopher
      World Wide Web
    What forms of information does one find on the 'Net?
      CMC texts
      Graphics
      Audio
      Video
    What kinds of information does one find on the 'Net?
      Text (sent)
        Private
        Public
      Text (retrieved)
        Through FTP, Gopher, World Wide Web
      Images
        WWW sites
        Downloadable image files
    What is the content of such information?
      Social

Entertainment
Informational
Facts
Opinions
Scholarly
Legal
Consumer information
Advertising

At this point you're probably thinking (or saying out loud), "Phew, there's a lot there!" And, as detailed as this outline may appear, the list is hardly exhaustive. If we break down the issue "Should the Internet be censored?" we'd have to consider the various perspectives on the issue in addition to the various components of the key terms. Even if we divide the perspectives into a fairly unsophisticated triad of pro, con, and "in some cases yes, in some cases no," we could create an equally rich list of possible areas of analysis.

Pro censorship of the 'Net:
  Who are these people?
    Conservatives
    Liberals
    Church leaders
    Government officials
  Why are they in favor of censorship?
    Protect community standards of decency
    Protect rights of victims of hate speech
    Protect values of democracy and capitalism
  What do they want to censor?
    Pornography
    Hate speech
    Radical speech
    "Dangerous" speech
  What forms to they want to censor?
    Texts
    Images
  Why do they want to censor the Internet?
    Certain controls on other types of media have always been used.
    The Internet is wide open where children can access harmful information.

We could, of course, expand this analysis twofold if we thought through the perspectives of those who are anticensorship and those who take a middle perspective. And, as we noted earlier, an effective analysis would complicate the issue beyond the pro/con/synthesis perspective.

We have to wonder, then, whether we could write a detailed, 1,000- to 1,500-word analysis on the issue "Should the Internet be censored?" Given the fact that the outlining we've done, which doesn't include the pro and synthesis perspectives, is almost 400 words, it seems unlikely that we could actually explain the ideas, offer examples, and conduct an analysis of those ideas in 1,000–1,500 words. Such a broad topic might be appropriate for a book!

So, ultimately, the issue "Should the Internet be censored?" fails the third test. It is much too broad for a detailed and effective analysis. This is not to say the issue should be abandoned, but it needs to be narrowed and focused.

Step 3: Narrowing the Issue

As the previous example shows, you need to craft your issue to make sure it is phrased in such a way that it can be debated by reasonable people in a logical fashion, that it doesn't presume some larger agreement, and that it is narrow enough to deal with effectively. Our "Should the Internet be censored?" example passed the first two tests but failed the third. Clearly, the issue needs to be narrowed.

To do so, we would have to look at the broad range of possibilities that exist and choose a certain combination of those aspects to combine into a narrowed issue. In our example, we learned that the types of ideas, texts, and images that might be censored could include pornography (which could be further broken down into hard core, soft core, child pornography, heterosexual, homosexual, bisexual, etc.), hate speech (which can be further broken down into racist, sexist, xenophobic, etc.), or politically radical information. We could, therefore, narrow our issue considerably to "Should pornography be censored on the Internet?" We could narrow the topic even more if we made a distinction between text and images by asking, "Should pornographic images be censored on the Internet?" Finally, we could narrow it even further if we consider the way the information is distributed. For example, we might decide to make a distinction between information that is sent between individuals, point to point—such as a private E-mail message—and information that is broadcast either by one person sending a message to a whole group or by just making the information publicly available to anyone who wants to come and get it, such as on a World Wide Web site or an FTP archive. Then we might consider the following issue: "Should private E-mail containing pornographic language be censored?"

Here are some procedures that will help you narrow your issue:

- Consider what you learned about the topic from your background reading. Chances are that some of what you read revealed to you ways the issue can be focused.

- Analyze your issue by asking as many questions as you can about each of the keywords. Then, ask questions about the answers to your questions until you flesh out all the possible areas of analysis.
- Collaborate with your peers, on-line or in a face to face discussion, and share your issues. Your goal is to test one another's issues using the questions and principles offered earlier.

Step 4: Collaborative Activity: Using Your Local Learning Community to Explore the Issue

Now that you have narrowed your issue, you might consider turning to your local learning community to help you explore the issue. Even though your classmates may not be "experts" on your topic, as literate, educated members of our culture, they will have at least some passing knowledge of your topic, and you might find a few who have extensive knowledge. Also, because your learning community consists of a variety of individuals who might represent a wide range of beliefs, opinions, and perspectives on your issue or some aspect of it, your community provides an excellent place to test some ideas.

The general goal and purpose of this step is to share your narrowed issue, or question, with your peers and invite them into a debate on the issue. Again, depending on the technological context of your community, you have a couple of options for this step.

Option 1: Face-to-Face Debate

- Determine whether your community will group people by shared interests, that is, people who are all interested in "censorship and the Internet," or randomly with little regard for the content of their issues. The benefit of the first option is that because these people have already done considerable background research and reflection on the issue, they might be able to engage in a more informed debate. The second option, on the other hand, could offer some more diversity of ideas because people unfamiliar with the topic will be forced to think more divergently.
- Gather into small groups of three people each.
- Have one person read his or her issue aloud. The person whose issue will serve as the topic for the debate should be prepared to take notes.
- As a group, brainstorm all the possible positions on the issue that could exist. Write down those possible positions.
- As a group, brainstorm all the various arguments, reasons, and potential examples and evidence that might be used as support for a pro position on the issue.
- After the group has exhausted all the possible pro arguments, take each argument or reason and play devil's advocate by brainstorming several possible counterarguments.

- Continue this cycle of brainstorming possible positions and counter-arguments until you feel you've exhausted the possibilities.
- As time permits, repeat the procedure for each member of the group.

Option 2: CMC Debates

The goal of conducting on-line debates with your classmates is the same as that described in option 1: to explore as divergently as possible potential positions, arguments, and reasons surrounding the debate that grows out of your issue. The benefits of debating the issue on-line include being able to preserve a transcript of the debate and eliminating the need to meet in the same place at the same time to conduct the debate.

- As a large group, decide which CMC medium you will use. You may want to use E-mail or a synchronous chat program such as an IRC channel or a MUD/MOO or some other real-time conferencing program.
- Decide when and where you might conduct the debate. If you decide to use E-mail, for example, you may decide to conduct the debate over an extended period outside class. If you decide to use a real-time conference, you may want to dedicate class time to "meet" in a virtual space; or, if you have access to the virtual space outside of class, you and your group members may decide to meet on-line at a particular time outside of class convenient for all of you.
- Once you've made these preliminary decisions about time, place, and media, use the suggestions offered earlier in the face-to-face debate instructions to structure the activity.

ACTIVITY 10.4: Analyzing the Issue

To this point you have identified a topic, explored your own knowledge, shared your knowledge with others and thus perhaps learned more about your topic, conducted some background research to learn even more about the topic, transformed the topic into an issue, and tested and narrowed the issue. You are now ready to analyze the issue. For this activity, you will begin your first draft by opening a new word-processing file and addressing the questions offered in the next several steps. You should know in advance, however, that the following questions do not constitute the exact or final outline for or structure of your draft. The questions are designed, rather, to help you think through the analysis. As you go through the steps of analyzing your issue, you will learn, undoubtedly, that certain weaknesses in your analysis will arise because you won't have enough information to address some of the analytical questions. Thus, it is quite likely that during the analysis process itself, you will find the need to conduct more research. Although your initial research efforts provided some general background knowledge (depending on how much time and effort you dedicated to the first round of research, you may already have found highly detailed and focused information that fulfills your needs), this time around your research may involve looking for very specific kinds of information to fill in some gaps in your knowledge. The final step of this activity, therefore, will lead your through some focused research.

Step 1: Creating a Context for the Issue

One of the key features of an effective analysis is sharing with your readers the context of the issue. Answering the following questions will help you flesh out the context. If your answers to any of the following come from information you gathered during your research, be sure to include direct quotations, paraphrases, summaries, *and* the appropriate citation information. Doing so will prove useful as you develop and revise your draft.

- What is the issue? (Remember to state it as a question.)
- What is the history of the issue? For example, censorship has been an issue for a long time, but censorship of the Internet has only been an issue during the last several years when affordable, improved technology and the relative ease of use of the World Wide Web has made access to vast amounts of information relatively simple.
- When did it become an issue? Have any recent events related to your issue catapulted the issue into the public arena?
- What makes it an issue? In other words, what causes the controversy? As we've demonstrated with the censorship example, various individuals and groups have different interpretations of the laws and different belief systems about what constitutes decency.
- What is the current state of affairs concerning the issue? Has some new law been passed? Has some new government or private industry report related to your issue been published recently? Has a new book related to your issue been published and generated national discussion or debate?
- What are the various perspectives on the issue as you have defined it?

Step 2: Analyzing Perspectives on the Issue

As a result of your background research, exploration of your own knowledge of the issue, and debates with your classmates about your issue, you have probably been able to identify at least three and hopefully more perspectives or points of view on the issue. To keep these straight in your mind, you might want to label the different perspectives A, B, C, and so on. Write out your responses to the following for *each* of the perspectives you've identified.

- How would you summarize perspective A? For example, you could represent the anticensorship position thus: "Those who oppose censorship on the Internet do so on the grounds that all forms of expression are protected by the First Amendment."

- Who represent(s) or follow(s) this perspective? During your research, did you come across any editorials or arguments espousing a particular perspective on your issue? Do people who take this position on your issue generally belong to other groups—political, ideological, religious—whose belief system influences its members' points of views on the issue?
- What are the reasons people who believe in this position use to support their opinions?
- How do they make their arguments? In other words, do they make arguments based on reason, statistics, and empirical proof, or do they argue from faith?
- Why do you think they have the point of view they do?
- How do they critique the opposition's point of view? It is useful to understand how the proponents of one position critique other positions because you can then understand more about the issue.
- How does the opposition critique this point of view? Understanding how those who disagree with the proponents of this point of view will help you better understand the strengths and shortcomings of the position.
- On what points of definitions, belief systems, and so on, does this perspective differ from the other perspectives?
- What do you consider to be the strengths and shortcomings of this position?

Remember to complete these questions for all the real and potential positions on the issue.

Step 3: Developing a Controlling Idea

You have now completed the bulk of the analytical, critical thinking work. You have come up with a topic, done some background research, turned your topic into an issue and narrowed that issue, and analyzed the various debates and perspectives surrounding it. Now you need to reflect on everything you've read, thought about, and written to come up with a controlling idea that will serve as the anchor and focus for your analysis.

In short, your controlling idea will serve as what some people call a *thesis statement.* Because you are writing an analysis, the controlling idea needs to serve as a synthesis of the debate and the various perspectives surrounding the debate. Your thesis statement, which may be more than one sentence, needs to be broad enough to embrace the scope of the issue and narrow enough to notify the reader of the parameters of the analysis. What follows are some sample thesis statements that might appear in an analysis of the issue "Should pornographic images be censored on the World Wide Web?"

Example 1

"There is much debate over the issue of censoring pornographic images on the World Wide Web."

In some ways, this statement works—it does inform the reader that there is a debate, and it does tell the reader that the analysis will focus on a particular kind of information—pornographic images—on a particular aspect of the Internet—the World Wide Web. The statement can be improved, however, because it doesn't go far enough. Merely stating that there is a debate gives little indication of what you might analyze in the paper. Your reader will be better served if you give more information about the range of perspectives and the causes of the debate.

Example 2

"The question of what, if anything, should be done about pornographic images on the World Wide Web has generated a heated debate among those who represent a wide range of opinions. Some people believe that all forms of expression are protected by our First Amendment rights. These people oppose censorship in all its various forms. Those who support censorship of pornographic images believe pornography exploits women and children, exposes minors to morally corrupt behavior, or violates local community standards of decency. Between these two extremes exist those who argue for various levels of control of questionable materials."

This example is stronger because not only does it focus the issue and announce that there is a debate, but it also describes the range of perspectives on the debate. There is, however, still room for improvement because this example doesn't forecast for the reader the complex reasons for the debate. Here is a further revision to consider.

Example 3

"The question of what, if anything, should be done about pornographic images on the World Wide Web has generated a heated debate among those who represent a wide range of opinions. Some people believe that all forms of expression are protected by our First Amendment rights and therefore are against censorship in all its various forms. Those who support censorship of pornographic images believe pornography exploits women and children, exposes minors to morally corrupt behavior, and violates local community standards of decency. Between these two extremes exist those who argue for various levels of control of questionable materials. The debate is complicated not merely because people have different beliefs on pornography and censorship generally but also because no clear agreement exists on three basic issues: What constitutes pornography? How broadly or narrowly should the First Amendment be interpreted? How do the new ways of making pornographic materials available on the Internet affect our current laws?"

This example works on a number of levels. It focuses the topic, announces a debate with a wide range of opinions, and articulates the major causes of the differences in opinion. It also effectively forecasts for the reader what to expect from the analysis by offering an implied road map of the points of analysis.

Here are some suggestions for coming up with a controlling idea for your issue.

- Reread your research notes and the various documents you've produced during the preceding steps, especially the work you did earlier to analyze the various perspectives.
- Write down all the various perspectives, and compose a sentence or two about each in which you summarize their position.
- Reflect on common points among the perspectives. Do the groups at least agree on various definitions of the problem? Do they agree with one another up to a certain point, such as that a problem needs to be addressed, but diverge when it comes to causes of or solutions for the problem?
- Reflect on the differences among the positions. Do they disagree from the outset because of different belief systems? Do they disagree because they define and interpret the problem differently?
- Write your controlling idea with the goals of
  — summarizing the issue,
  — identifying the range of perspectives on the issue,
  — identifying the major points of disagreement that cause the debate, and
  — charting a road map for your readers so they can anticipate where your analysis will take them.

Step 4: Conducting Follow-up Research

During your exploration and analysis of your issue, you probably came across questions you couldn't answer or got the sense "Hmmm, if I just had some statistics on X, I could really strengthen this part of the analysis." For example, while researching the "censorship on the Internet" topic, you might have read sources in which people built their arguments on the basis of the First Amendment. It is quite possible, also, that these people failed to explain or cite the First Amendment and were working from commonly held (and perhaps erroneous) assumptions about it. If you don't know the text, intent, and spirit of the First Amendment and the history of interpretations and applications of it, you will probably need to learn more about it firsthand before you can analyze and evaluate arguments based on it. Or, as you've conducted your analysis, you might have realized you haven't achieved a balance among the various perspectives. Your background reading might have provided you with a number of pro censorship resources but a shortage of anticensorship resources. Thus, your follow-up research would focus on finding such resources to achieve a better balance.

Here are some suggestions for determining how to focus your follow-up research:

- Evaluate the types of sources you've come up with thus far:
  — How many "opinion pieces"—official position statements, argumentative essays, editorials—have you used?
  — How many relatively objective reports—original research reports, summaries of original research reports, news reports in magazines and newspapers—have you used?
- Evaluate the sources of your information:
  — How many of your sources come from newspapers? Are those newspapers local (your town's newspaper) or national (e.g., the major papers from big cities like the *New York Times,* the *Washington Post,* the *Wall Street Journal,* etc.)? If the local paper did a story on computers and education, it will most likely focus on a local school to appeal to the interests of local readers. If a national paper did a story on computers and education, it would focus most likely on national trends to appeal to wider audience.
  — How many of your sources come from popular magazines, and what is the level of sophistication and "seriousness" of those magazines? You can evaluate the seriousness of magazines by looking at the ratio of text to advertisements (more serious magazines often have fewer advertisements than do popular magazines), the lengths of the articles (are they short blurbs or fully developed essays?), and the kinds of advertisements (are the advertisements promoting consumer goods and luxury items with high-concept art and four-color layout, or are they less consumer oriented and more staid?). Are the magazines the kinds you can buy at the supermarket checkout stand and focus on entertainment and pop culture (*People*) or news (*Time, Newsweek, U.S. News and World Report*), or are they the kind you'd buy at book and magazine stores (the *New Republic,* the *Economist,* the *Atlantic Monthly*)?
  — How many of your sources come from the Internet? Remember that Internet users have high-level interest in the Internet, and some have a vested interest in its growth. You might find more anti–Internet censorship sources than pro–Internet censorship among those who see the Internet as a positive phenomenon.
  — How many of your sources come from "scholarly" publications, those that are written by and for experts in a particular field? One way to identify such publications is that they rarely include advertising, and

when they do, the products are focused on the professional needs of a very narrow audience.

- Now that you have evaluated the sources you have referred to, is there a balance among them in type (report/argument) and media (newspaper/magazine/scholarly/Internet)? If not, you may need to explore more information about your issue in some of the other forms.
- Evaluate the analytical work you've completed thus far. Are there any "holes" in your knowledge about some aspect, fact, or point of view about the issue? For example, if you have never read the First Amendment, you might need to look it up. If a major point of your analysis hinges on Supreme Court rulings on pornography or censorship, you might have to conduct a search on Supreme Court rulings.

ACTIVITY 10.5: Composing Your Analysis

The time has come to write your first complete draft. Assuming you have followed many of the procedures described so far, you have now created a number of documents and notes that will serve as the bulk of your first full draft. Because you have completed a very thorough invention process, the task ahead involves selecting information and then arranging that information into a logically and coherently sequenced analysis. To better understand what information to select and how to arrange it, you'll need to give some thought about your audience. Having a target audience in mind will help you select the appropriate details and information and arrange them appropriately. Your first step, therefore, is to conduct an audience analysis.

Step 1: Audience Analysis

Developing a clear understanding of your potential readers is important for several reasons. First, understanding how much they already know about your topic will allow you to gauge how much background information you'll need to share, how many details and definitions you'll need to provide, and what kinds of connections among ideas you'll need to make. Unless you are writing for a magazine that, through market analysis, has a well-developed definition of its readers or an academic journal in which you can assume a high level of expertise among the readership, you are always in a position of having to construct your audience somewhat artificially. That is, because you are writing in a school rather than a professional setting at this point, you have more control over your target audience. The key issue for you is that once you've decided on an audience, throughout your analysis you must be consistent in the kinds of information you provide and the language and style you use. What follows is a series of issues to consider when analyzing your audience:

- The assignment as described at the beginning of this project identified your audience as "college-educated" readers. As such, we might assume that they are people who can understand fairly sophisticated language and analyses. They respect critical thinking. As a group, they probably keep up with current events through newspapers and have passing but informed knowledge of a wide range of topics and issues. They probably do not, however, have deep knowledge of your particular issue.

- Evaluate the level of interest potential target audiences may have in your issue. In other words, who would be most interested in reading about your issue? For instance, if you were writing about "censorship and the Internet" (a more focused version of this issue, of course), a wide range of potential readers exists. Parents who want to let their children explore the Internet might be interested in learning more about the issue. Teachers who would want to allow their students to use the powerful tools of the Internet would be very interested. School, college, and university administrators who have to make decisions about permitting Internet access would need to learn more about the issue. Lawyers, particularly those who deal with freedom of expression issues, would need to understand the issue. And, of course, those who dabble in the forms of information that might be censored would be interested to learn about their rights and liabilities. Each of these potential audiences, however, would have different motivations for reading an analysis of your issue, and each would expect different foci and kinds of information. Given the information you already have on your issue, which of the vast potential audiences you've identified could you address most appropriately?

- Evaluate the prior knowledge of potential target audiences. Writing an analysis of "censorship and the Internet" for parents would require different kinds of information than writing one for lawyers. Because the First Amendment and various interpretations of it probably lie at the center of the controversy, you would have to gauge how much prior knowledge about the First Amendment your potential target audiences have. Among a group of parents, you'd have to assume a wide range of knowledge, from almost nothing to almost everything, so you'd probably have to spend a generous amount of time explaining it. If, on the other hand, you were targeting lawyers who specialize in freedom of speech issues, you probably need not spend a great deal of time explaining the First Amendment.

- Evaluate how the prior knowledge of potential target audiences compares with your own. Basically, your potential readers could know more, the same, or less than you do about your issue. And, to further complicate matters, your audience may know more, the same, or less than you on particular aspects of your issue. An audience of parents may know less than you do on both issues of censorship and the Internet, whereas an audience of lawyers may know more than you do about legal issues, but they may know less than you about the Internet. People such as you, your classmates, for example, may share your general knowledge about the Internet as a result of sharing your ride this semester on the information superhighway but less than you do about the legal issues. So, the parent audience would need lots of explanation about both legal issues and the Internet, the lawyers would need less background information on the legal issues and more on the Internet, and your peers would need less background information about the Internet and more about the legal issues.

- Reflecting on the information you have gathered and the knowledge you've gained as a result of it, think about the range of potential audiences you've come up with as a result of your thinking about these considerations and any other possible audience constraints (e.g., your instructor may have defined an audience for you), and generate an audience analysis statement along the lines of the following example: "My target audience will be limited to parents of young Internet users. I assume they want to know more about the issue of censoring pornographic images on the World Wide Web because they want to know how safe the Internet is for their children; what the government, Internet users, and Internet access providers and Internet software vendors are doing to make it a safe place for minors; what their rights are as parents; and what roles they might take in making the Internet safe for their children. Because these parents may have only a passing knowledge of the technology and the legal issues, I will have to provide thorough background information and definitions about Internet technology and how it is and can be used and the legal issues concerning freedom of speech, censorship, and the various forms of control of controversial information."

Step 2: Outlining the Draft

Now that you have a focused issue and audience in mind, you may find it useful to construct a tentative outline for the structure of your draft. Note that we used the term *tentative* to describe this outline—the final structure of your draft may very well change as you actually write it. While constructing your outline, you will need to consider *what* your target readers will need to know, *why* they need to know it, and *when* they will need to know it. So, for example, before you analyze the range of points of view surrounding your issue, you need to share with your readers the whole range of possible positions. And, before you tell them the whole range of issues, your readers may need to know why such a broad range exists, that is, what causes the controversies that surround your issue. What follows is a sample outline for an analysis of censorship of pornographic images on the World Wide Web. Remember, also, that the outline does not necessarily represent actual paragraphs of a draft but rather broad, general sections. Some sections may take only one or several paragraphs to flesh out, depending on the issue and the audience.

   I. Context of the issue
      A. What is the history of the issue?
      B. Why is it an issue?
      C. What are the range of possible—real or imagined—positions on the issue?
      D. How are these positions related to one another—that is, on what do they agree and on what do they diverge?
      E. What is your controlling idea or thesis?
   II. Necessary background information (Note: What you consider "necessary background information" has everything to do with how you have defined your audience.)
      A. What is the Internet?
         1. The technology
           a. Hardware
           b. Software
           c. Wide-area network
         2. CMC
           a. Asynchronous
              1. E-mail
              2. Usenet
              3. Electronic bulletin boards
           b. Synchronous
              1. Internet relay chat
              2. MUDS/MOOs
              3. Chat rooms
         3. Information sharing
           a. FTP
           b. Gopher
           c. World Wide Web
         4. Forms of information on the Internet
           a. Text
           b. Graphics
           c. Audio/video
      B. What is censorship?
         1. History of censorship
           a. First Amendment and freedom of speech and expression
           b. What has counted as "speech and expression"?
           c. Interpretations of First Amendment
              1. Supreme Court
              2. Local rulings
         2. Pornography
           a. What is pornography?
           b. What are the current interpretations and laws?
           c. What are latest proposals?

III. Articulation and analysis of points of view
   A. What is position A?
      1. What actual or types of individuals or groups adhere to this position?
      2. Why do they believe what they do?
      3. How do they argue their position?
      4. Who do they criticize, and how do they do it?
      5. Who disagrees with this position, and what critiques and counterarguments do they offer?
   B. What is position B?
      1. What actual or types of individuals or groups adhere to this position?
      2. Why do they believe what they do?
      3. How do they argue their position?
      4. Who do they criticize, and how do they do it?
      5. Who disagrees with this position, and what critiques and counterarguments do they offer?
   C. What is position C?
      1. What actual or types of individuals or groups adhere to this position?
      2. Why do they believe what they do?
      3. How do they argue their position?
      4. Who do they criticize, and how do they do it?
      5. Who disagrees with this position, and what critiques and counterarguments do they offer?
   D. What are positions D, E, F, G, and so on (if applicable)?
IV. Conclusion
   A. Summary of the analysis
   B. Predicted future of the issue
      1. Predictions on which point of view may prevail
      2. Predictions on how issue will affect society as a whole

Step 3: Composing the Draft

Your outline has provided you with a general road map, if you will, of the points you are going to visit as you unfold your analysis. Using your outline as your *tentative* organizing structure, write out your analysis keeping the various considerations in mind:

- *Keep your focus.* The controlling idea you worked so hard to articulate and narrow should serve as your anchor. Every point you make and every piece of supporting evidence you offer should relate to and contribute to explaining and supporting your controlling idea.
- *Keep your audience in mind.* Be sure you explain ideas clearly, fully, and in logical sequence. In a sense, you are taking readers on a journey through the issue, and you are the tour guide. Do all you can to make

sure they don't get lost. Because they are critical readers (that's not to say they are hostile readers but rather those who value rigorous critical thinking and who lose faith in a "tour guide" who overgeneralizes or makes leaps in logic), keep in mind that with every word, sentence, paragraph, and major section of the analysis, such readers are looking for the logic of your analysis. Make believe your readers are sitting on your shoulder and whispering in your ear "Why are you telling me this?" "Why are you telling me this now?" and "So what?" If you can answer the questions "I am telling you X because you have to understand it to understand Y, and I am telling you X now because I will build on it to make point Z," then you will be addressing the readers' needs.

- *Support generalizations with evidence.* It is necessary to support all general statements with examples and evidence to illustrate or "prove" your generalization. If, for example, you make the generalization that "According to those who favor censorship, the number of children who have access to pornographic materials has risen over the last five years," you would need to offer statistical information to illustrate the rise in number of children who have access to the Internet.
- *Strike an appropriate balance among generalizations and details.* Of course, any analysis that relies on a string of generalizations without detailed support would prove inadequate. So too would an analysis that is akin to a shopping list or outline of statistics, quotations, and examples without generalizations that tell your readers what the details mean.
- *Document your sources.* When quoting a spokesperson for a particular point of view, citing a statistic, or otherwise incorporating into your analysis ideas and information that are not your own, use appropriate documentation style.
- *Make appropriate transitions among your ideas.* If you think of your task as taking your readers on a journey through your issue and you are the tour guide, you can think of transitions among ideas like the brake lights and turn signals on your car. If you had several carloads of people following you in a caravan and only you knew the way, you would need to make sure your brake lights are working so the caravan didn't crash into you when you slowed or stopped, and you would need to use your directional signals to indicate left or right turns.

ACTIVITY 10.6: Revising Your Analysis for Content and Structure

Now that you have completed a draft, this would be a good time to share that draft with peers to get some feedback. As has been the case at this stage on previous projects, you have the option of giving and receiving feedback in small or large face-to-face or on-line groups, depending on how much class time you have to dedicate to this stage of the project or what kind of CMC system is available to your community. Consult

Chapter 2, Activity 2.3; Chapter 6, Activities 6.2 and 6.5; and Chapter 8, Activity 8.4, for an array of guidelines for organizing the feedback process.

No matter what flavor of the feedback process you choose, it is still important that you reflect on your own draft to help you make sense of both what you've accomplished thus far and what you want to accomplish on future drafts. Reflecting on your progress to date also helps you prepare the draft to share with your peer reviewers.

Step 1: Reflections on the First Draft

Open a file in your word processor and address the following:

- What parts of the process involved in writing this paper, from exploring a topic to writing this draft, went best for you? Describe those parts of the process in some detail, offering reasons they went well.
- What parts of the process thus far have proved most challenging? Why?
- Remind yourself of your purpose. In twenty-five words or less, summarize the point about your issue that you are trying to make.
- Remind yourself about your audience. Have you provided them enough information about your issue so that they will understand what you are analyzing? Have you used language appropriate for the audience and purpose? Have you provided appropriate amount and type of details to support your assertions?
- What are the successful aspects of your draft thus far? Describe in some detail what works and why.
- What are some of the areas that need improvement in the current draft? Describe in some detail what areas you want to improve and why.
- If you were to share this draft with readers, what questions might you ask them? What kind of feedback would you like?
- Articulate for yourself a revision strategy that includes what you feel the draft still needs and what you plan to do to make the essay more effective.

Step 2: Preparing Your Draft for Peer Reviews

Your reflection process will help you prepare your draft for the peer review process. Append to your current draft an assessment of what you think works in the draft and a list of questions you would like your reviewers to address as they review your draft.

Step 3: Giving/Receiving Feedback

Read your peers' drafts (depending on how your peer review process has been organized) twice: once silently and again aloud. Then, use the following items to guide your written feedback.

- Initial responses
  — What are the best parts of the draft?
  — What did you find most interesting?

— What was the best passage or detail of the draft?
— What was the best-written passage?
— What did you learn about the issue?
- Describing the draft
  — Write a fifty-word abstract of the draft.
  — Construct an outline of the draft, using a Roman numeral for each part of the essay (i.e., introduction, body, conclusion), a capital letter for each paragraph, and an Arabic numeral for each supporting detail.
- Evaluating the draft
  — Is the draft "analytical" or more descriptive or argumentative?
  — Were there any points where you got "lost" in the draft? What might have caused your confusion?
  — Look at the outline you wrote. Does it flow logically from point to point, or does it seem that some parts might be re-arranged?
  — Evaluate the quality of the analysis. Are various possible and real points of view identified and articulated? Has each of the possible positions been adequately analyzed? How might they be better analyzed? Take a few moments to think about the issues as if the writer was portraying your point of view. Take a few moments to play devil's advocate for each of the points of view. Can you come up with different and perhaps better points of analysis?
  — Evaluate the balance of the analysis. Are all potential points of view equally represented and supported, or do some get greater emphasis? If so, what effect does this imbalance create on you as a reader? If you recognize imbalances, be sure to identify them to the writer and indicate why you think the imbalance exists and suggest ways the writer can strike a better balance among the various perspectives.
  — Evaluate the development. What else do you think you need to know to understand the draft better? Did you find any unsupported generalizations or unsubstantiated claims? Any generalizations, assertions, or claims that could use *better* support? Are the details used judiciously?
  — Evaluate the language and style. When you read the draft aloud, did you stumble over any phrases? Did you notice any drawn-out sentences that left you nearly breathless? Did you notice any short, choppy sentences that might have created a staccato, telegraphic rhythm? Is the level of formality and sophistication appropriate for the audience?
- Revision ideas
  — What are those good parts of the draft the writer might build on?
  — In general, what are the areas of improvement?
  — In detail, what do you believe the writer needs to do improve the draft? For example, does the writer need to add more information? Where? What kind? Cut out some details? Which ones? Why?

Step 4: Making Sense of Feedback You've Received

Read your peers' responses carefully and consider the following items:

- Were all the comments clear? Which did you not understand? Did reading the comments make you wonder about other aspects of your draft?
- Reply to the E-mail feedback you received from your peers by asking for clarification of their comments. If one reader pointed out one problem with your draft and the others didn't, you might ask the others to look at the same section again to see what they think. Having now read the feedback from your peers, do other questions occur to you? E-mail your peers with those questions.
- How were your peers' comments similar to those you made about the draft in your reflective statement?
- How are the critiques similar? In other words, are there certain features of your draft all your readers liked? Did they have similar comments about the content, structure, or style of your draft? List all the common comments.
- How are the critiques different? Did they comment on different aspects of your draft? Did one applaud you for a section, whereas another reader identified that same section as an area of improvement? If you do get contradictory comments on the same aspects of your draft, what might that mean? Make a list of all the areas of improvement or contradictory comments.
- What did you learn about writing an effective analysis from the critiques of your writing partners' drafts? Was there anything you said about their drafts that might equally apply to your own?
- Reflect on the lists you've made and on what you noticed in your peers' drafts, and develop a revision strategy for yourself. You might begin this strategy by completing the following phrases:
  - — What my readers most appreciated in my draft was . . .
  - — According to my readers, the areas of improvement for my next draft include . . .
  - — In my next draft I plan on doing . . . because . . .

Step 5: Revise Your Draft

Revise your draft based on the feedback you've received.

Step 6: Reflecting on Your Revisions

First, write a new reflective statement about the most recent draft by considering the following. Be sure to append your reflective statement to the draft before sharing it with your peers.

- What did you change to create this most recent draft, and why did you do so?
- What is your favorite part of this draft?

- What other revisions are you planning on making?
- Are there certain sections you want a particular type of help on?
- Are there particular issues you want your readers to focus on?
- If you had had more time to prepare this draft, what would you have done differently?

Step 7: Sharing Second Drafts

Exchange your draft with the same or new peer critics either in hard copy or electronic file or as E-mail or an E-mail attachment. Peer critics should use the criteria described in step 3 to generate feedback on this most recent draft.

ACTIVITY 10.7: Revising for Style and Correctness

After two or more rounds of peer review and revisions, your analysis should be taking shape in terms of its content and structure. And, as you've been revising, it's very likely you have paid some attention to language, style, and correctness. Complete the following steps to fine tune your analysis.

Step 1: Reading Aloud to "Hear" Your Draft

Read the draft aloud slowly, either to yourself, a classmate, friend, or family member (or have one of them read it to you), and listen for the following:

- Do you hear any "echoes," that is, certain words that are used over and over in close approximation to one another?
- Do you or your reader stumble over any words or phrases? Stumbling may indicate missing words or awkward constructions.
- Do certain sections sound telegraphic? Mark those passages and see whether you can revise them to eliminate choppy phrases and incomplete sentences that may be fragments.
- Do certain sections leave you or your reader breathless? Mark those passages and see whether you can revise them to be less wordy.
- Do some sections sound droning and monotonal? Check those passages to see whether you can vary the styles and lengths of a group of sentences so that the rhythm is more varied.

Step 2: Checking the Documentation

Chances are good you employed references to write your analysis. If you have not done so during the drafting stages, now is the time to check the style, appropriateness, and correctness of your citations. You can do this individually or collaboratively.

- Which documentation style have you decided to use (i.e., Modern Language Association [MLA], American Psychological Association [APA], Chicago, etc.)?

- Have you used the appropriate citation techniques for the style you have chosen?
- Have you provided an alphabetized "Works Cited," "References," or "Bibliography" page formatted according to the documentation style you have selected?

Step 3: Spellcheck and Proofread

Remember to use your word processor's spelling checker to seek out and correct typos, misspellings, and repeated words.

ACTIVITY 10.8: Sharing Your Analysis

The final activity of this project is sharing your analysis with real readers. Once again, depending on the technological setup of your institution, you have a number of options.

Option 1: Sharing Hard Copies

Print several copies of your final version, and distribute them to the peers who read the various drafts of your analysis. If your peers shared their drafts with you, be sure to send them an E-mail message with your thoughts on the final result of all your hard, collaborative efforts. When replying to your peers' final versions, you need not offer additional critical feedback. Just tell them your favorite parts, what you learned that you didn't know before, and so on. By praising their work and offering them a virtual pat on the back, you increase your chances of receiving favorable reviews of your analysis.

Option 2: Sharing Electronic Texts

By now you have plenty of experience sharing texts electronically. As when you shared your drafts, you can do one (or more) of the following:

- Send your final version to reviewers (including any E-mail correspondents you might have established as you conducted your research) as E-mail or E-mail attachments. When you receive final versions from others, be sure to reply with sincere words of praise and encouragement.
- Post your final version as an article on a newsgroup if your teacher has set one up for your class.
- If you have the technological access and ability at this point to construct your own site on the World Wide Web, "publish" your analysis there. Chapter 5 offers a brief introduction to constructing Web pages. In Chapter 12 you will find more resources to help you construct a Web site of your work.

PROJECT 7: ARGUING CONTROVERSIAL ISSUES ABOUT THE INFORMATION SUPERHIGHWAY

Objectives

- To write a 1,000- to 1,500-word academic argument about a controversial social, political, or cybercultural issue

Technological Requirements

- A word processor
- Access to on-line research sources including on-line library catalogs, Gopherspace, and the World Wide Web
- Access to a computer-mediated communication system such as a local area network or wide area network E-mail system or electronic conferencing system.

Participant Prerequisites

- Mastery of skills and concepts of analysis presented in Chapter 10, Project 10.6
- Basic knowledge of conducting research on-line, including (see Chapter 4 for information about these techniques):
  — Searching on-line library catalogs using Boolean search techniques
  — Searching Gopherspace using Archie and Veronica
  — Searching the World Wide Web using search engines
- Basic knowledge of using asynchronous CMC (newsgroups, E-mail groups) to share information

Overview

Argumentative writing could be considered the highest form of academic discourse. Why? Argument is the way you join, contribute to, and otherwise represent yourself in the various ongoing conversations—academic, civil, political, and social—you will engage in as a student, professional, and citizen in a democratic society. Learning to argue well indicates an intellectual coming of age, when you take your place at the big table of knowledge makers. Much of the writing you have done in school thus far could be classified as "writing to learn" and "writing as testing." You have engaged in writing-to-learn activities to *use* writing as a tool to help you figure out how to do something and to capture your knowledge on paper. You have used expository writing to explain ideas to others—usually your teachers. You have written essay exams and book reports to show others, again usually your teachers, how much you have learned about something. You have written analyses to demonstrate your critical thinking abilities and to analyze what others have thought about an idea or an issue. The time has come for you to take your stand; the time has come for you to contribute to the ongoing conversations of our culture.

Much of the writing you have done involved various aspects of writing that you will incorporate into argumentative writing. Writing arguments is where it all comes together, so to speak: you will need to employ your best expository writing, critical thinking, and analytical skills to construct an argument that appeals to your audience's sense of logic and establishes your authority to speak intelligently on the topic.

This project is designed to lead you through the critical thinking and writing processes involved in writing an academic argument. For a number of reasons, we recommend you continue pursuing the issue, or some version of the issue, that you analyzed in Project 6. First, to argue well you need to know what you are talking about; you need to establish your authority on the issue. Developing such deep knowledge requires much time for research, reflection and contemplation, and critical thinking to uncover all the various aspects of the issue and arguments surrounding it and to think them through logically to discover strengths and weaknesses of various arguments. Only after such a process can you decide for yourself what version of which arguments you will make. Because you have already done much of this intellectual work in Project 6, we recommend you build on that knowledge to construct an argument. If your learning community chose not to do Project 6, you would do well to refer at least to those activities and steps to help you find something to write about, turn your topic into an issue and narrow that issue, conduct background research, and analyze the issue. As we will explain in more detail, academic argument requires careful and thorough analysis, so if you haven't already analyzed an issue in Project 6, or if you decide to change your issue, you will need to go through the steps of analysis.

The Assignment

Write a 1,500- to 2,000-word academic argument about an issue of your choosing for a college-educated audience. Your community, including your instructor, may decide to negotiate the actual length. You should remember that "depth" is more important than the number of words or page length. The issue can grow out of some aspect of cyber culture (e.g., intellectual property rights, censorship on the Internet, the appropriate roles of technology in education, etc.) or something relating to our larger, general culture (e.g., equal rights, gun control, economic inequities, etc.). If you completed Project 6, "Analyzing Issues," we recommend you continue to pursue that issue or some aspect of it. Your college-educated readers will expect

- a comprehensive explanation of the context of the issue (i.e., what is it, and what are its history and causes?);
- a focused and clearly written statement of the problem;

- a focused and clearly written statement of your position on the issue (your controlling idea);
- a detailed, logical, and well-supported defense of your position;
- an articulation of potential and real counterarguments to your position and defense;
- an analysis of the strengths and shortcomings of those counterarguments;
- an analysis of how your position is in some way more reasonable, logical, or tenable than the counterarguments;
- evidence that you have researched the issue, used those sources effectively, and appropriately documented the sources you do use; and
- conventions of standard written English and a formal writing style appropriate for an academic audience.

Features of Academic Argument

Informally, argument means different things to different people. In everyday life we often think of an argument as a hostile interaction—one that can be emotionally charged and bordering on violence—between two people, such as when you get into an argument with your parents or with a spouse or significant other over money ("You spent how much?!"), divisions of labor ("I cleaned the toilet last time! When are you going to take a turn?"), or personal issues ("You're not going to wear a nose ring while living in my house!"). Unfortunately, and wrongly, we often equate "argument" with fighting. Although it shares with more popular notions of argument some characteristics such as differences of opinion, a statement of a position, and explanations and defenses of that position, formal, academic argument is the tool of rational debate. Its goal is not to "get your way" by overpowering those who disagree with you but rather to employ logical analysis to examine an issue or problem critically—a way to think through a problem and come up with a reasoned explanation or solution.

Another distinction we must make is that between *argument* and *persuasion*—two terms that, informally, are often used interchangeably. Again, these two terms share certain characteristics. In both argument and persuasion a controversy over some issue exists, as do clearly distinguishable positions and explanations and defenses of the positions. The goals of argument and persuasion, however, differ in sometimes subtle ways. The goal of an argument, to state it somewhat loftily, is to seek truth (or at least a mutual understanding among people) through logical reasoning. You could argue logically, for example, the issue "Will investing X amount of dollars in educational technology improve the writing abilities of high school students?" because that question can be researched, tested, analyzed, and argued logically. Persuasion, on the other hand, is more often interested in getting people to *act*, to do something because the persuader wants them to do it, and logic may not always be the basis of a persuasive appeal. So, for example, a toothpaste company will try to convince you to use their toothpaste by making you believe that the product gives you sex appeal. Or a fast-food company will try to persuade you to buy their hamburgers because they are more delicious. In neither case can logic and fact establish the truth of the claim. Instead, the persuasion depends on how strong an emotional impact the text can have on the reader or viewer.

Argument and persuasion differ not only in their goals but in their techniques. You can use any of three basic ways—called *appeals*—to influence an audience or make your ideas attractive to an audience. The ethical appeal, or ethos, refers to the way the authority of the speaker or writer can influence the audience. You will find many examples of the ethical appeal in the persuasive techniques of print and media advertising. Companies often use highly recognizable and popular celebrities, for example, to "pitch" their products. So, you may hear a famous actress promoting a particular telephone company or a sports figure promoting a certain cereal. These spokespersons, of course, probably have no technical expertise about the product (other than what they learned from the company that has hired them), but because they are celebrities and have reached a high status in our culture, we associate the product with our positive images of the spokespeople. Such spokespeople do not strive to teach us the truth about the products but rather to persuade us to buy them. Academic arguments use ethos, of course, but they use a different kind of ethical appeal. Instead of relying on celebrity status or sex appeal, ethos in an academic argument is established by the credibility of the writer based on her depth of expertise as demonstrated by what she has to say about the issue, the rigor of her critical thinking, and the quality of her writing.

Another appeal commonly used in persuasion is *pathos,* or the appeal to the emotions. In advertising, once again, you will find numerous examples of products that play on, and sometimes prey on, people's sympathies, inadequacies, or fears. When you see a fast-food commercial that depicts a father and his little girl sharing quality time together in a restaurant, the commercial is designed to play on people's sentimentality. The commercial implies, "Our restaurant and food will provide happy moments for parents and children who get little time together in this busy and chaotic world." Such commercials rarely speak to the product's nutritional value or quality. Another example includes home security devices that depict burglars breaking into an elderly person's home, an event that causes fear in most people. The implication, of course, is if elderly people buy a home security system, particularly the one being advertised, they will be safe and sound. Rarely do such commercials offer statistical evidence that the particular product will in fact stop burglars. And, if they do, the logical appeal of the statistics, which may or may not be verifiable, is secondary to the emotional appeal. In academic argument, the pathetic appeal is rarely used, and when it is, it is most often employed to personalize an abstract problem so that readers will take interest in it. Academic arguments appeal first to the intellect. Writers are expected to provide evidence for their positions, and most readers do not regard most emotional appeals as evidence—only as motivation. Thus, emotional appeals are secondary in academic arguments.

The final appeal, *logos,* or the logical appeal, is the cornerstone of the academic argument. In general, two major forms of logic exist: deductive and inductive. In deductive logic, conclusions are drawn from generally accepted beliefs. These beliefs are referred to as *premises.* The most basic structure of deductive logic is the *syllogism,* a statement of major and minor premises— ideas about which the vast majority of people agree—that follow from one to the other to a logical conclusion. A classic syllogism is one offered by Aristotle:

> All humans are mortal. (major premise)
> Socrates is human. (minor premise)
> Socrates is mortal. (conclusion)

This syllogism works only because the major premise is an accepted truth: all people die. The minor premise takes a specific example of "human" in the form of another accepted truth: Socrates was indeed a human being. And from it, we can logically conclude that Socrates is mortal or, better stated, was mortal! He did, in fact, die about 2,400 years ago in 399 B.C. The syllogism works because once the reader accepts the premises, he cannot rationally deny the conclusion.

In inductive logic, conclusions are drawn from observations and evidence rather than generally accepted truths or beliefs. You will see examples of inductive logic in the scientific and legal worlds. For instance, scientists often observe phenomena (e.g., cancerous skin lesions), hypothesize possible causes (overexposure to the sun), and run experiments to test the hypothesis, to find evidence that refutes or confirms the hypothesis. They do not work from a general truth, "The sun causes cancer," and build a syllogism around the major premise. Rather, they base their conclusions on scientific observations of people who develop skin cancer. In the legal world, one in which we presume people are innocent until proven guilty (a major premise of our culture), police officers and lawyers need to draw their conclusions of guilt or innocence based on evidence. Because we as a culture believe in innocence until proven guilty, we require that guilt be established as a result of an investigation, which includes the gathering of evidence and a logical analysis of that evidence.

Although the strongest arguments are constructed with both deductive and inductive logic, as you construct your argument, you might think of yourself as an investigator in the inductive mode whose job is first to observe, gather, and analyze evidence, and then to draw conclusions based on that evidence.

Some Considerations and Advice about Critical Thinking and Argument

Although the previous definitions of argument, persuasion, ethos, pathos, logos, deduction, and induction can sound somewhat technical, the fact is you have considerable experience with all the concepts already. You have had plenty of real-life experiences arguing and persuading and using the various appeals. The big step you might have to take, therefore, is using of the concepts and techniques consciously and strategically. Most likely, the biggest leap you will have to make as a critical thinker is in how you envision the relationship between conclusions and evidence.

You've heard (and we hope fully believe in) the expression "Everyone has a right to their opinions." You might have also heard, however, the saying "Not all opinions are equal." Some opinions, which Aristotle called "unexamined opinions," are the result of people forming their opinions based on a lack of knowledge about the issue on which the opinion is held. Such opinions are not always wrong, but they are less likely to be respected because they are conclusions with no inductive or deductive basis. Other opinions—the more highly respected ones—grow out of either deductive or inductive logic, or both. The opinions are not arrived at just because someone else believes them or because they are based on hearsay, rumors, or partial knowledge; they are arrived at as a result of critical thinking. Today, we call these opinions *judgments.*

Sometimes the leap from unexamined opinion to judgment is a big one, especially if your opinion is about something close to your heart or personal experiences. So, for example, you might hold the opinion that using word processors will help everyone become better writers because word processing made your work as a writer easier and better. It would be difficult, and a logical fallacy, however, to make a generalization for the whole population based solely on your personal experience. And sometimes our own opinions are shaped by those held by people we respect or admire. It is not unusual, for instance, for young people to base their political opinions on those of their parents. If, therefore, parents believe in conservative ideals such as small government and free-market economy, their offspring might hold similar opinions. On the other hand, young people might develop opinions opposite to their parents' *just because* their parents hold them!

Sometimes, also, writers can construct weak arguments because they start with their opinions, which may be unexamined, and let the opinion and their desire to "prove" it right control the entire critical thinking process. When writers start with opinion, a temptation arises to research selectively and only to look for and use evidence, examples, and arguments that support the opinion. The writer who works in this way is not then investigating a problem with the goal of arriving at a reasonable, logical conclusion and thus is not thinking broadly, deeply, and openly.

So why, finally, is the judgment or argument drawn from analysis of evidence superior to the unexamined opinion? Because there are many negative consequences of unexamined opinions in the real world. If as a professional you are asked to develop a sales strategy or argue for one manufacturing technique over another one, you will be wise to form your opinion based not on what you *believe* will work but rather on what you infer will work based on a thorough investigation. Even if your investigation leads you to unpopular opinions and recommendations, the truth, for better or for worse, will help people make better decisions.

To make this leap, then, from the unexamined opinion to the informed argument, one that results from rigorous critical thinking, you will seek solutions to problems and not mere support for your opinions. Thus, you will need to keep in check the opinions you have on an issue before you have investigated it as thoroughly as time and resources permit. If you are lucky, your investigation and critical thinking will confirm your initial opinion. But keep your mind open, because your investigation will probably force you to alter and even change totally your opinion, and sometimes doing so will cause confusion and frustration and perhaps prove stressful and painful. Sometimes you will be lucky enough to have your research confirm a formerly unexamined opinion. Other times, your research will lead you to replace an old unexamined opinion with a new and better informed one that grows out of critical thinking. Both those outcomes are victories. The only defeat lies in being uninformed.

One final word of advice. The days when one person could know all there is to know about a topic are long gone. Our culture constantly revises its "truths" and "facts" as a result of newly found information or new ways of interpreting that information. The same will happen to you. Have the courage to change and refine your opinion each time you read or hear something new about your issue. At some point you will just have to make the best conclusion you can based on the information you have been able to gather, digest, and analyze in the time you have. What is more important than your actual position at this point is how critically you think about it and how well you demonstrate that critical thinking.

ACTIVITY 10.9: Finding Something to Write About

Throughout this book you have learned about and practiced various techniques for developing topics, turning those topics into issues, and narrowing those issues into ideas you can address adequately in 1,500–2,000 words. The purpose of this section, then, is not to take you through all those steps again but rather to remind you of your options.

Step 1: Revisiting Your Issue from Project 6

If you completed Project 6, you engaged in a thorough process of brainstorming possible topics, selected several in which you had an initial interest, chose one and turned it into an issue, tested the issue, researched the issue, and analyzed it. If, however, you or your class did not complete Project 6, you might turn to it now and complete Activities 10.1 and 10.2.

Even if you did complete Project 6, for a number of reasons you may not want to write an argument about that exact issue, but rather some version of it. So, for example, while analyzing the issue "Should pornographic images be banned from the World Wide Web?" you might have developed a heightened interest in the Communications Decency Act. Your argument, therefore, now might deal with the issue, "Should the Communications

Decency Act be repealed or overturned?" Completing the following items will help you decide on something to write about.

- Freewrite about Project 6. Are you still interested in the issue? Why?
- What did you learn about the issue that surprised you?
- What did you believe about the issue before you did your research?
- What do you believe now?
- If what you now believe is different from what you believed before, what caused that change?
- If you remain committed to the issue you analyzed in Project 6, skip the next step. If you feel you want to pursue a different issue for the project, complete the following steps.

Step 2: Developing an Issue Out of Other Previous Experiences

Throughout this course you have explored the information superhighway in a number of ways. You've read about it and issues that surround it on the Internet itself through computer-mediated virtual communities, your informal browsing of and focused research on the World Wide Web, and what your peers have written about in their various papers, ones they shared with you as drafts and final versions. Your instructor may even have assigned a number of readings. Take a few minutes now to freewrite on the following items:

- Dig through your memory to recall all the virtual places you've visited this semester, all the reading you have done, all the writing you have completed, and all the conversations you've engaged in. For example, if you've completed all the projects in this book thus far, you would have
  — introduced yourself to your new classmates via computer-mediated communication;
  — worked collaboratively with a classmate to write a handout, quick note, or brochure about some aspect of your school's technological landscape;
  — joined a computer-mediated virtual community and written a narrative about some aspect of it;
  — written a discourse analysis of some virtual community you joined;
  — explored electronic texts—CMC, FTP, Gopher, the World Wide Web—and read them critically;
  — written an analysis of some controversial issue; and
  — collaborated, both verbally and on-line, with classmates and perhaps even writers at other schools;
  — learned how to use a host of computer tools.
- After you complete your list, reflect on your experiences thus far:
  — What was the most interesting, disturbing, or thought-provoking conversation—oral or on-line—you have been part of this semester? Can you recall any flame wars that you were either part of or witness

to? Did any people or events really get under your skin, cause you to brood over them outside class, inspire you to tell your dorm mates or family members about them?

— What was the most interesting, disturbing, or thought-provoking essay shared with you by your peers?

— What was the most interesting, disturbing, or thought-provoking E-text or print text you read this semester?

— Throughout this course, you have been asked to think about different ideas and in different ways as compared with what you might do and how you might do them in a traditional English class. What have been the best parts of your learning experience this semester? Which have been the most frustrating? For example, whereas many people see many virtues in collaborative learning, computer-mediated communication, hypertext, and the World Wide Web, others, either before or after experiencing these things firsthand, wonder about what is lost and about new drawbacks. Does the extra time, effort, and logistics of collaborative learning make it better or worse than your previous educational experiences, which might have focused on individual learning? Is on-line communication really better than or different from face-to-face interaction? Is hypertext a better way to construct texts? Is the World Wide Web a better way to get information?

• Taking an inventory of what you've experienced this semester and reflecting on those experiences may have dug up for you more topics and issues that you might argue for this project. Take a few minutes now to reflect on all your options, evaluate your level of knowledge and interest in each, and select one to pursue.

• If you have chosen a topic or an issue different from the one you analyzed in Project 6, refer to Activities 10.2 and 10.3 in Project 6 for advice and techniques for turning a topic into an issue and narrowing that issue.

ACTIVITY 10.10: Exploring the Issue

Now that you have settled on a tentative issue for your argument, you will need to explore the issue in a number of ways. First, you will want to take inventory of everything you know about the issue already. If you've stuck with the issue you analyzed in Project 6, you've already developed a wealth of information. If you have decided to write about a different issue, remember that you will most likely need to conduct some background reading and research to get a better understanding of the issue. If you are starting from scratch, you'll want to return to Project 8, "Writing to Read Critically," and step 3 of Activity 10.2 in Project 6, "Analyzing Issues," for techniques on conducting research. Then, you'll need to explore your beliefs on the issue to formulate a *tentative* position statement or thesis about the issue. We use the term *tentative* very consciously. Remember that an argument needs to draw its conclusions from investigation and analysis of the issue. It is not unlikely that while you start with a position based on your beliefs, you may need to revise or perhaps even reverse your position based on what you learn as you develop the argument. Part of your exploration will also involve looking at the argument from various perspectives as a way of testing your position. Looking at the issue from various perspectives not only allows you to keep your mind open to various perspectives but also helps you discover possible objections and counterarguments to your position, ones that you will need to analyze and refute as you construct the argument. Also, as you discover potential objections and counterarguments, you may find gaps in your knowledge and thus may need to conduct some further research to gather data, facts, and other information to support your argument further. The following steps lead you through the process of exploring the issue.

Step 1: Exploring What You Know and Believe

Exploring what you already know and what you believe about an issue will help you flesh out your argument, analyze why you believe the way you do, and help you identify gaps in your knowledge and understanding about the issue. Open a word-processing file, type in the following items, and respond to each one as thoroughly and in as much detail as you can. Note that not all the items may pertain to your particular issue. We urge you, therefore, to revise the items and create new ones as they occur to you.

- What do you know about the history of your issue? In other words, what historical events created the issue?
- What has made your issue an issue? What events have occurred, or what ideas and beliefs have clashed to create the controversy?
- What are the various ways the issue has been defined? For example, censorship does not mean the same thing to everyone, and because of different definitions of key terms and the issue itself, different perspectives and positions arise.
- Who are the "players" in the controversy? Has there been a clash among various groups who share certain beliefs? Are there any notable, famous, or nationally recognized people who created the controversy or who have contributed opinions and arguments about the issue? Whom does the controversy affect?
- What are the various positions on the issue? Clearly, there will be pro and con sides to the issue, but a range of other perspectives might also exist. How many of them do you know about?
- How do those who hold the various positions on the issue argue their positions? In other words, what reasons do they offer, and what examples, evidence, and data do they use to support them?

- Why do you think those who hold various perspectives believe as they do? Do you find evidence of political, religious, legal, or cultural belief systems influencing various perspectives?
- What is *your* position on the issue? If you were asked today what should be done about your issue, how would you respond and why?
- *Why* do you believe how you do? Is your position based on your political, religious, or cultural belief system? Is your position based on your inquiry and analysis of the issue?
- Look through what you've written thus far. What do you believe to be the gaps and blanks in your knowledge about the topic? In other words, what do you believe you have to learn more about to help flesh out the background context of the issue, to support your position on the issue, to develop the counterarguments, and so on?

Step 2: Composing a Tentative Position Statement

You know from your previous writing experiences that any essay needs to make an assertion that serves as the controlling idea—the main idea each major point of your essay will define, explain, and support. In an argument, you can think of your thesis as a proposition, a position statement, an assertion. In your previous writing experiences, also, you might have thought of a thesis statement in terms of a single sentence, but an effective proposition or position statement may actually consist of several sentences. A strong proposition

- states your position,
- helps the reader anticipate the complexity of the issue, and
- helps the reader anticipate the major reason or reasons for the position.

By way of example, let us explore several possible position statements.

Example 1
   "The Internet should not be censored."
   In some ways this example could work. It is concise and offers a clear statement of the writer's position. However, it does not allow the reader to anticipate the complexity of the issue, and it does not help the reader anticipate why the writer is taking the position she is.

Example 2
   "The Internet should not be censored because any form of censorship undermines First Amendment rights."
   This version of the position statement is stronger because it not only offers the position but also makes clear to the reader the major reason or principle on which the position is based. The position could be improved, however, if it also helped the reader anticipate the complexity of the issue.

Example 3

"The controversy surrounding censorship of the Internet grows out of competing beliefs about what constitutes pornography, how standards of decency are determined, what role various forms of government should play in issues of censorship, and the traditional conflict between the individual's rights to freedom of speech and the need to protect the moral values of those who object to pornography. Because one of the cornerstones of American democracy—the First Amendment—protects freedom of speech, the government must not censor the Internet because censorship of any kind threatens to undermine the very foundation of American culture."

As you can see, this statement is much more complex. It offers some context for the issue, states the position very clearly, and also shares with the reader the underlying principle on which the position stands.

As we noted earlier, the position statement you generate now is tentative. It represents your best and clearest assertion *at this time.* As you shape and refine your argument, you will probably find that you need to revise the structure of the statement. You may even decide to revise your position altogether. But at least for now you have a controlling idea in place.

Step 3: Engaging in Devil's Advocate Debates

Constructing a reasoned argument involves exploring various potential perspectives surrounding an issue, analyzing those real and potential perspectives, and drawing a conclusion, which becomes your position, from that analysis. Thus, it is not enough to state your position and develop several reasons to support only your position. You need to explore as many alternative positions, possible objections, and counterarguments to your position as you can. How do you learn about such objections and counterarguments? Of course, as you've done background reading and conducted research, you probably came across some competing perspectives, and you'll want to draw on those readings as you construct your argument. Another effective technique for exploring the issue is by engaging in a devil's advocate dialogue, either verbally or on-line, with peers. Generally, speaking, to play the devil's advocate is an exercise in consciously opposing any point of view. During this exercise you will need to decide whether you will work in a face-to-face or computer-mediated peer group, exchange with your peers position statements, and conduct debates surrounding the issue.

Option 1: Face-to-Face Devil's Advocate Debates

- Gather into groups of three to five members. Smaller groups will give each member more time to offer her or his issue up for debate; larger groups will often lead to a greater diversity of ideas. The composition of the groups should be taken into consideration, also. For instance, people could be grouped based on their shared interests. Several people writing on similar topics would bring a wealth of knowledge to the debates. You could, however, also arrange groups so no two experts on the same topic work together. Although the other devil's advocates might not have depth about the particular issues, nonexperts can offer fresh perspectives and bring up elements of the issue that people very close to it might not be able to imagine.

• Each group member should take a turn sharing, either in writing or verbally, a brief context or background of her or his issue and position statement. The other group members then serve as devil's advocates. Doing so may prove difficult at first because some group members may find that they agree with the writer's position, but remember that as the devil's advocate you are role playing here. Regardless of personal beliefs, each member of the group should propose as many counterarguments as possible and offer reasons, examples, and evidence to support them.

• The writer whose position statement serves as a catalyst of the debate should take careful notes, as this exercise will yield many potential counterarguments for possible use in her or his argument. After each person has offered as many counterarguments as possible, the writer should take some time to defend her or his position in light of the counterarguments. Repeat the exercise for each person in the group.

Option 2: On-Line Devil's Advocate Debates

As a group, determine which type of computer-mediated communication technology you will use. Using a real-time conferencing program during class time offers the immediacy of a face-to-face debate and, in many cases, will permit you to capture a transcript of the dialogue. Using an asynchronous CMC technology, such as E-mail, will allow you and your peers to conduct the debate over an extended period of time. Whichever technology and technique you use, shape what you do with the technology around the following procedures:

• Determine how many people will be in how many groups. If using a real-time conferencing program, you will probably want to set up different channels, rooms, or subconferences for each group. If using E-mail, you will want to set up mail groups for each one.

• Have someone in the group type in his or her position statement (or copy and paste in from the file you created when you composed your tentative position statement) and send it to the entire group.

• All other members of the group offer as many oppositions and counterarguments, with reasons and supporting evidence and examples, as they can come up with.

• As the counterarguments come in, the writer should defend his or her position within the context of the counterarguments by pointing out their shortcomings and offering reasons, evidence, examples, and other forms of support for his or her position.

• Repeat the procedure for each member in the group.

Step 4: Exploring Arguments, Reasons, and Counterarguments

As a result of your background reading and research, your personal exploration of your knowledge and beliefs, your own critical thinking about arguments and counterarguments, and your engaging in debates with devil's advocates, you have generated much data and a plethora of ideas. You might find yourself swirling in a whirlpool of supportive and contradictory ideas, and you might also have found that your tentative position has been challenged so strongly that you no longer know what you believe about your issue. This is natural. This is good. Your idea is maturing, growing, and becoming more complex. Now you need to try to make sense of it all. This step leads you to reflect once again on your position and leads you through a procedure for making sense of all these ideas.

• Create a new word-processing file and type in the following items. Note: The reasons 1, 2, and 3 and the counterarguments A, B, and C are arbitrary. The actual number of reasons and counterarguments will depend on how many ideas you have. Don't limit yourself now, and don't worry about ranking them in any particular order of importance or significance. Also, be careful to realize you're not creating an outline for your paper here. The purpose of this step is merely to let you see what you have in some sort of organized fashion.

My position:
    Reason 1:
        Support for reason 1:
        Analysis of reason 1:
    Reason 2:
        Support for reason 2:
        Analysis of reason 2:
    Reason 3:
        Support for reason 3:
        Analysis of reason 3:
    Counterargument A:
        Support for counterargument A:
        Analysis of counterargument A:
    Counterargument B:
        Support for counterargument B:
        Analysis counterargument B:
    Counterargument C:
        Support for counterargument C:
        Analysis of counterargument C:

- Now complete the form you've just created in as much detail as possible. Remember, it is very likely you have more than three reasons and more than three counterarguments. In the "support" categories, you want to include as much evidence as you have at hand. Such evidence might include statistics, anecdotal evidence, examples, and opinions of authorities on the subject. When conducting the analysis of each reason or counterargument, be sure to question the validity of the data or statistics you have used (where does the data come from? how accurate is it? who generated the statistics? what hidden biases might you uncover?) and the potential biases of the expert sources (why do the experts believe what they do? what are their political, religious, ideological affiliations? what commercial interests do they have?). Also consider how threatening to your position the counterarguments might be. Are the reasons given by those who oppose your position more logical, reasonable, more compelling, more valid, less biased than your own reasons? You might find that the support for the counterarguments is stronger than that for your position. If you believe this to be the case, you might consider conducting more research to find information you need to better support your argument.
- Reflect on all the arguments and counterarguments you have generated, and test your position in light of them. Does your position still seem tenable? If not, do you need to revise your position statement? Do you need to change your position altogether?
- Using the Cut and Paste functions of your word processor, take some time to "play" with the arrangement of the reasons and counterarguments.
  - Play with a couple of logical sequences for the reasons behind your argument. Which reasons seem to be prerequisites for other reasons? Which reasons seem to be more important, and which seem less important?
  - Play with a couple of logical sequences for the counterarguments. Which reasons seem to be prerequisites for other reasons? Which reasons seem to be more important, and which seem less important?
  - Play with the relationships among your reasons and the counterarguments. Which counterarguments are best aligned with which of your reasons?

ACTIVITY 10.11: Writing the First Draft

Activities 10.9 and 10.10 led you through a thorough process of inventing your argument. You are now ready to write your first draft. As you begin, you will need to take some time to consider your audience. Knowing your audience will determine what you say. The audience dictates how much and what kind of information you will share, how you will arrange it, and how you will say it, that is, what tone and what level of formality you will use.

Step 1: Audience Analysis

Audience, those who will read your argument, is on the surface an easy concept. In reality, however, the notion of audience, especially in school writing, is a rather complex one. Writing in "the real world" is sometimes made easier because writing on the job, for example, has a very well-defined audience. If your supervisor asks for a report on your work in progress, you know the audience—what she expects to hear and how she expects to hear it. If you were writing a marketing proposal for potential clients, your audience would be pretty clear. You know who your potential clients are, what they need, and so on. If you were writing for a magazine, you would have available to you much demographic information on the subscribers—income level and education level, for instance—that would tell you much about how and what they think about and find appealing.

Things are not so clear in school writing, however. Although you may be writing this argument because your instructor assigned it to you, you are not writing "to your teacher." Indeed, your teacher is one member of your audience, a representative of your audience who will judge the quality of the work, but thinking of your teacher as the sole reader is too narrow. You would err also to think of your audience as "a general audience of anyone who wants to read the essay." To write a focused argument, you need to construct your intended audience. We recommend you write out an audience analysis based on the following considerations:

- Assess your potential audience's age and education level. What can you infer about their expectations of your argument? For a college-educated audience to take your argument seriously, for example, they would expect a certain kind of tone (formal), language (sophisticated diction), and intellectual rigor (balanced and thorough critical thinking). Such readers would privilege certain kinds of arguments (academic) and supporting evidence (objective data, logical reasoning, and conclusions drawn from research) over persuasive techniques supported by anecdotal evidence and relying on the pathetic or ethical appeal.
- Assess your potential audience's prior knowledge on the issue. Does your intended audience have more, the same, or less knowledge than you do on the issue? This is important to know because how much and what you say to an audience of experts in an area is much different than how much and what you say to an audience of novices.
- Assess your potential audience's attitude toward the issue. Does your intended audience share your belief system? Certain issues, particularly those that grow out of political or religious convictions, don't cause disagreement because of the "facts" but because of the differences in the ways people interpret facts based on their belief systems.

- Assess your potential audience's position on your issue. Is your intended audience likely to agree, disagree, or have no opinion about your position on the issue? Making this distinction early is crucial. Shaping your argument for those that agree with you is akin to "preaching to the converted." If such readers already agree with you, you wouldn't have much occasion for debate. On the other hand, those who disagree with you based on their political, ideological, or religious beliefs will not be swayed by arguments that grow out of conflicting ideological perspectives. On any issue, however, there are people who don't know enough about an issue to have formed an opinion or who keep their minds open awaiting more information so that they can draw their own conclusions. In general, you probably want to focus on this latter group.
- After you have considered these issues, write a brief statement that characterizes your intended audience.

Step 2: Writing the Argument

You've given much thought to your position on the issue, your reasons and evidence, possible counterarguments, and intended audience. You are now ready to write your first draft. Your goal with this step is to compose your argument from beginning to end as fast as you can.

- Set aside an hour or longer, during which time you will write a draft of the argument from beginning to end. Don't get too hung up just now on style and correctness. If during the composing you realize you need more support for one of your reasons, just skip by it. You can strengthen the individual components of the argument during later revisions.
- Review all your notes to refresh your memory.
- Begin a word-processing file.
- Write the history and context of your issue.
- Write out your position.
- Develop your reasons and support.
- Offer the counterarguments and analysis of those counterarguments.
- Write a "closing argument" that analyzes and summarizes all the evidence on various sides of the issue. The analysis, of course, should result in a logical and reasonable defense of your position.
- If you are using information you gathered from your research, do make sure you document that information—use an appropriate and accepted citation style—as well and correctly as you can at this time.

ACTIVITY 10.12: Giving and Receiving Feedback on the First Draft

By now you should have the most fully articulated version of your argument to date. By nature it is rough. Various sections may be more developed and better supported than others. The sequence of ideas could be more logical. Some transitions from one idea to another may be better than others. And grammatical errors and stylistic glitches may exist. It will be a good idea at this point in the project, then, to get—and give—some feedback. The following steps help you prepare your draft, offer advice for sharing the drafts, structure your feedback, and make sense of the feedback you've received.

Step 1: Preparing the Draft for Critiques

- First, reread your entire draft critically, and respond in writing to the following:
  - What parts were easiest to write or came to you most naturally? Which parts do you feel most confident about?
  - What do you believe to be the strengths of the draft?
  - What parts were most difficult to write? Which were the most confusing to you even as you were writing them?
  - What do you believe to be the areas of improvement for this draft?
  - Which parts would you like most help on, and what kind of help would you like?
- Use the reflection on your draft to compose a brief (150- to 200-word) statement that you will attach to your draft and share with your peer critics, a statement that will help them structure their feedback. In your statement, tell your peers about
  - your issue,
  - your position,
  - your intended audience,
  - your favorite parts of the draft,
  - your greatest concerns about your draft, and
  - the kind of feedback you would like. You might ask your peer critics specific questions about your draft to help them structure their feedback.
- Copy your statement and paste it as a preface or introduction to your draft so your peer critics can read the statement before reading the draft. Save the new document, which now includes your draft and your reflective statement.

Step 2: Sharing Drafts

You have several options for sharing your drafts with your peers.

- Determine the size and makeup of your peer groups. Because providing quality feedback takes considerable time, you should keep the groups rather small, perhaps three to five people. You will also want to consider if you want to gather yourselves into groups that share similar issues (e.g., all group members are arguing some issue related to education and technology), or you may want to gather into groups of people who know very little about one another's topics. The homogenous or "similar issue" grouping can be useful because all peer critics will have prior knowledge about the issue and thus might better understand its complexity. Groupings made up of people who know very little about one another's issues can be useful because they represent a certain segment of the audience and thus could add insights and perspectives overlooked by those close to the issue.

- Determine when you will share drafts and provide feedback. Your group may decide to use class time to conduct critiques or do them as homework over several days.
- Determine how you will share drafts. Your options include exchanging printouts of the drafts or exchanging the drafts electronically. Your decision will be based on the technological context of your setting.
- Once you have considered these variables, exchange drafts.

Step 3: Providing Feedback

The role of peer critics at this point in the project is not to "correct" the draft but rather to provide feedback about the content and structure of it. The following items will help you structure the feedback you will provide to your peers.

- Read the draft, including the writer's reflective statement, all the way through once.
  — Write your initial reaction, your gut response.
  — What sticks out in your mind?
  — What was your favorite part of the draft?
- Read the draft all the way through a second time. Write out a brief summary of the argument, starting with a statement of the issue, the writer's position, and an overview of the major arguments and counterarguments.
- Evaluate the content of the draft.
  — Does the writer provide enough information to establish the context of the issue?
  — Is the issue clear to you?
  — How clear is the position?
  — Does the draft include several arguments in support of the writer's position?
  — Do each of the reasons offer adequate, appropriate, and concrete support in the forms of examples, data, expert opinions, and so on?
  — Does the draft include several counterarguments? Are those counterarguments addressed and analyzed effectively, or does the writer bring them up and dismiss them without analysis?
- Evaluate the structure of the draft.
  — Do arguments flow logically from one idea to another, or does the line of development jump around and switch jarringly from one direction to another?

— Do the arguments seem arranged in any particular order from most important to least or vice versa?

— Are the counterarguments arranged logically?

— How effective are the transitions among ideas, paragraphs, and sections of the argument?

- Evaluate the audience awareness of the draft. Read over the part of the writer's reflective statement that focuses on the intended audience.

— Do you believe that audience is the most appropriate one for this issue and argument?

— How well has the writer shaped the argument for that audience?

— Is the kind of support and evidence appropriate for the intended audience?

— Is the tone and language appropriate for the intended audience?

- Evaluate the language and style. When you read the draft aloud, did you stumble over any phrases? Did you notice any long sentences that left you nearly breathless? Did you notice any short, choppy sentences that might have created a staccato, telegraphic rhythm? Is the level of formality and sophistication appropriate for the audience?

- Reflect on your responses to these items, and draft your critique by addressing the following items. Remember, when writing out your critique, be as detailed and thorough as possible. Don't just say, for example, "Your second reason needs more support." Say, "Your second reason didn't advance your argument because you didn't offer any supporting evidence. I think it would be stronger if you could offer some census data to help the reader understand how many people the issue affects" or "If I were making this argument, I would mention X, Y, and Z."

— Begin your critique with positive reinforcement about the successful elements of the draft.

— Copy, paste, and revise your summary of the draft as the second part of the critique that will follow the positive features of the draft.

— What are the major areas of improvement? What parts left you wishing you were given more information? Which arguments and counterarguments seemed underdeveloped or lacked adequate and detailed support? How could the draft be revised to better address the needs of the intended audience?

- Because your feedback needs to be understood and interpreted by the writer, you will want to make sure the feedback is well written. Reread your comments aloud to yourself, spellcheck, and otherwise get it in the best shape possible. Then, using the technique you and your group decided on—exchanging hard copy or E-texts via file sharing or CMC— share your feedback with the writer.

ACTIVITY 10.13: Revising Your Argument for Content and Structure

Now that you have written a draft based on your research and exploration of your issue and your position on the issue, shared your draft with peers, and given and received feedback on first drafts, you need to reflect on what you've learned thus far about your draft and draw on those reflections to revise the argument. The following steps will lead you through the process.

Step 1: Reflecting on the Feedback You Received

Read your peers' responses carefully and consider the following items:

- Were all the comments clear? Which did you not understand? Did reading the comments make you wonder about other aspects of your draft?
- If your peers used E-mail to critique your draft, reply to the E-mail feedback by asking for clarification of their comments. If one reader pointed out one problem with your draft and the others didn't, you might ask the others to look at the same section again to see what they think. Having now read the feedback from your peers, do other questions occur to you? E-mail your peers with those questions.
- How were your peers' comments similar to those you made about the draft in your reflective statement?
- How are the critiques similar? In other words, are there certain features of your draft all your readers liked? Did they have similar comments about the content, structure, or style of your draft? Make a list of all the common comments.
- How are the critiques different? Did they comment on different aspects of your draft? Did one applaud you for a section while another reader identified that same section as an area that needs improvement? If you do get contradictory comments on the same aspects of your draft, what might that mean? Make a list of all the areas for improvement or contradictory comments.
- Often, reading other's drafts will reveal to you ways of developing an argument that you didn't think of yourself. What did you learn about writing an effective argument from the critiques of your writing partners' drafts? Was there anything you said about their drafts that might equally apply to your own?
- Reflect on the lists you've made and on what you noticed in your peers' drafts, and develop a revision strategy for yourself. You might begin this strategy by completing the following phrases:
  — What my readers most appreciated in my draft was . . .
  — According to my readers, the areas of improvement for my next draft include . . .
  — In my next draft I plan on doing . . . because . . .

Step 2: Testing Audience Awareness

As we noted earlier in this chapter, what you say, how much you say, and how you say it are all determined by audience. You need to first ask yourself the following questions, answer them the best you can based on the feedback you've received and your own reflections, and revise your draft accordingly.

- First, return to your original thinking and analysis of your intended audience for your argument.
- As your argument unfolded, do you still believe your intended audience is an appropriate one or the best one? Might your draft actually have grown in a way appropriate for a different audience? If so, you will need to decide whether your original audience is still the best one or the one you want to target or if you want to revise your argument for a different audience. Making this decision now is crucial as a clear conception of your target audience is necessary to evaluate the criteria that follow.

Step 3: Testing the Context of the Issue

Take a close look at the section, probably the introduction, that lays out the context of the issue for your readers.

- How appropriate, given your target audience's needs, is the amount of background information you have offered? Could it be that you've given too much information so that your readers have to wade through a page or more of context before they get to the point of the argument? Or does the opposite situation exist? Did you launch right into your argument without providing your readers with enough context so that they understand the history of the issue and what makes it an issue?
- Have you made the issue appealing to the reader? In other words, why should they care about the issue? Have you offered them a way to connect with the issue? If the issue is an abstract concept such as "Does computer-mediated communication lead to addictive behavior?" you might offer an anecdote—a short, illustrative story—about the harrowing experiences of a real person who has succumbed to the seduction of on-line existence. Or, if you are arguing about the sociological perils of the widening gap between those who have access to technology and those who do not, you might offer some startling statistics that illustrate the gap. If the issue is one that generates debate because of ideological perspectives, you might offer quotations that contradict or conflict with one another.

Step 4: Testing the Proposition

During the prewriting for your first draft, you gave much consideration to your proposition, but as you developed the draft, you might have discovered and explored perspectives and approaches you hadn't considered during prewriting. Or the relationships among your ideas might have emphasized or deemphasized ideas you originally believed to be more or less important. Again, this is a natural part of the composing process. As you revise, you will need to evaluate your original proposition to see how it holds up in light of where the argument actually went.

- Revisit Activity 10.10, step 2, in this project to review the criteria for a strong proposition, and evaluate your proposition in light of that criteria.

- Does your proposition still help the reader anticipate the complexity of the issue?
- Does your proposition still state your position clearly?
- If necessary, revise your proposition to reflect more clearly and accurately what you've actually developed in your argument.

Step 5: Testing the Logical Flow and Development

You might think of your job as a writer somewhat similar to that of a tour guide. You are taking your readers on a journey. You know better than your readers do where you are going and what the points of interest are along the way. You also know the best way to get where you are going. You would be an ineffective tour guide, however, if you sped up past some relatively important points of interest and spent too much time at some relatively minor points of interest. You would be an inefficient tour guide if you took those who are following you first to one side of town, then to another town, then back to the other side of the original town, and then someplace altogether different. In other words, your tour would lack a sense of direction and focus. Test to see whether you have taken your readers on a logical, clear, focused, and unified journey by addressing the following items:

- Are the reasons for your arguments supported fully through logical constructions, examples, and evidence, or have you just offered assertions without any supporting evidence?
- Do the supporting details and evidence actually support what you are trying to support, or do they inadvertently contradict or confuse your point?
- Have you offered a counterargument for each of your arguments?
- Have you offered analyses and/or refutations of those counterarguments that demonstrate how the counterargument fails to weaken your argument?
- Have you arranged your arguments and counterarguments in a logical sequence, or do you (and your readers) get a sense that the ideas jump around without any sense of connections?
- Have you used effective transitions among ideas and paragraphs to help your readers understand the relationships among those ideas?
- Have you offered a "closing argument," so to speak, that offers an analysis of how in the light of the evidence offered during the draft your position is stronger than others?

Step 6: Writing the Second Draft

After you have completed this analysis of your first draft, you are ready to revise it. Take into consideration everything you've learned about your draft from your peers, your instructor, and your own reflections on and analysis of the draft. This will be the strongest version of your argument thus far, one that will probably remain as the bulk of your final version, so you'll also want to pay close attention to the following as you compose the second draft:

- Integrate your sources appropriately. When using sources, you might find it tempting to sort of dump meaty quotations into your text. To use sources effectively, however, take this advice:
  - Don't overuse long block quotations. Synthesize, summarize, and paraphrase others' ideas as much as possible, keeping direct quotes to a minimum.
  - Don't drop quotes in without explanation and just expect readers to understand how the quote, statistics, and so on, support your point. You need to integrate sources by either directly stating or implying how the quotation or statistic is related to the point you're trying to make.
- Document your sources appropriately. Consult a handbook or look up on-line the appropriate technique for citing sources, depending on what style you and your instructor have determined you should use (see Chapter 13 for help finding instructions for documenting sources). In most cases, you could expect to use American Psychological Association (APA) or Modern Language Association (MLA) styles.

ACTIVITY 10.14: Sharing Second Drafts (Optional and Recommended)

When second drafts are complete, and if time permits, you and other members of your learning community may want to engage in another round of peer critiques, especially if you made significant revisions between the first and second draft. If your group does decide to conduct another round of peer critiques, repeat Activities 10.12 and 10.13.

ACTIVITY 10.15: Revising for Style and Correctness

After two or more rounds of peer review and revisions, your argument should be taking shape in terms of its content and structure. And, as you've been revising, you have very likely paid some attention to language, style, and correctness. Complete the following steps to fine tune your argument.

Step 1: Reading Aloud to "Hear" Your Draft

Read the draft aloud slowly, either to yourself, a classmate, friend, or family member (or have one of them read it to you), and listen for the following:

- Do you hear any "echoes," that is, certain words that are used over and over in close approximation to one another?
- Do you or your reader stumble over any words or phrases? Stumbling may indicate missing words or awkward constructions.
- Do certain sections sound telegraphic? Mark those passages and see whether you can revise them to eliminate choppy phrases and incomplete sentences that may be fragments.

- Do certain sections leave you or your reader breathless? Mark those passages and see whether you can revise them to be less wordy.
- Do some sections sound droning and monotonal? Check those passages to see whether you can vary the styles and lengths of a group of sentences so the rhythm is more varied.

Step 2: Checking the Documentation

Chances are good you employed references to write your argument. If you have not done so during the drafting stages, now is the time to check the style, appropriateness, and correctness of your citations. You can do this individually or collaboratively.

- Which documentation style have you decided to use (e.g., MLA, APA, Chicago style)?
- Have you used the appropriate citation techniques for the style you have chosen?
- Have you provided an alphabetized "Works Cited," "References," or "Bibliography" page formatted according to the documentation style you have selected?

Step 3: Spellcheck and Proofread

Remember to use your word processor's spelling checker to seek out and correct typos, misspellings, and repeated words.

ACTIVITY 10.16: Sharing Your Argument

The final activity of this project is sharing your analysis with real readers. Once again, depending on the technological setup of your institution, you have a number of options.

Option 1: Sharing Hard Copies

Print several copies of your final version and distribute them to the peers who read the various drafts of your analysis. If your peers shared their drafts with you, be sure to send them an E-mail message with your thoughts on the final result of all your hard, collaborative efforts. When replying to your peers' final versions, you need not offer more critical feedback. Just tell them your favorite parts, what you learned that you didn't know before, and so on. By praising their work and offering them a virtual pat on the back, you increase your chances of receiving favorable reviews of your analysis.

Option 2: Sharing Electronic Texts

By now you have plenty of experience sharing texts electronically. As when you shared your drafts, you can do one (or more) of the following things:

- Send your final version to your draft reviewers (including any E-mail correspondents you might have established as you conducted your research) as E-mail or E-mail attachments. When you receive final versions from others, be sure to reply with sincere words of praise and encouragement.

- Post your final version as an article on a newsgroup if your teacher has set one up for your class.
- If you have the technological access and ability at this point to construct your own site on the World Wide Web, "publish" your analysis there. Chapter 5 offers a brief introduction to constructing Web pages. In Chapter 12 you will find more suggestions for constructing a Web Site of your work.

11

WRITING IN THE DISCIPLINES

Now we want to begin the process of thinking about academic writing, about both the kinds of writing we do in college and the ways that writing may carry over once we've left college for the workaday world. As in earlier chapters, you'll develop this knowledge collaboratively, by exploring the ways writing functions in different disciplines, looking at how writers in different fields of study and work address their readers, and so forth.

WRITING **FOR** *A* **DISCIPLINE**

Let's begin with an example. A common genre for writing in various social sciences and natural sciences is the research report, or lab report. Here the writer uses a basic format to meet the reader's expectations about what the report will contain and how the report will progress from part to part. This format is widely known as IMRAD, which only *sounds* like it should be a division of the Strategic Air Command. Actually, it stands for Introduction, Methods (and Materials), Results, Analysis, and Discussion—the principal parts of the research report. Writers in the social and natural sciences use IMRAD because the parts, taken together, present all the important information and analysis from a scientific study and because, once readers are accustomed to reading in the IMRAD format, they can find the information they want quickly and easily. Here, then, we have laid out a heuristic for the research report. If you have occasion to write such a report, in this or some other class, you could easily type the heuristic into a word-processing file and use it as a framework for composing your first draft.

The first step is to break the paper into all the pieces required in the report—abstract, title, introduction, materials and methods, analysis, discussion, and works cited. The second step is to ask questions or generate prompts that will lead you to include the information each section should contain. Finally, you can begin to write by answering whichever questions seem easiest to answer. Beginning this way allows you to gather steam, to get a lot of words on paper before you get to the harder parts. It also allows you to echo the way the professionals write, since they typically begin with materials and methods—the easiest section to write—and continue from there, looping back, eventually, to write the introduction and abstract, once they know what they want to introduce. Once you've entered the information into your heuristic, then, you can delete the questions and add whatever you need to add to make the prose clearer, more coherent, and more effective. Voilà! You'll have finished your first draft!

ACTIVITY 11.1: Inventing the Social Science Research Report

Note: We have not forgotten how to count. The section numbers below remind you of the *final* order for the sections in the report. Drafting them in the order they are listed, rather than in their numerical order, will make writing the report easier. Then you can cut and paste the items into the numerical order, so that they will appear in the way a reader needs to see them.

4. Materials and Methods

   - What *materials* did you use in your experiment or study (lab equipment, furniture, objects, physical space, etc.)?
   - What people, animals, or other organisms did you use as *subjects* in your study? How many? How did you select them? What characteristics of these subjects were important to the outcome of your study or experiment?
   - What *procedure(s)* did you perform on or with your subjects, or using your materials? Here you provide a step-by-step process description of *what you did*, going into enough detail to allow a reader to duplicate your actions.

5. Results

   - What data did you gather? Save the discussion of significance or importance for later. Just report the facts here, in whatever form will make them most accessible, most understandable, for your readers.
   - What factors were most significant in producing the results your experiment or study produced? For instance, if all the snakes you studied went to sleep at 10°C, then that temperature would be a significant factor in producing the observed behavior.
   - What data establish those factors as significant?

- Report—don't discuss—whether those data support or refute your hypothesis.
- In more advanced science or social science classes, you may need to include some statistical analyses of the various significant factors; if you need to do so, that analysis would go here in the results section.

6. Analysis

- What is your hypothesis?
- Why do the data confirm or contradict that hypothesis?
- What have you found out? What does that result mean? You will probably answer these two questions more than once in the report, because you may well have come to more than one conclusion about your results. For each conclusion, report what you found, and then interpret the finding. Tell why the finding matters. In the drafting stage, write down all the *possible* conclusions and their interpretations, in whatever order they occur to you as you study your data. Later on, you will use Cut and Paste to rearrange these conclusions into a logical, understandable order, and you may want to delete some of the minor ones in order to focus on the major findings.
- What larger questions or problems does your study, your results, help answer, solve, or understand? How has your study contributed to answering the research question with which you began your study? How has your study helped understand or solve the problem you set out to examine?
- How does this study relate to other, similar studies that you find in books, articles, and other publications dealing with your topic?

7. Discussion

- What are the limitations of your study? What does it *not* demonstrate?
- What are the flaws in your own research? If you do not identify and deal with them here, others will.
- What are the next steps researchers need to take in examining the question or problem that is central to your study? What further research will help solve or understand the problem?

3. Introduction

- What was the problem of interest in your study?
- What was your research design? This part calls for *naming* your research design (double-blind study, naturalistic observation, etc.) rather than describing it, which you do in the materials and methods section.
- What other research has been done on your question or closely allied questions? Briefly describe these studies, giving just enough

information for readers to understand how other research bears on your own study or experiment.

- What is your hypothesis, the statement that your study or experiment was designed to test? What results did you expect from your study? Why did you expect them? How did you develop your hypothesis?

1. Title

   - What is the main idea of your research? Be certain that the title you settle on contains the main idea, stated clearly, accurately, and smoothly.

2. Abstract (100–200 words)

   - What was the purpose of the study or experiment?
   - What methodology did you use in the study?
   - Who/what were your subjects or the objects used in the experiment?
   - What procedures did you use to gather your data?
   - What were your results?
   - What were your conclusions?

8. Works Cited

   - What sources do you *actually* cite (mention) in your report? List them alphabetically, using the format specified by your teacher or common to your field.

Using this heuristic, you will be able to draft one example of a widely used discipline-specific genre. **However,** a word of caution: Even a form as stable and widely used as the research report will have local variations, so be alert for specific differences from field to field, from class to class, or, later on, perhaps from professional journal to professional journal.

WRITING IN THE DISCIPLINES

ACTIVITY 11.2: Exploring Writing in the Disciplines

As you progress through college, you will probably have an opportunity to experience writing in a variety of disciplines. You'll take courses in the humanities, social sciences, and natural sciences. Perhaps you'll also take courses in applied sciences (engineering, nursing, etc.). Ultimately, you'll settle on a field of concentration—your major. There you'll learn to think and write in ways that practitioners in the field recognize and value. Once you learn that, you'll be a member of that discourse community, you'll be able to talk with others in the field in ways that will lead them to recognize that you are "one of them." And—no small factor—you'll be able to understand what they write and what they say, too.

The steps listed here can be carried out as individual assignments, or as stages of one larger assignment. Each step leads you to understand one aspect of writing in the discipline you'll choose for your focus. As you share that information with your classmates, you'll become familiar with writing in a variety of disciplines, and you'll gain a significant amount of knowledge about writing in your own chosen field.

Step 1: The Interview

For this assignment, you will interview someone in your major field, someone who is farther along the career path than you are now. This could be a professor or a TA in one of your other courses, or you might know of someone who is actually doing what you hope one day to do. At any rate, you want to choose someone who has graduated from college and who is pursuing the career path you hope to follow, either by teaching about it, studying it further as a graduate/professional student, or actually getting paid to do it. Talk to that person at some length.

Ask the subject

- how he or she uses writing in his or her job or studies,
- what kinds of writing he or she does,
- how much writing he or she does,
- how much freedom he or she has in choosing topics,
- whether he or she typically writes alone or in collaboration with others,
- what audiences he or she writes for,
- what sorts of deadlines he or she works under,
- what percentage of time on the job would he or she estimate is spent writing,
- what tools he or she uses in doing the writing,
- how important writing is to his or her success in the job,
- whether he or she was a "good writer" in college, and
- whether that training helped on the job.

In addition, you may want to develop some questions that are specifically related to the field. Think of a set of questions that will really give you a good idea of the role writing plays in the field you've chosen for a career. Avoid questions that can simply be answered yes or no. The more you can keep your subject talking, the more you will find out—and the more fun you will have conducting the interview.

After you've conducted the interview, write a two- or three-page report about the role of writing in your field of study. Upload these reports to your class's E-mail list to start a discussion about writing that the class can continue over a longer time. Once you've uploaded your own report, spend some time reading and reacting to reports your classmates have uploaded. Take this occasion to do some informal peer review. Ask questions, seek clarification, note comparisons or contrasts, point out surprising information, and so forth.

Step 2: The Professional Journals

Find the most prestigious professional journals for your chosen field of study, the ones your professors are just dying to publish in or the ones no one in the field would ignore. In the field of composition, those would be *College Composition and Communication* and *College English*. For a medical doctor, these might be the *New England Journal of Medicine* and *Lancet*. For other fields, you'll find at least two major journals that are written by and addressed to specialists in the field. Analyze these journals in at least two ways:

1. Browse through the most recent two volumes (i.e., the last two years' worth) of each journal, taking note of what kinds of articles appear there.

   - What are the major topics being discussed?
   - What *kinds* of studies, methods, and so on, are prevalent?
   - How would you describe the writing in the journals?
   - Does it differ from one journal to the other?
   - Do the writers seem to use one or a few identifiable formats or genres?
   - What does the journal contain besides articles?

2. Select two articles that interest you the most and read them.

   - How would you describe the writing?
   - What sort of reader do the writers seem to be addressing? In other words, how have they constructed their reader in order to address that reader's needs?
   - Based solely on your reading of these two articles and your more general analysis in item 1, how would you describe writing in your discipline?

After you've finished this process, write a **two- or three-page** report about the characteristics of writing in your field of study, as they are revealed in the two journals. Upload your report to your class's E-mail list to start another discussion about writing that the class can continue over a longer time. Again, after you've uploaded your own report, take some time to read and react to your classmates' reports in the same way you did in step 1.

Step 3: Popular Magazines

Locate a popular magazine that deals with issues in your field, one that is addressed to a general audience rather than to professionals or specialists in the field. Examples of such magazines are *Popular Mechanics, Psychology*

Today, Science, Popular Science, Nature, National Geographic, and *Smithsonian.* Perform the same two-step analysis on these magazines that you did for the journals in step 2.

1. Browse through the most recent two volumes (i.e., the last two years' worth) of each magazine, taking note of what kinds of articles appear there:

   - What are the major topics being discussed?
   - What *kinds* of studies, methods, and so on, are prevalent?
   - How would you describe the writing in the magazines?
   - Does it differ from one magazine to the other?
   - Do the writers seem to use one or a few identifiable formats or genres?
   - What does the magazine contain besides articles?

2. Select two articles that interest you the most and read them.

   - How would you describe the writing?
   - What sort of reader do the writers seem to be addressing? In other words, how have they constructed their reader in order to address that reader's needs?
   - How does that audience differ from the one the journals addressed?
   - Based solely on your reading of these two articles and your more general analysis in item 1, how would you describe writing in your discipline?

After you've finished this process, write a **two- or three-page** report about the characteristics of writing in your field of study, as they are revealed in the two journals. Upload your report to your class's E-mail list to start another discussion about writing that the class can continue over a longer time. Again, after you've uploaded your own report, take some time to read and react to your classmates' reports in the same way you did in steps 1 and 2.

Step 4: The Virtual Community

Steps 1, 2, and 3 have taken you through the traditional ways practitioners in a discipline interact: on the job (your interview), as expert to expert (your survey of a professional journal), and as expert to layperson (your magazine survey). Today, technology has added more media for interaction. This step asks you to look at the ways practitioners interact on-line, in electronic mail groups, in Usenet groups, or even on MOOs or IRC channels. In Chapters 3 and 10 you learned how to access these virtual communities, and you may already have participated in one or more of them. So those projects may have given you a head start on this one.

Basically, you should join an electronic community that relates to the field of your planned major concentration. If you have not yet experienced such a community, then you should look back at Chapters 3 and 10 so that you can know what is involved. Also, those chapters contain references on how to locate the communities that relate to your interests. Observe the community you've joined, focusing on the following, at least:

- How do the people in the group communicate?
- How do they write?
- What assumptions do the writers there seem to make about their readers?
- How do the topics here compare or contrast with the topics you found in the journals? In the magazines?
- How would you describe the tone of the exchanges?
- How would you describe the level of usage in the on-line community?
- Does the community have a FAQ file? If so, what does it tell you about the community?
- What is the writing like? How does it compare with the writing you found in the journals and magazines?
- How do the messages in this on-line community compare with messages in other communities you've joined?
- In what ways do the communications in this group seem related to or determined by the discipline?

After you've finished this process, write a **two- or three-page** report about the characteristics of writing in your field of study, as they are revealed in the discipline's on-line community(-ies). Upload your report to your class's E-mail list to start another discussion about writing that the class can continue over a longer time. Again, after you've uploaded your own report, take some time to read and react to your classmates' reports in the same way you did in earlier steps.

Step 5: Websites

A second prominent way that technology has added to the media in which practitioners within a discipline communicate is the World Wide Web. The Web provides another locus for exchanging traditional texts, of course, but it is also a medium for exchanging information in new forms (as multimedia documents, e.g.) and for sharing collaboratively developed data instantaneously. The Web, or something like it, is also likely to become the principal medium for exchanging the kinds of information that we only find today in journals and magazines. Therefore, understanding how practitioners are beginning to communicate on the Web is important to understanding the roles writing plays in the discipline you've chosen for a major.

Start a search on keywords in your discipline. You could search on the name of the discipline itself (engineering, psychology, philosophy, etc.), but you will probably want to narrow your search. Identify a specific interest (computers and writing, e.g., comets, schizophrenia) and search the

Web for that term. Then explore the sites you find, focusing in particular on the following:

- How do these Web sites compare with ones you examined in earlier chapters?
- What are the main kinds of information contained in the Web Sites?
- What seem to be the primary purposes for having Web Sites in your discipline?
- Who manages these Web Sites? Are they maintained by acknowledged experts or amateurs?
- How valuable are these Web Sites likely to be to experts in the field?
- What kinds of text do you find in the Web Sites? Words only? Graphics? Multimedia documents?
- How would you describe the rhetorical characteristics of the Web Sites in your discipline? How do they address the reader? What do the Web spinners seem to assume about their readers?

After you've finished this process, write a **two- or three-page** report about the characteristics of writing in your field of study, as they are revealed in the discipline's Web Sites. Upload your report to your class's E-mail list to start another discussion about writing that the class can continue over a longer time. Again, after you've uploaded your own report, take some time to read and react to your classmates' reports in the same way you did in earlier steps.

Step 6: Possible Essay Topics

Looking back on all five of the steps and your classmates' reports, write an essay in which you explore some issue involved in these reports/discussions. You can use your own materials and the reports and discussions as source material for your essay; that is, you can quote or cite each other. You should find an issue that interests you. Don't feel limited by the examples here. They represent only a few of the possibilities.

Examples of Possible Topics

The importance of writing in a specific field
The importance of writing in preparing for a career
The differences between academic writing and writing in popular magazines
How audience affects writing, using examples from the workplace, academic/professional journals, and popular magazines
How writing helps make knowledge in a field or in general
What kinds of writing are important in a particular field
What writing instruction in college ought to focus on
What it means to be *literate* in your chosen field
What role technology plays in communications in your field

How similar or dissimilar communications in your field are in different media (journals, magazines, E-mail lists, Web Sites, etc.)

What sort(s) of reader or audience writers in your field seem to
construct and to address

The rhetoric of your field

What you hope to get out of your college education, given what
you've learned about how your field works

How our educational system might better address the needs of students as they prepare for careers

Once you've worked your way through these steps, you should have a
sound basic understanding of writing in your field. As you work your way
into that discourse community, you'll want to pay particular attention to
the ways people there make and report knowledge (and those two activities are not as separate as they may seem). In most fields, you'll find texts
about the kinds of writing that are common in the field, so in addition to
the work you've done here, we encourage you to "read more about it."
Your library will have or be able to get these books for you.

12

WRITING FOR THE WORLD WIDE WEB

There is perhaps no more exciting development on the information superhighway than the World Wide Web. It offers access to a vast range of information—texts, digital images and sounds, and videos—in a graphical and hypertextual way. Highly successful and popular browsers such as Netscape Navigator and Microsoft Internet Explorer make navigating the Web as simple as clicking on a hyperlink. Hundreds, perhaps thousands, of new Web Sites—commercial and personal ones—come on-line every day. As more and more countries around the world build or improve their Internet infrastructures, a ten-year-old in Ann Arbor, Michigan, can conduct research on wombats on a Web Site in Australia. Search engines, the tools that allow users to search for specific information on the Web, are becoming more numerous, more powerful, and easier to use and thus make the seemingly random array of information more accessible and usable to everyone on the Web.

How people use the Web mimics many of the cultural institutions—economic, civic, political, educational—of the near past. Entrepreneurs have set up on-line mail-order catalogs and virtual malls. Businesses, advertisers, and public relations firms use the Web to set up virtual billboards on the shoulders of the infopike. A vast array of interest groups have set up Web Sites to distribute information about social and political causes. Politicians have set up Web Sites to share information with their constituents and to help their reelection campaigns. Newspapers, magazines, and books are going digital. Libraries are going on-line. And, of course, many educators and educational institutions are exploring ways the World Wide Web can be used to teach everything from art and anatomy, to writing and zoology, to preschoolers and senior citizens.

For some the Web represents the new world, the new frontier, and just as with previous land rushes for new, unclaimed territories, the Web and its possibilities generate unbridled enthusiasm and cynical scorn. Information technology entrepreneurs trip over one another and themselves racing to find a new way to make money on the Web by either developing the latest, greatest "killer app," that software application that will change the way people do things (and make lots of money for the inventor!) or creating and providing services most people don't yet even know they want or need. Such entrepreneurism is driven by the daily news in the business press of wildly inflated stock sales of companies that have yet to make a profit (or even sometimes a product), college students becoming instant millionaires, and futurists' utopian forecasts that echo of the nineteenth-century gold rush: "Thar's gold in them thar hills!" and "Go West (Web?), young (wo)man!"

On the other hand, all the hype and excitement over the World Wide Web is softened by often well-founded critiques of the Web. Some critics argue that much of the available information is useless or inaccurate. Others claim that despite the potential for equal access and participatory, interactive communication among people—types of communication that could effectively undermine the stranglehold big government or big business have on society—the Web merely will become the television of the twenty-first century, with all the negative connotations of such critiques. Others see it becoming nothing more than a big advertising medium. Some have already forecast the death of the World Wide Web as we know it.

The fact is, no one really knows for sure what the Web will become. In the short half-decade since the Web became known to the general population, it has been transformed from a text-based environment used primarily by computer technology specialists to one in which Web weavers—be she a lone individual sharing her poetry with the world or working in the advertising department for General Motors—"publish" hypermedia documents that integrate text, graphics, audio, and video and thus contribute to the vast database of human knowledge. Where once, in the long, dark past of a couple of years ago, the Web was used just to display documents, today the Web can facilitate computer-mediated communication. Video conferencing through the Web will be a given soon. Change in the technological world is not merely inevitable; it occurs faster and faster all the time.

So, what does all this mean for you, the writer, in the information age? Well, as you've already discovered, the Web becomes a virtual library from which you can gather information and, through critical analysis of that information, broaden and deepen your knowledge. Just as important, however, is that the Web can become your own private printing press, so to speak. You can use the Web to share your knowledge with an audience of readers that include not only your classmates but also, in theory, all the millions of people who cruise the infohighway.

This chapter includes three projects designed to help you create a presence on the World Wide Web. Project 8, "Analyzing Web Sites," will help you learn how to create effective Web Sites by analyzing some that work and some that don't. This writing-to-learn activity will help you understand some rudimentary design and construction issues and techniques you will need to construct your own useful and rhetorically effective Web Site. Project 9, "Publishing Your

Work on the World Wide Web," will introduce you to techniques for accomplishing much of what you have tried to accomplish in traditional essays, that is, communicate effectively with a given audience to accomplish a certain goal, through an HTML hypertext. Project 10, "Constructing a Webfolio" will help you put together a World Wide Web portfolio of the work you produced during your semester in this writing course.

As you begin this final chapter, you should keep in mind that we are providing you with an introduction to concepts and techniques of writing for the World Wide Web. We will provide you with adequate principles, concepts, and rudimentary techniques, but given the scope of this book and the rapid advances in World Wide Web innovations, we cannot pretend to claim you will become advanced Web weavers. As your interest in producing Web pages grows, you will need to consult various World Wide Web and HTML guides, available both on the Web itself (and we provide you the URLs for many of these) and in books in your library or local bookstores. As with anything else in the high-tech era, your willingness and ability to be a self-motivated and adventurous learner is more important, ultimately, than being a knower.

PROJECT 8: ANALYZING WEB SITES

Objectives

- To analyze World Wide Web pages
- To learn the rhetoric and structure of Web pages
- To write critiques of Web Sites

Technological Requirements

- A word processor
- Access to World Wide Web
- The latest versions of World Wide Web browsers such as Netscape or Internet Explorer

Participant Prerequisites

- Intermediate Internet literacy skills including knowledge of
  — how to use a Web browser and
  — how to search for Web documents
- An ability to conduct critiques and discourse analyses on texts
- Reading of Chapter 5, "Constructing Texts On-Line"

Overview

Web pages can range from relatively simple documents that merely display traditional, linear text to highly complex and attractive hypermedia documents that include numerous hyperlinks between parts of the document and to other documents anywhere on the World Wide Web. Such advanced pages might include background colors and images, tables, colorful graphics and digitized photos, and video clips. In other words, they can range in visual quality from the equivalent of a typed manuscript to a high-concept multimedia presentation one might see on a nightly newscast. The former is relatively easy to construct; the latter becomes a far more complex affair requiring the Web weaver to know much about advanced techniques of using HTML, constructing image maps, and graphic design. Although bells and whistles are attractive and appealing, the most effective Web pages can be measured by the same criteria as a traditional text: the appropriateness of the document in terms of audience and purpose. One of the best ways to learn how to construct your own Web pages and build your own Web Sites is to study, examine, and critique Web Sites that already exist.

The Assignment

Write a 500-word critique of a Web Site of your choosing using evaluative criteria your learning community generates as a result of your collaborative analysis of sample Web Sites. Your learning community, including your instructor, may decide to write several shorter critiques to fulfill this assignment. Or, instead of or in addition to writing a critique of an individual site, you may want to write an analysis of several sites and compare and contrast them. Your critique(s) should take into account the perceived audience and purpose of the Web Site and how well the Web page fulfills the purpose and needs of the target audience.

ACTIVITY 12.1: Finding Professional Sites to Critique

To this point in the course, you have had numerous opportunities to explore the World Wide Web, and as a result you have seen lots of Web pages, the good, the bad, the ugly. You have a number of options available to you to find Websites to study and evaluate.

Option 1

Reflect on all the Web sites you might have visited this semester. Which did you like? Which did you dislike? Which did you find most helpful? Which were the most attractive? Make a list of those sites and share them with your fellow learning community members in a CMC message.

Option 2

A number of individuals and organizations have started awarding "best of" and "worst of" the Web. Here are URLs for a number of these sites:

"Best of" Sites
   "Best of the Web Awards"
         http://www.yahoo.com/Computers_and_Internet/Internet/
         World_Wide_Web/Best_of_the_Web/index.html

"Cool Site of the Day"
   http://cool.infi.net/
"Walcoff's Best Websites of 1995"
   http://webwise.walcoff.com/bestof95/

"Worst of" Sites:
"Mirsky's Worst of the Web"
   http://mirsky.com/wow/Worst.html
"Useless Pages"
   http://www.chaco.com/useless
"Mediocre Site of the Day"
   http://pantheon.cis.yale.edu/~jharris/mediocre.html

ACTIVITY 12.2: Developing Evaluation Criteria

Step 1: Examining Sites

- Look at a minimum of five sites on each list, so that you'll get an idea of the range of criteria the compilers employed. Be sure to examine closely any site that appears on more than one of the lists.
- Write a list of criteria that you feel accounts for the reasons the sites are listed as "best" or "worst."

Step 2: Investigating Prescribed Evaluation Criteria

Obviously you are not the first person or group of people to determine criteria for successful Web Sites. Chapter 5 in this book offers a brief overview of HTML and Web design, and we recommend that if you haven't read it already to do so at this point in the process. Also, a number of Web Sites exist that provide design criteria. Take some time to check out the following sites:

Jeffrey M. Glover's "Top Ten Ways to Improve Your Homepage"
   http://206.65.104.194/~jmg/improve.html

"Web Style Manual" by Patrick Lynch at the Yale Center for Advanced Instructional Media (This one also has extensive links to other HTML and homepage style guides and documentation.)
   http://info.med.yale.edu/caim/StyleManual_Top.HTML

Step 2: Developing Descriptive Criteria

Look at those lists and try to decide on what criteria the people compiling those sites included each item. What follows is a list of variables you might consider when developing criteria:

- Purpose
  — What do you perceive as the purpose of the site? Advertising? Entertainment? Informational? Educational?
  — Does it fulfill that purpose adequately?
  — How does it fulfill its purpose or how and why does it fail to fulfill its purpose?

- Audience
  - — Who do you perceive to be the audience for the site?
  - — Do you suspect visitors would need to be novices or experts in the topic the site addresses?
  - — Do you suspect the visitors need to know much or little about WWW technology to use the site effectively?
  - — How effectively do you suppose the site fulfills the needs of the audience?
- Content
  - — Does the page offer content or is it dominated by links to other links?
  - — Does the page deliver the kinds of information it promises, or implies it will based on the title?
  - — Is the page well written, or is it fraught with misspellings, ungrammatical sentence and phrase constructions, and unfocused, disunified, unclear writing?
- Appearance
  - — How many colors does the site employ?
  - — Does the site employ graphics? If so, with what effect? Are they employed as mere decorations, or do they add meaning to the page?
  - — How attractive is the page? Is it cluttered? Does it look "designed"? Is it easy on the eyes with logical flow among the components (text, graphics, art, columns, etc.), or is it a jumble of small fonts and tight text that forces you to squint?
  - — Does the background create an adequate contrast to the text, or does the text fade into the background colors or graphics?
- Accessibility
  - — How long does it take to load the page?
  - — Is the document readable by the browser you are using, or does viewing the document require the most recent version of a particular browser or a special application like an audio or video player?
- Navigability
  - — Is the document or site "chunked" effectively? That is, are you forced to scroll through a long page, or are you offered hyperlinks to screen full-length nodes? Are there too many links to small nodes?
  - — Do all the links work, or do they lead to error messages?
  - — Do all the links take you where they imply they are going to take you?
  - — Are you offered several ways to navigate the site? In other words, does the site rely on an image map or graphic buttons only, or does it also offer you text-based links?
  - — Does the site offer you multiple ways to get around the site, that is, to return to where you started, or are you led on a one-way path farther and farther away from your starting point with only your

browser's "back" or "home" button to get you back to where you began?

Step 3: Developing Communal Evaluation Criteria

- Share your lists in class or post them in your class's E-mail group.
- Face to face or on-line, conduct a discussion to arrive at a fairly comprehensive listing of criteria for "best of" and "worst of."

ACTIVITY 12.3: Evaluating Noncommercial and Academic Sites

Test the comprehensive list of criteria against what you might call "substantial" Web Sites, ones that clearly move beyond the commercial to provide intellectual content, push the boundaries of hypertext or multimedia, or create an artistic experience.

Step 1: Finding Noncommercial and Academic Sites

Here are some Web Sites to check out as you explore the Web for sites like the ones we're suggesting:

"Rhetnet"
  http://www.missouri.edu/~rhetnet/
"Kairos"
  http://english.ttu.edu/kairos/
"Computer-Mediated Communication Magazine"
  http://www.december.com/cmc/mag/current/toc.html
"Post-Modern Culture"
  http://jefferson.village.virginia.edu/pmc/
"HotWired"
  http://www.hotwired.com/
"Discovery Channel Online"
  http://www.discovery.com/
"Hegirascope: A Hypertext Fiction" by Stuart Moulthrop
  http://raven.ubalt.edu/staff/moulthrop/hypertexts/hgs/
  hegirascope.html
"The Electronic Frontier Foundation"
  http://www.eff.org/

Step 2: Exploring Noncommercial and Academic Sites

- Look at—*explore*—these sites.
- Compare what you see here with the list of criteria you developed in steps 1 and 2.
- How do these sites expand your sense of the criteria you might use in evaluating Web Sites?
- What is different about these sites from the "best of" and "worst of" lists?

- Revise your original list, adding, amplifying, deleting, changing whatever you need to change for your criteria to accommodate these new texts.

Step 3: Revising Evaluation Criteria

Post your revised criteria to the class's E-mail group, or distribute copies of the criteria in class. In a face-to-face or electronic discussion, negotiate the new criteria until you again arrive at a "consensus" set of criteria.

ACTIVITY 12.4: Evaluating Student-Written Web Sites

Dozens, scores, and perhaps hundreds of writing and writing-intensive courses are now using the World Wide Web as a communication and publishing medium. You can learn much about how to construct your Web Site by exploring, evaluating, and critiquing those student-constructed Web Sites that already exist.

Step 1: Finding Student Web Sites

Here are a number of URLs that will give you leads to on-line writing courses, most of which include samples of student work. Point your browser to several of the following, and browse until you find a group of appropriate student-constructed Web Sites.

"The Alliance for Computers and Writing"
http://english.ttu.edu/acw/

"Writing Classes on the World Wide Web" by Steve Krause
http://ernie.bgsu.edu/~skrause/WWW_Classes/

"Writing for the World" by Keith Dorwick
http://www2.uic.edu/~kdorwick/world.html

"Writing the Information Superhighway" (not this book but a writing course that inspired this book designed and taught by Wayne Butler and Rebecca Rickly)
http://www.lsa.umich.edu/ecb/infohighway.html

Step 2: Developing and Refining Evaluation Criteria

As you explore some student-produced texts, repeat steps 2 and 3 in Activity 12.2 and steps 2 and 3 in Activity 12.3.

- What are the kinds and quality of texts you find in these locations?
- How do the criteria have to change to accommodate these texts?
- How do these texts expand your ideas about the Web?
- Revise your criteria again, and post the new list to the class's E-mail group.

ACTIVITY 12.5: Writing Your Web Site Critique

Now that you've reached this point, you have developed some significant evaluation criteria to use as you write your Web Site critiques.

- The first set of criteria address the overall quality of Web Sites. This set, though limited in scope, does help you understand what makes Web Sites communicate.
- The second set helped you understand how to use the Web to communicate substance, to engage in important issues, even how to use the Web to conduct a critique of the Web. These Web Sites probably came closest to the kinds of sites you'll use as models for academic work, so this set of community standards will be important in understanding how your work in this class will be evaluated, and it will be useful as you move into other courses where you'll use the Web.
- The final set of criteria, based on the student texts, probably relates most closely to the criteria that will be used in this class to evaluate your texts and your overall performance. No one expects perfection, but everyone expects to see you working hard to meet the criteria for excellent work. The first step, of course, is to discover and understand those criteria. You're on your way!

Step 1: Select a Web Site to Critique

Because you will be attempting to create a Web Site of your own for this writing class, it would probably serve you well to critique a Web Site most like that you are going to create yourself. Therefore, choose one or several student-constructed Web Sites you have come across during the last activity. You may want to choose sites

- produced by students most like yourself in terms of type of educational institution, age, and geographic location;
- that address topics related to those in which you have an interest; and
- that look like site(s) you aspire to create yourself.

Step 2: Evaluate the Web Site

- Review the evaluation criteria your learning community generated, keeping the specifics in mind.
- Read, browse, and navigate the Web Site in its entirety. As you go through the site, take notes about the following:
  - *Appearance:* Is it laid out attractively, clearly, and logically? Are graphics, backgrounds, and images used? If so, are they used meaningfully, or do they serve as decorations?
  - *Navigability:* Did you find it easy or difficult to work your way through the site? Did all the links work? Did the site give you several options for getting around in it? If you got lost, where did you, when did you, and why did you?

— *Content:* What are your initial impressions about the content of the site? Was it well written? Were the E-texts unified, coherent, and developed appropriately? What did you learn about the topics and issues?

Step 3: Prewriting Your Critique

Now that you have reflected on evaluation criteria, browsed the Web Site(s), and taken notes on your initial impressions, respond to the following items to prewrite your critique:

- What do you perceive to be the purpose of the site?
- Who do you perceive to be the audience for the site?
- How well do you think the site fulfills the needs of its perceived audience and purpose?
- What do you like most about the site(s)? Were you impressed by the appearance? By the technological sophistication? By the quality and the content? Write down as many strong points about the site as possible.
- What areas of improvement did you find with the site in terms of the appearance, writing quality, and content? Why do you believe these features or components seem to be flawed to you? Be sure to be as concrete as possible. Write down which links didn't work, for example, or which graphics seem to detract rather than add to the site.
- If you were constructing the site, what would you have done differently and why?

Step 4: Audience Considerations

Before you begin drafting your critique, take some time to think through or discuss with your learning community, on-line or face to face, the intended audience for your critiques. Will you be writing them with the idea that only other members of your learning community—people who did not construct the sites—will read the critiques? If so, you may have the room to be objective and highly critical. Or, do you have any plans to share the critiques with the Web weavers themselves (which may be possible if the Web weaver has included his or her E-mail address on the site)? Do you plan on "publishing" your critique as part of your own or your learning community's Web Site? In both of these cases, you will want to keep in mind that while the Web weaver will appreciate knowing that someone on the Web has read his or her work seriously, you don't want to insult that person with harsh criticism or a hostile tone. Keep in mind that you too will soon be "published" on the World Wide Web, and thus you don't want to contribute to creating a hostile environment that will serve to undermine the universal communication possible on the information superhighway.

Step 5: Draft the Critique

Draft your critique from beginning to end. You may wish to follow this general outline:

- What are your evaluation criteria? Of course, you need not repeat all the criteria your learning community has developed, but, in general, what principles for successful Web Sites are you using? Do you intend, for instance, to focus on aesthetic, technological, or rhetorical issues? What critical lens(es) are you using?
- Which site(s) are you critiquing and why? You may want to include the URL(s) in your final version.
- Offer an overview of the site: Is it an individual E-text, a Webfolio, a resource site? What is its purpose? What is its intended audience? What do you know about the Web weaver?
- What are the strong points of the site? What are your favorite aspects? Offer an appropriate number of examples, illustrations, and supporting details to support your generalizations.
- What do you perceive to be the areas of improvement? Why do you believe they are areas of improvement? How would the site be stronger if the Web weaver could or would be inclined to follow your suggestions? Again, offer an appropriate number of examples, illustrations, and supporting details to support your generalizations.
- What else might you say about the site? Would you recommend it to others? How does it compare to other sites you have examined?

ACTIVITY 12.6: Revising and Sharing Your Critique

Throughout this course, you have participated in various processes for sharing drafts, either electronically or face to face; giving and receiving feedback on the content, structure, style, and correctness of the drafts; and reflecting on the feedback you receive to revise your drafts. If these techniques have not yet become integrated into your writing process and the writing practices of your learning community, please consult the sharing drafts, giving and receiving feedback, and revising activities of previous chapters.

PROJECT 9: PUBLISHING YOUR WORK ON THE WORLD WIDE WEB

Objective

- To compose World Wide Web pages

Technological Requirements

- A text editor
- An HTML editor
- A World Wide Web browser such as Netscape, Internet Explorer, etc.
- Access to a World Wide Web server

Participant Prerequisites

- Intermediate Internet literacy skills including basic understanding of HTML
- Reading of Chapter 5, "Constructing Texts On-Line"

Hot Web Sites for Project 9

In this project you'll be creating your own HTML files that can be read on the World Wide Web. Check out some of the following sites to learn all about it!

HTML Editors

"Yahoo! HTML Editor Page"
http://www.yahoo.com/Computers_and_Internet/Internet/World_Wide_Web/HTML_Editors/

HTML Authoring

"Putting Information on the World Wide Web" by the World Wide Web Consortium
http://www.w3.org/pub/WWW/Provider/Overview.html

"Guides to Writing Style for HTML Documents"
http://union.ncsa.uiuc.edu/HyperNews/get/www/html/guides.html

"A Beginner's Guide to HTML"
http://www.ncsa.uiuc.edu/General/Internet/WWW/HTMLPrimer.html

"HTML Quick Reference"
http://kuhttp.cc.ukans.edu/lynx_help/HTML_quick.html

"How Do They Do That with HTML?"
http://www.nashville.net/~carl/htmlguide/index.html

Web Page Style Guides

"Web Style Manual" by Patrick Lynch
Yale Center for Advanced Instructional Media
http://info.med.yale.edu/caim/StyleManual_Top.HTML

"Writing HTML: A Tutorial for Creating WWW Pages"
Maricopa Center for Learning and Instruction
http://www.mcli.dist.maricopa.edu/tut/index.html

"The Ten Commandments for Writing HTML" by Sean Howard
http://www.visdesigns.com/design/commandments.html

"Top Ten Things Not to Do on a Web Page"
http://cast.stanford.edu/cast/www/donts.html

"The HyperTerrorist Checklist of WWWeb Design Errors"
http://www.mcs.net/~jorn/html/net/checklist.html
"Top Ten Ways to Improve Your Homepage" by Jeffrey M.
Glover
http://www.winternet.com/~jmg/Improve.html

Overview

Throughout this book, we have been urging you and other members of your on-line writing and learning community to share your revised documents with one another—in hard copy, through computer-mediated communications technologies, or on the World Wide Web. With this project, you will have the opportunity finally to start publishing your electronically produced but traditionally structured, linear essays, critiques, and arguments on the World Wide Web by converting those linear texts into hypertexts. In reality, experienced Web weavers don't necessarily first write formal essays and then reconstruct them as hypertexts. They do, however, plan what they will write and consider their purposes and audiences. Indeed, once you become experienced enough with hypertext theory and structures, hypertext markup language, and the various HTML editors and filters, you too will actually be able to compose in HTML. Based on our experiences of working with Web novices, we are convinced it is easier to begin with electronic versions of essays you've already completed—ones that are focused and unified, well developed, well written, and proofread—as a starting place to learn the basics of HTML, Web page layout, and hypertext theory and design.

Our goal with this chapter, then, is not so much to show you how to write sophisticated hypermedia on the World Wide Web but rather how to publish your thoughts on-line. Along the way, however, as you begin converting your linear texts into ones that have links both to sections within your document and to other documents out on the Web, you will begin to think of the differences between the logic and structure of your linear essays and the logic and structure of hypertexts. Likewise, as you strive to make your pages more attractive by adding backgrounds, images, graphics, and so on, you will start thinking not only of the techniques involved in getting a graphic to appear right where you want it, but also of the effect of that graphic on the meaning you are trying to communicate to your readers.

The Assignment

Convert one of the projects you've completed for this course into a World Wide Web document. If you and your learning community intend to create "Webfolios" (see Project 10) as your final projects for the course, you will want to convert several of your linear electronic documents into hypertextual World Wide Web documents.

Getting Started with the Basic Structure of an HTML File

Before you begin tagging your text in HTML, let's review briefly the basic structure and most immediately useful tags. Every HTML file must include three basic elements. First, you must identify the entire document as an HTML file by beginning the file with the tag <HTML> and ending the file with </HTML>. Every HTML file should also include header information, text that won't be displayed by a browser but that provides necessary information, like the title of the page that will be displayed in the title bar of the browser. Information within the header will begin with a <HEAD> tag and end with a </HEAD> tag. Finally, the body elements of your document will be enclosed in the body section, which begins with a <BODY> tag and closes with the </BODY> tag.

```
<HTML>
<HEAD>
Header information such as the title of the page
</HEAD>
<BODY>
The main text of your essay will appear in the body section.
</BODY>
</HTML>
```

Each of the sections of a basic HTML document will also include other elements. The header will include the title of the page—the one you want to appear in the title bar of the browser. The title text will be tagged thus: <TITLE>Your Title Text</TITLE>

The body of the document will include several elements. First, you will probably want to use headings. You can use HTML to display headings of six different sizes, with <H1>**Sample Heading**</H1> being the largest and <H6>Sample Heading</H6> being the smallest. Browsers will display the text in the headings in larger, bolder type and automatically skip a line between the heading text and the text before and after it. The body, too, should include information about the author of the document and when the document was created or last revised. Such information would begin with the tag <ADDRESS> and end with </ADDRESS>

In the body, you would also use a number of tags to create line breaks, paragraph breaks, and horizontal lines between elements of the document. To create a line break, all you need to insert is a <BR> tag at the end of a line. To create a break between paragraphs, all you need insert is the tag <P> at the end of a paragraph of text. To have the browser display a simple thin gray or black line between elements of your document, all you need insert is <HR>. Note that the line break, paragraph break, and horizontal line tags do not require the opening tag.

So, now our template would look something like this:

```
<HTML>
<HEAD>
<TITLE>Education and the World Wide Web</TITLE>
</HEAD>
<BODY>
<H1>Education and the World Wide Web</H1>
<H3>by Frank Cerra</H3>
In the beginning, there was the World Wide Web and so on and so forth and
so on and so forth etc., etc., etc.<P>
...In conclusion, I believe the World Wide Web will change everything
because, because, because and so on and so forth and so on and so
forth.<P>
<HR>
<ADDRESS>
Frank Cerra <BR>
3614 Corlear Ave.<BR>
Beacon, NY 12345<BR>
email: fcerra@beacon.edu<BR>
</ADDRESS>
<HR>
Revised 8/3/96<BR>
</BODY>
</HTML>
```

When displayed in a browser, this HTML document would look like the illustration on p. 274. Notice that the text between the <TITLE> tags is displayed in the browser's title bar, that the text ("Education and the World Wide Web") between the <H1> tags is larger than the text ("by Frank Cerra") between the <H3> tags. Notice too the break between the first sentence of the "essay" and the last is the result of the <P> tag, the horizontal lines the result of the <HR> tags, and that the address text between the <ADDRESS> tags is italicized.

Indeed, there will be much more to learn about HTML, but now you know enough to at least publish your document on the Web. In activities later in this project, we'll work on making your Web page more sophisticated.

ACTIVITY 12.7: Gathering Documents, Resources, and Tools

Before you actually begin converting one of your documents into a Web page, you will need to do the following:

- Read Chapter 5, if you haven't already, to arrive at a basic understanding of HTML and Web page design issues.
- Find on the World Wide Web a number of on-line guides to HTML and designing Web pages. We offer the URLs for a number of excellent sites at the beginning of this project. Browse through these sites to see

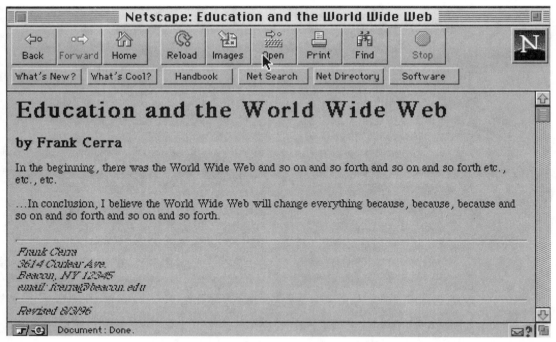

Netscape Communications, the Netscape Communications logo, Netscape, and Netscape Navigator are trademarks of Netscape Communications Corporation.

which one(s) best suit your needs. Also, if your school supports a World Wide Web server and offers students access to it, it very likely also provides some sort of on-line help and tutorials for setting up Web Sites. Check out any local resources you can find.

- Develop a fairly advanced understanding of the technological context of your learning environment. You have already had several opportunities to learn about where you can set up a home page in Activity 5.1 in Chapter 5 and Project 2 of Chapter 7, "Documenting the Local Landscape." If your learning community completed those projects and activities, someone in your class probably knows whether your institution runs a Web server, how to access it, and how to build your homepage on it. If your learning community hasn't yet developed that knowledge, return to those projects and activities now to learn about your institution's support and access to the World Wide Web.
- Determine what ASCII text editor, HTML editor, or commercial Web page production tools are available to you.
- Gather all the electronic texts, including E-mail archives, electronic conference transcripts, and word-processed documents, you have produced this semester. Make sure you have them on a hard disk, a floppy diskette, or a shared server file space. *Make sure you have backups of all*

your files, and particularly the most important ones! You will be manipulating your files extensively as you tag them in HTML, and you want to be working on copies rather than your originals, just in case the files get lost, corrupted, or otherwise damaged.

- Select one of your best, nearest-to-completion documents, perhaps the most recent version of one of the projects you've completed for this course.

ACTIVITY 12.8: Tagging Your Text with HTML

During this activity, you will use HTML tags to allow a Web browser to display your document. In the first step you will convert your word-processed document to a text-only or ASCII text; in the second step you will open the file in an HTML or plain-text editor, and then you will incorporate the basic tags into your document so it can be displayed by a browser.

Step 1: Preparing Your Word-Processed Document

- Open the document you are going to convert with the word processor you used to create the document.
- Use your word processor's Save As command (or the equivalent) to save your document as a text-only or ASCII file. *Be sure to give the text only version of your file a slightly different file name. If you don't, you will replace your formatted word-processed document.*
- Quit your word processor.
- Launch a simple text editor (TeachText or SimpleText on Macintosh or Notepad in Windows, e.g.) or HTML editor you have available to you.
- Open the document you saved as text-only or ASCII.

Step 2: Tag Your Text

- Insert the <HTML> and </HTML> tags at the very beginning and end of your file.
- Insert the <HEAD> tag on the line after the <HTML> tag.
- Create the title by typing in the title of your essay between <TITLE> and </TITLE>.
  Note: Because this is the title the browser will display in the title bar, it is better to use the title of your essay rather than "Project 2" or the file name of the document. People should be able to tell from the title bar text what the document is about.
- On the line after the title, close the heading by inserting the </HEAD> tag.
- If your essay currently has a title, surround it with the heading tag of your choice, probably <H1> and </H1>. If you have chosen an essay you have not yet titled, now would be a great time to come up with one!
- Type in your "byline" surrounded by tags for a smaller heading, such as <H3> and </H3>.

- Insert after each paragraph of your current essay a paragraph break mark <P>.
- At the end of the essay, insert a horizontal line break with the <HR> tag.
- Create an address section by imitating the previous model.
- Close the body of the document with the </BODY> tag.
- End the entire document with the </HTML> tag.
- Save your HTML file by giving it a unique file name with the extension .html.
  For example, if you are using the essay you produced for Project 8 in this book, your file might be named proj8.html.
- Where you ultimately save your file is very, very important. You will need to save the HTML file in a particular directory on a World Wide Web server that allows others on the Web to access your file. You will need to consult your instructor or local technical staff to learn where and how to do so. However, you can see what your document looks like on any computer that has a Web browser. All you need do is copy your file to the hard disk of a machine that has a browser and open the file off the hard disk. The browser will display the file exactly as it will appear to others on the Web once you put it where they can get access to it.

ACTIVITY 12.9: Making Your Document More Sophisticated

Congratulations! If you have gotten this far, you are probably now published on the World Wide Web. If you've been successful, millions of people can now access your document and learn what you know and believe about your topic. Once you recover from the thrill of instant worldwide publication, you will probably notice a couple of things about your document compared to others on the Web. At this point, yours is not hypertextual—it's probably one long text readers have to scroll through. You have noticed during your sojourns on the Web that lots of sites have colorful backgrounds and snazzy graphics. Yours is probably comparatively bland and relies much more on text than it does on graphics and images. Indeed, you have a long way to go to becoming an advanced Web weaver, but the following steps will help you make your document more hypertextual and colorful.

Step 1: Making Your Document Hypertextual: Internal Links

There are two primary reasons you would want to make hyperlinks in your document. Because using a browser as an electronic page turner or scroller is antithetical to the purpose and power of hypertext, you want to create for readers ways to choosing paths through your document. That is, you can use links from one part of your document, especially if it is a long one, to another part of your document. You will also want to make links to documents external to the one you're creating. The most concrete example would be citations of sources you might have used for your essay.

Let's say, for instance, you incorporated into your project information you learned about from another Web Site. In a traditional paper, you might include a parenthetical reference (Smith 1980, p. 45) that implies to the reader that if they went to the end of the paper, they would find a works cited or references page that would list in alphabetical order all the sources you used in the paper. If the reader wanted to track down that source herself, she would have to go to the library to find the original. On the World Wide Web, however, you can make an external link directly from your document to the Web source itself. Now if the reader wants to peruse the original source, she can just click on the link you've created. In this step we will walk you through the process of making internal links so readers can jump from place to place within your document.

Go through your document and create logical headings for each section. If, for example, you were tagging Project 2 in which you created brochures or handouts documenting various elements of your technological landscape, you would already have a document that includes different categories such as "Overview," "Terms You Should Know," "Procedures," and so on. Remember, to create a heading in an HTML document, you need to surround the term or phrase with the <H#> and </H#> tags, where the # is 1–6 to identify the different sizes you want the heading to be displayed.

Now that you have broken up your document into various headings, you can create a table of contents of those headings. Each item in the table of contents will appear on a bulleted list with links to the various sections of your document. Let's look at this example. You'll notice that Frank has created a bulleted list that begins with the tag <UL><LI> and ends with the tag </UL>. Each of the items on the list—"Introduction," "Technical Terms," "Procedures," and so on—is preceded by <A HREF = "#text">. So, the line

```
<LI> <A HREF = "#Technical Terms">Technical Terms</A>
```

tells the browser to display the term "Technical Terms" as an item on the bulleted list and make that term a hyperlink to a part of the HTML document called <A NAME = "Technical Terms"</A>. A person browsing this document, then, could click on "Technical Terms" and would be taken to that part of the document.

You'll notice also before the table of contents actually begins, there appears the line <A NAME = "Table of Contents"</A>. That line is there so someone reading the document could jump from one section back to the table of contents.

```
<HTML>
<HEAD>
<TITLE>Using Netscape</TITLE>
</HEAD>
<BODY>
<H1>Using Netscape</H1>
<H3>by Frank Cerra</H3>
<HR>
<A NAME = "Table of Contents"</A>
<H4>Table of Contents</H4>
<UL> <LI> <A HREF = "#Introduction">Introduction</A>
<LI> <A HREF = "#Technical Terms">Technical Terms</A>
<LI> <A HREF = "#Procedures">Procedures</A>
<LI> <A HREF= "#Getting Help">Getting Help</A>
<LI> <A HREF = "#Other Sources">Other Sources</A>
</UL>
<HR>
<A NAME="Introduction"</A>
<H2>Introduction to Netscape</H2>
Netscape is a World Wide Web Browser. One uses it so on and so forth and so
on and so forth because because because because because.........<P>
Return to <A HREF = "#Table of Contents">Table of Contents</A>.
<P>
<HR>
<H2>Technical Terms</H2>
<A NAME="Technical Terms"</A>
There's lots of jargon on the World Wide Web. You have to know URLs, http's,
and other acronyms. Here are a few of the most important ones defined for
you.......<P>
Return to <A HREF = "#Table of Contents">Table of Contents</A>.
<P>
<HR>
<ADDRESS>
Frank Cerra <BR>
3614 Corlear Ave.<BR>
Beacon, NY 12345<BR>
email: fcerra@beacon.edu<BR>
<HR>
Revised 8/3/96<BR>
</BODY>
</HTML>
```

Let's see how the HTML document here would look in a browser. The next example shows how the bulleted list appears in Netscape. The underlined terms are links to points within the document.

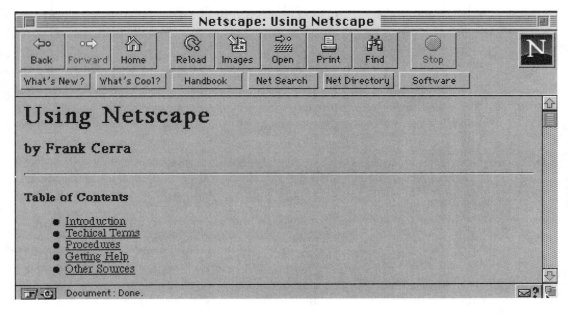

If you were to click on "Introduction," the browser would take you to the "Introduction to Netscape" section, as seen here:

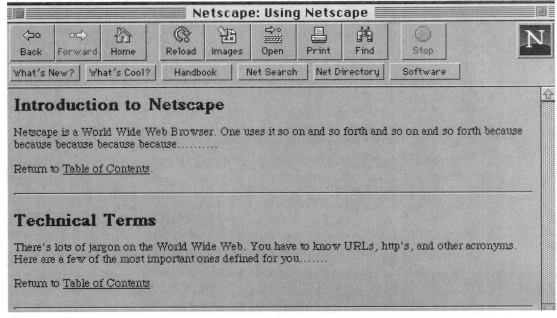

Netscape Communications, the Netscape Communications logo, Netscape, and Netscape Navigator are trademarks of Netscape Communications Corporation.

If when you completed the "Introduction to Netscape" section you didn't want to scroll down to the next section ("Technical Terms") that would appear in a linear sequence, you could click on "Table of Contents," which would take you back to what you see in the first graphic. You would then have the option of clicking on the "Getting Help" link, for example.

Do you realize that this procedure can be used for offering your reader not only hypertextual links to various parts of your text but also to create a link between a parenthetical citation (Smith 1980, p. 45) and the works cited section of your document?

Some Considerations on Working with Long Documents

The procedure described here for creating links within a single document to allow readers to navigate it hypertextually is effective up to a point. Using this procedure requires the browser to load the entire file, and the longer the file gets, the more time it will take to load—an especially annoying occurrence if your readers are paying by the minute. At some point your documents will grow to a length that you will want to break the sections of your document into individual HTML files that are connected with a number of links. The procedure you would use for doing so is similar to the one described in step 2.

Step 2: Making Your Document Hypertextual: External Links

To this point you have created a rudimentary hypertext in the sense that you've made links from one part of your document to another. In doing so, you have created for your readers ways of navigating your text in other than a linear fashion. In this step we'll focus on how to make links between your document and others on the World Wide Web.

Making External Links

To make links to other documents on the World Wide Web, you have to create *anchors* or *hyperlinks* in which you create a tag that tells the browser to jump to a particular URL when a user clicks on the term associated with that URL. The basic structure of a hyperlink is <A HREF="URL of place linking to">text</A>. The browser displays the "text" part underlined or in a contrasting color or in some other way to indicate to the user that the "text" is a hyperlink to elsewhere.

So, if you wanted to make a link to the popular search engine Lycos, for example, the hyperlink would look like the following:

```
<A HREF = "http://lycos.cs.cmu.edu">Lycos</A>
```

Here you will find an excerpt from an HTML file that shows how hyperlinks are integrated into a paragraph of text:

```
<H2>Format</H2>
You will construct a World Wide Web hypertext (using
<A HREF="http://www.ncsa.uiuc.edu/General/Internet/WWW/
```

HTMLPrimer.html">HTML</A>) in which you gather through <A HREF =
"http://akebono.stanford.edu/yahoo/">Yahoo</A>, <A HREF =
"http://lycos.cs.cmu.edu">Lycos</A>, <A HREF =
"http://webcrawler.cs.washington.edu/WebCrawler/WebQuery.html">
WebCrawler</A>, the U of Michigan's Clearinghouse for <A HREF =
"http://www.lib.umich.edu/chhome.html">Subject-Oriented Internet
Resource Guides</A> and other Internet research techniques as many
URLs as you can, read the contents of the links, and link those links
together with text you write that would help a browser or reader of
your hypertext make sense of those links. <P>

Now take a look at how the browser displays the paragraph:

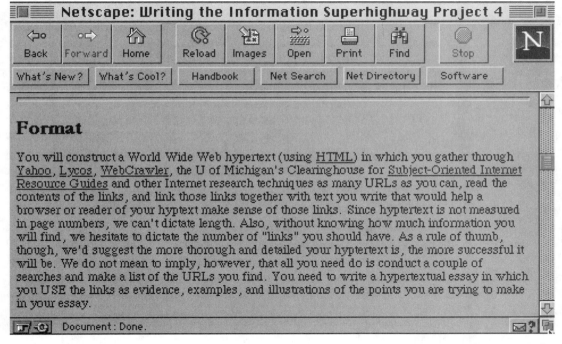

Netscape Communications, the Netscape Communications logo, Netscape, and Netscape Navigator are trademarks of Netscape Communications Corporation.

Now you try it with your document.

- First, identify some part of the project you are converting into a Web page that would lend itself to creating an external link. Did you, for example, in writing the handout for Project 2 refer to URLs of on-line resources? In Projects 6 and 7—"Analyzing Controversial Issues" and "Arguing Controversial Issues"—did you make references to World Wide Web sites? If so, you can now make hyperlinks to those sites.

- Create a hyperlink using the technique described earlier.
- Save your HTML file again. Make sure you save it as a text-only or ASCII file.
- Load your file into your browser. If you've created the hyperlink properly, the term or phrase you used for your text should be underlined. If it is not, go back and check the syntax of your hyperlink to make sure you've followed the procedure, punctuation, and symbols completely.
- Click on the highlighted or underlined term or phrase and see whether it takes you to the proper Web Site. If it does, congratulations! If not, check the URL to make sure you've gotten it right and check the format for the hyperlink again.
- Continue creating external hyperlinks wherever and whenever they seem appropriate. You will find you can make external hyperlinks from your works cited page, to Web Sites that deal with similar issues or topics as your own, and so on. Your first impulse will be to make too many links. Although doing so will give you plenty of practice, you will also make your document overly difficult to navigate. Create hyperlinks judiciously!

ACTIVITY 12.10: Revising Your Hypertexts

To this point you have probably been focusing more on the technical aspects of converting a linear text into a World Wide Web hypertext. Now it is time, however, to evaluate and revise the document based on its rhetorical effectiveness. It is time to share Web documents and give and receive feedback on them.

Step 1: Giving/Receiving Feedback

You have spent a good portion of your time this semester critiquing E-texts and Web Sites. Revisit the work you and your learning community peers did during Projects 5, "Writing to Read Critically," and 8 "Analyzing Web Sites," to remind yourself of the kinds of criteria you've developed as you've become a more and more critical participant of cyberculture. The following procedure will help you and your peers evaluate one another's Web pages.

- Either orally or via E-mail, share the URL of your newly created Web page with two or three members of your learning community.
- Browse the Web document carefully and take notes while you're considering the following:
  — What is your favorite aspect of the site? Did your peer find a way to integrate colors and graphics with good effect? Are the links logical? Do they work?
  — Evaluate the technical aspects of the document. Do all the links work? If not, which ones? View the source and see whether you can

find out why the link doesn't work. Is the anchor syntax incorrect? Is the URL typed wrong?

— Evaluate the navigability of the document. Did the Web weaver give you a number of options for navigating the site, or did you have to read it as if you were reading a linear text? Did the hyperlinks offer you ways to get back where you came from, or did links keep taking you farther and farther away from your starting point with no easy way back?

— Evaluate the unity and coherence of the document. As you have discovered, a linear text has one type of logical flow, whereas a hypertext might employ different types of logical connections. As you navigated the hypertext, did you get lost or confused? Where did you get lost?

— What did you learn about constructing a hypertext from your peers' efforts that you wished you could have incorporated into your hypertext?

— If you were going to revise your peers' hypertexts, what would you do differently and why?

• Review your responses and notes to the preceding items, and compose a critique of your peers' Web Sites.

• Exchange critiques face to face, on hard copy, or via computer-mediated communication.

• Reflect on the feedback your site has received, and articulate a strategy of what you hope to improve about your hypertext.

Step 2: Revising the Document

• Use the feedback provided by your peers and what you learned about hypertext from evaluating your peers' work to
  — fix what doesn't work,
  — improve the rhetorical effect of the document,
  — improve the unity and coherence of the document, and
  — improve the navigability of the Web document.

• Here is a list of other elements and features you may want to add to your Web document. To learn how to accomplish these, consult one of the Web Sites listed at the beginning of this project or one of the ones cited later. Also, remember you can always "View Source" through your browser. So, if you find a feature on some other Web Site that you like, you can view the HTML document for that page to determine how the effect was created.

  — Experiment with logical and physical styles or those things that can be done to the appearance of the text, including emphasizing and strong emphasizing text and bolding and italicizing text.

  — If you've used a lengthy block quote in your document, figure out how to format it properly.

— Add graphics and in-line images.
— Add background colors.
— Add your E-mail address as a hyperlink.
— Add a counter so you can see how many visits have been made.
— Register your Web Site with the various search engines. By doing so, you will be added to the worldwide directory of Web weavers.
— If you've already created a homepage, make a link between your homepage and your hypertext document or essay.

WHERE DO YOU GO FROM HERE?

Projects 8 and 9 provided you ample experience to develop an intermediate level of knowledge about the rhetoric of Web design and the basics of HTML. Now that you've experimented with building a Web page on one document, you might want to consider converting the other projects you've created this semester into World Wide Web documents. In fact, in the next project, "Constructing Webfolios," we will suggest you build a Web Site of all the work you've produced this semester.

PROJECT 10: CONSTRUCTING A WEBFOLIO

Objectives

- to build an assessment Webfolio

Technological Requirements

- text editor
- HTML editor
- World Wide Web browser such as Netscape, Internet Explorer, etc.
- access to World Wide Web server

Participant Prerequisites

- advanced Internet literacy skills
- intermediate web weaving and HTML skills
- read Chapter 6, "Assessing Writing"
- completed Projects 8 and 9

Hot Web Sites for Project 10

In this project you will be constructing a Webfolio of your work. Check out the following Web Sites for potential models of the kind of work you may want to do yourself.

The Alliance for Computers and Writing
 http://english.ttu.edu/acw/

Writing Classes on the World Wide Web by Steve Krause
 http://ernie.bgsu.edu/~skrause/WWW_Classes/

Writing for the World by Keith Dorwick
 http://www2.uic.edu/~kdorwick/world.html

Writing the Information Superhighway by Wayne Butler and
Rebecca Rickly
 http://www.lsa.umich.edu/ecb/infohighway.html

Overview

OK, let's start with an admission: we all hate grades and grading. Yes, yes, yes, there are a few teachers out there who like grading, and there are students (probably those who always get As!) who like getting grades, but for the most part, we feel safe in saying giving and receiving grades for homework, individual essays, and courses is a drag. But why do we all hate it so much? From your perspective, that of the student, the grading of writing often seems arbitrary and subjective. In many cases, course grades might reflect an average of a half-dozen or so "final" products, but often there is no way to take into account all the freewriting, drafting, peer critiques, writing to learn activities, and undocumentable contributions to the learning experience. You might often feel outside the grading process, too. That is, you may never before have had an opportunity to add your two cents to the determination of your grade.

Instructors often abhor grading, too. First, it is awfully time-consuming, and time is a premium during a semester. Most writing teachers would rather spend their time working with writers or talking about writing than sitting alone at home or in the office, often late at night, pouring over essays. And, when teachers grade, they can rarely read for pleasure and celebrate and enjoy the successes of a well-wrought, provocative, and lyrical essay. When teachers grade, they often have to look for what's wrong with a text rather than with what's right about it. Grading essays tends to put the emphasis on the grade rather than the communicative act of writing. When essays are graded, it is natural for a writer to start thinking in terms of "what do I need to do to make this B+ an A–" rather than "How can I make this draft have more rhetorical impact on my readers?" And, because the teacher tends to be the sole grader, student writers tend then to write for the teacher or for the grade.

Historically speaking, grades are problematic because they tend to emphasize products rather than processes. They tend to be top-down and one-sided; that is, the teacher does the grading with little or no input from the writer. Also, they fail to capture all the subtleties of the experience of becoming a writer.

What might be done about this? Let's eliminate all grades! It would be nice, wouldn't it? But it's not likely to happen. What we can do, however, is work with alternative forms of assessment. If you read and worked through Chapter 6, "Assessing Writing," you know something about portfolio assessment and community standards already. And, if you've been following most of the steps in the various writing projects, particularly those in which you and your learning community peers—including your instructor—derived evaluation criteria collaboratively, evaluated one another's work, and reflected on the evaluation you've received, you are already familiar with many of the components of portfolio assessment.

In a nutshell, portfolio assessment entails three basic tenets: collection, selection, and reflection. First, the writer needs to *collect* all her work, which could include more than just final versions of essays and products. You know that during a writing course, especially one like this one, you've written many drafts, writing to learn texts designed to help you read critically and make sense of your learning experiences, peer critiques, and formal and informal E-texts such as E-mail and contributions to real-time conferences. Of course, collection is only the first step. It wouldn't suffice to merely hand in a big fat folder (or a 1.5-megabyte diskette) crammed with everything you wrote over the semester. You need to *select* from your collection a group of texts. How many and what kind can often be negotiated among the writer, the instructor, and the learning community. But it still would not be enough for a writer to hand in to the teacher a folder of one third of her entire collection. To make the evaluation process—the grading process—an interaction, a transaction, between the writer and instructor, the writer needs to have a voice in the process. The writer needs to *reflect* on what she's done, why she's made the selections she has, and what she makes of her learning experiences and growth as a writer. Such reflection, then, creates a conversation between the writer and instructor about assessment.

Doing all this on the World Wide Web, of course, adds another dimension to the process. Because of the hypertextual nature of the Web, a writer can better make connections among the processes and products and create alternative navigational trails through her corpus. If the portfolio concept enriches the notion of assessment, hypertextual portfolios—Webfolios—can add even more sophisticated textures and further promote the assessment transaction between grade givers (instructors) and grade receivers (student writers).

The Assignment

As your final project for the course, create a Webfolio of your work. Your learning community, including your instructor, will need to negotiate which selections will be mandatory and which will be optional. Your learning community, too, will need to negotiate evaluation criteria. Your Webfolio must be more than merely a collection of your E-texts; it should also create connections among your texts to show the relationships among them. You will also need to include a reflective or self-evaluation Web page that will help your readers (remember, your instructor will not be the only one perusing your Webfolio) to navigate your Webfolio, make sense of it, and evaluate it.

ACTIVITY 12.11: Arriving at Evaluation Criteria

Before you and your learning community can decide what to include in a Webfolio, you will need to come to some consensus about what your community, including your instructor, of course, deem important and valuable.

Step 1: Discussing Evaluation Criteria

In a face-to-face or computer-mediated discussion (E-mail, Usenet, real-time conference), your community should consider the following items to get you thinking about evaluation criteria:

- What are the strengths and weaknesses, benefits and drawbacks, and rewards and frustrations of traditional grading systems from your perspective, as either a writer or an instructor?
- From your perspective as a writer or an instructor, what is most important: the writing and learning process one goes through to arrive at a product or the product itself? If you believe they are equal, how so?
- What makes for a successful product? Length? Breadth? Depth? Effect on an audience? Fulfillment of purpose? Fulfilling the assignment? Beauty? Style? Correctness?
- What makes for a successful process? Loyalty to writing process (prewriting, drafting, revising, etc.)? Number of drafts written? Number and kind of revisions? Loyalty to peer review process?
- From your perspective, what is more important: mastery of one type of writing (analytical, e.g.) or competence in a range of different types of writing (narrative, analytical, argument, hypertext, etc.)?
- From your perspective, what is more important: mastery of traditional, linear print texts or competence with hypermedia digital texts?
- From your perspective, what is more important: masterful demonstration of flawless products or an increased awareness of the complexities of rhetorical situations (audiences, purposes, media, and content) that you might be able to articulate but have not yet been able to demonstrate through effective, polished writing?
- How much should class participation count? What should count as class participation? Contributions to oral conversations? Contributions to on-line discussions? "Acts of altruism" in which some community members offer solicited or unsolicited assistance to others? How should class participation be measured?
- How much should peer critiques count toward a course grade? How should quality be measured?

Step 2: Articulating Criteria

As a group, reflect on the preceding conversation and articulate criteria for evaluation. Someone or a group of community members should draft the criteria and share them electronically with the rest of the community for revision and approval.

ACTIVITY 12.12: Developing Selection Criteria

The previous activity should have led your community to derive a set of evaluation criteria. You now need to first take an inventory of what you've produced this semester and then determine what selections from that inventory might be selected to best demonstrate community members' fulfillment of the evaluation criteria.

Step 1: Individual Inventory

- Gather together your notebooks, folders, and computer diskettes, and take an inventory of everything you've done during the course.
- Organize all the files and papers by project, putting everything in chronological order.
- Write out a list of your inventory. If possible, send an electronic copy of your personal inventory via E-mail to all other members of the community.

Step 2: Community Inventory

It is quite possible that some people in the community completed more or fewer projects, sent more or fewer E-mail messages, or did a better or worse job of keeping track of all their work.

- If members of your community shared their inventories via E-mail, read one another's inventories closely.
- As a group, create a master inventory of all possible activities, projects, E-mail discussions, and so forth.
- Were there any communal texts, that is, E-mail conferences, real-time conferences, Usenet groups? Are those still active? If not, have they been saved or archived? If so, where are they available?
- Compare your personal inventory with the group's. Are you missing anything? Could you track down the missing texts? Could you make up some of the work you might have missed?

Step 3: Developing Selection Criteria

- Compare your community's evaluation criteria with the inventory of activities, projects, and texts (hard copy and digital, individual and communal).
- As a group, determine a set of mandatory submissions, ones everyone will include in their Webfolios. Your instructor will probably have much to say about this category. For instance, your community might

have completed five of the projects in this book, and your teacher may require that you include at least three of them in the Webfolio. Or, she may require a couple of specific ones, like an analysis of a virtual community, an analysis of a Web site, and an argument.

- As a group, determine optional selections. Your class may decide to leave what kind and how many optional texts up to individuals, or your group may decide on a maximum number and type of optional texts. Remember, more is not necessarily better. The more you include in your Webfolio, the more you have to talk about in your reflective essay. On the other hand, the more you include, the more you can demonstrate about yourself and the richer your Webfolio can become.

ACTIVITY 12.13: Selection through Reflection, Reflection on Selections

You will use personal reflection in two distinct ways in this activity. First, you will reflect on the work you've done this semester as a way of selecting E-texts for your Webfolio. Second, once you make your selections, you will write a reflective, self-evaluative essay to pull together your Webfolio.

Step 1: Selection through Reflection

- Take a few days, or as much time is available to you, and read through your entire inventory of texts, including but not limited to
  - — your drafts of formal projects;
  - — the most recent, complete versions of your formal projects;
  - — the peer critiques you wrote;
  - — responses to any readings you might have done for the class;
  - — your critical annotations of E-texts and Web Sites;
  - — all the CMC messages you sent and articles you posted, including both those you sent to your course-based virtual community and to those other virtual communities you might have joined during the semester; and
  - — all the communal texts, such as real-time electronic conferences, you contributed to during the semester.
- Which of the texts represent your proudest achievement during the course?
- Which represent your greatest frustration or failure during the semester?
- Which best represents your growth as a writer? How do those texts illustrate that?
- What was the best feedback you received as a writer this semester? Who was the source of that feedback?
- What does the body of your work reveal to you about you
  - — as a writer, including your strengths and your areas of growth;

— as a critical thinker and inquiring mind, including your strengths and your areas of growth;

— as a student, including your strengths and your areas of growth;

— as a contributing member of the learning community, including your strengths and your areas of growth; and

— as a citizen of cyberspace, including your strengths and your areas of growth?

• Review your community's selection criteria, and now select those texts you believe will best represent you in your final Webfolio.

Step 2: Reflection on Selections

The very act of reflecting as a way of making your selections has prepared you to write a reflective or self-evaluation essay that will serve to unify your Webfolio. As with any piece of writing, what, how, and how much you say in your reflective essay depends on your purpose and audience. Let's consider audience first. Because it is very possible that a major portion of your course grade may rest on your Webfolio, your instructor is certainly a key member of your audience. She may wish for nothing more than a rumination or reflection on your work, your progress as a writer, or your growth in terms of how you view the world or yourself. Or, your instructor might want you to write a self-analysis in which you argue for a course grade. Do remember, however, that your Web Site will probably be available to the whole world, so writing a reflective essay directed at your instructor only would not serve the larger audience of cyber citizens well. If this is an issue for your community, and it very likely will be, you will need to consider, perhaps, offering one entry into your Webfolio for your instructor and other members of your learning community and another one for cyber citizens at large.

Your purpose, too, will have much influence on what you say and how you say it. If your instructor invites you to make a case for a course grade, your task becomes persuasive, and you will probably want to employ your best analytical and argumentative skills. The best way *not* to earn a high grade is to write a poorly developed, supported, and written argument for a high grade, especially in a writing class! On the other hand, your purpose may be nothing more than offering a guided tour of your work in which you explain what you selected, why you selected them, why you wrote them, and what you learned from them or like about them. In any case, you along with the other members of your learning community will need to arrive at a consensus about the purposes and audiences for the reflective essay. Once you have done so, do the following:

• What is the major point you want to make about yourself, your intellectual growth, and/or your writing in your reflective essay? Because the reflective essay will likely be the first thing your reader sees, what tone do you want to set, what impression do you want to leave as she enters your Webfolio, reads, and perhaps evaluates and judges, your work?

- Of the E-texts you've selected, which ones best illustrate the points you want to make about your writing or yourself?
- How do those representative texts illustrate the points you are making?

Step 3: Drafting Your Reflective Essay

Draft your reflective essay, keeping in mind, of course, that it will become a hypermedia document that will probably include both internal and external hyperlinks to the selections in your Webfolio.

ACTIVITY 12.14: Constructing Your Webfolio

The time has come to weave your Webfolio. To do so, you'll have to get everything organized and make the appropriate hyperlinks among your HTML files.

Step 1: Getting Organized

- Get all the files you will use in your Webfolio into the same place, probably your WWW server directory or folder. These files will certainly include all the mandatory submissions such as your reflective statement and the formal projects your community decided to include. They might also include your optional submissions such as E-mail and other CMC files you've converted into text files.
- All those files need to be converted into HTML files using the techniques you learned in Project 10. Depending on how much progress you made as an HTML author this semester, some of your Webfolio pieces may be fully marked and browsable and others still need to be tagged.
- Be sure each file has a separate and unique file name, one that ends with the .html extension.

Step 2: Creating a Plan

Before you start weaving your Web, you'll need to consider where cybernauts will find your Webfolio and how they will get into it. Here are some possibilities:

- Perhaps your instructor has supported this course with a course Web Site. If so, she can set up a class roster on the course Web Site. Each student name on the course roster could then be a hyperlink to that student's Webfolio.
- Did you create a homepage earlier in the course when you went through Chapter 5? If so, perhaps your personal homepage could serve as the starting point of your Webfolio. If that's the way you'll go, you'll need to revise your homepage to add a hyperlink to the starting point of your Webfolio.

- You will need to create an entry way into your Webfolio. An argument can be made that your reflective essay would be a good place to start, especially if it provides a guided tour of your work. If the reflective piece, however, argues for a grade, a type of essay appropriate for your instructor or course audience but not necessarily for the rest of the cyber citizens, you might just offer a table of contents to the Webfolio that allows readers to begin where they wish.

Step 3: Weaving the Web

- If you wrote an effective reflective essay, one that uses the selections in your Webfolio as evidence to support the claims you want to make about yourself as a thinker, student, and writer, your task should be relatively simple. Each time you refer to a draft, final project, peer critique, E-mail message, or what have you, you will make a hyperlink from your reflective essay to the appropriate file.
- Remember you need to create clear and logical means of navigation for your readers. If in your reflective document you take them, through a hyperlink, to one of your projects, you will need to create a way to get them back. Thus, you may need to revise the project file to include a hyperlink back to the reflective essay.

ACTIVITY 12.15: Sharing Webfolios: Giving and Receiving Feedback

Once everyone in your learning community has put together a Webfolio, it is time to offer one another feedback before you put the finishing touches on the capstone experience of the course.

Step 1: Organizing the Process

- Organize yourselves into groups of three.
- Communicate with your feedback peers via E-mail or in writing the following:
  — The URL for your Webfolio
  — A self-evaluation of your site including what you like about it, what you still hope to do with it, and what kind of feedback or technical help you would like from your peers

Step 2: Offering Feedback

- You have critiqued enough Web Sites and been through the feedback process enough at this point to be able to generate high-quality critiques without going through a full-blown process of developing evaluation criteria. Before you begin your critique, however, revisit the evaluation criteria your community generated in Project 5, "Writing to Read Critically," and Project 8, "Analyzing Web Sites," and the early stages of this Webfolio process to prepare yourself to critique your peers' Webfolios.

- Read your peers' Webfolios very closely.
  — Attempt to use every navigational possibility made available to you.
  — Pay close attention not only to the appearance, technical aspects (do the links work and go where they're supposed to?), and the navigational ease (can you jump among texts logically?) but also to the quality of the writing itself.
- Write up thorough critiques of your peers' Webfolios, and share your feedback with them via electronic mail or by exchanging hard copies of the critiques.

ACTIVITY 12.16: Revising Your Webfolio

This is your last, best chance to put your best virtual foot forward and take your place in cyberspace. Your work will be published to the world. Future students may reference your work as a model for their own. Other thinkers and writers may read your work and reference you in their own work. You have joined the Docuverse. Take great care in these last several steps to serve yourself well.

Step 1: Reflecting on the Feedback Process

- Read and reflect on the feedback you received from your peers. What were the similarities among them? What were the differences?
- Do you have any more questions for them?
- What did you learn while critiquing their Webfolios that you might use to revise yours?

Step 2: Revise and Publicize Your Webfolio

Revise all aspects of your Webfolio.

- Consider all the feedback you received
- Implement all you've learned this semester about writing well, using HTML, and constructing hypermedia.
- Register your site with various search engines. Here are the addresses for two popular ones, Magellan and Yahoo!
  — **Magellan**
    http://www.mckinley.com/feature.cgi?add_bd
  — **Yahoo!**
    http://add.yahoo.com/bin/add?

APPENDIX A

DIRECTORY OF ON-LINE RESOURCES FOR WRITERS

The resources we've provided here were chosen because they enhance what this book delivers. These resources help you find information about writing, they help you learn more about writing on-line, and they help you reach the cutting edge of electronic text.

We also selected these resources because they are as reliable as possible. Today's Internet is a rapidly changing place. Often, sites are here today and gone tomorrow. We've tried to identify sites that will be around for a while—for at least as long as it takes our publisher to get this book into print and for you to use it. In a few cases, though, you will try to access one of these resources, only to find that it no longer exists or that it has moved and left no forwarding address. We've tried to resolve that problem, too, by establishing a Web Site for this book. So if you hit a dead end, fire up your Web browser and run a search for the Allyn & Bacon Web Site.

One final hint: if the address for a resource no longer works, and if the URL listed here provides no help, then run a Net Search, using the titles we provide later as the keywords. That should take you to the new address or to an updated version of a listed item.

As the sites change, as new resources come on-line, we'll do our best to keep up, and we'll post the latest and greatest on that Web Site. Then, as the book is revised, we'll incorporate the updated information into the next edition. In that sense, this book acts as a bridge between traditional, paper-based resources and life, as it were, on-line.

ON-LINE HELP FOR WRITERS

If you've worked through very many of the projects this book offers, you will have realized what a valuable resource other writers can be—as readers. In many cases, some of those other writers have located some of their expertise on-line. You can easily look up words in on-line dictionaries, find just the right word in an on-line thesaurus, access a minilesson about grammar and mechanics, or, in some cases, actually seek assistance from a real person— liveware. Here are some of the Internet's most valuable resources, along with a very brief description of what to expect from them.

http://www.lsa.umich.edu/ecb/OWL/owl.html

University of Michigan On-Line Writing Lab (OWL)'s Web-based setup allows linkage to other OWLs, dictionaries and other reference works, and information about Michigan's writing program. Writers can send a paper to English Composition Board–trained undergraduate peer tutors via a forms page that is easy to understand and use. **Caution:** As with any university-based resource, the home campus's students come first. Responses may take a while to come back. This OWL promises its campus clientele a turn-around time of twenty-four to forty-eight hours. If you're not enrolled at Michigan, you're likely to wait considerably longer.

http://www.missouri.edu/~wleric/writehelp.html

"Writing tips, guides, advice and stray bits of wisdom" from the University of Missouri's writery homepages. Like Michigan's, this OWL is interactive in the fullest sense. You can even "talk" with a tutor in real time by going to Missouri's MOO. Understandably, the tutors take care of Missouri students first. But the information resources are available to anyone.

http://www.rpi.edu/dept/llc/writecenter/web/net-writing.html

Rennselaer's OWL is resource-rich, though at this writing it does not provide contact with tutors. Its best feature is an extensive list of links to many on-line writing labs on the Web and in Gopherspace.

http://owl.english.purdue.edu/

Purdue's is the original OWL. It provides extensive grammar advice and a thorough—and ever-growing—list of on-line writing centers and resources.

http://www.uark.edu/depts/comminfo/www/study.html

"Study, Research, and Writing Skills," maintained by the University of Arkansas, provides general writing help and useful advice on writing in graduate school.

http://www.english.upenn.edu/~jlynch/writing.html

"Resources for Writers and Writing Instructors" aims to provide a compilation of on-line resources for writers and teachers of writing. As we write, the page is still developing; it's worth watching.

http://english.ttu.edu/acw/

The Web Site of the Alliance for Computers and Writing (ACW), this is the ultimate compilation of resources, people, courses, and programs. Its strength is completeness; its weakness is its sheer size. This site links to practically everything else in this list. If you're interested in writing and the Internet, the ACW Web Site is definitely the best place to begin.

WRITERS ON-LINE

http://www.uncg.edu/~agcowan/writers.html

"Internet Inkslingers" is a WWW site designed to provide a central location for writers of the world. Inkslingers provides on-line utilities for written submissions and postings of comments. Here writers interact in ways that go beyond the typical OWL's school setting and mission.

WRITING ON THE INTERNET

http://rs6000.adm.fau.edu/rinaldi/netiquette.html

"I'm Not Miss Manners of Internet," by Arlene Rinaldi, a guide for netiquette, covers topics such as E-mail, Telenet protocol, FTP, and the World Wide Web. Good general introduction, which users can follow up by reading the more specific suggestions in "Internet Resources," presented later.

http://www.daedalus.com/MBU/MBU.resources.html

MegaByte University (MBU-L) is an electronic mail list devoted to computers and writing. MBU is probably the most friendly of the mail lists. This Web-based "List of Electronic Resources" is a section of a larger MBU FAQ. This chunk deals specifically with resources for writing on the Internet. The list is updated several times a year, so it's a good place to look for more sites and other resources.

http://www.wimsey.com/~chrish/

"Circuit Tracers—Your Guide to Online Writing" is an on-line magazine and WWW launchpad dedicated to serving the needs of aspiring Netwriters.

RESOURCES FOR WRITING ACROSS THE CURRICULUM

General Resources

http://ewu66649.ewu.edu/WAC.html

Maintained by faculty at Eastern Washington University, "Welcome to the Writing Across the Curriculum Page" provides information on EWU's program, and it links to other WWW sites for writing. This site provides an extensive listing of places to go for information.

http://www.mala.bc.ca/www/wac/wac.htm

"Writing Across the Curriculum" is dedicated to helping students and teachers improve writing skills in classes other than English. The Web Site also suggests ways teachers can get more writing into classroom across the curriculum.

Writing in the Natural Sciences

http://www.wfi.fr/est/est1.html

"Resources for Teachers of English for Science and Technology," EST-L, is an E-mail forum for writing in science. This page also links to several other Web pages about science and writing.

http://www.welch.jhu.edu/publishing/sci.writing.html

"Scientific Writing," from Johns Hopkins University, provides links to books about scientific writing, along with on-line handbooks for science writers.

Writing in the Social Sciences

http://www.pol.adfa.oz.au/essay.intro.html

"Essay Writing for Students in Politics and Social Sciences," from the Australian Defence Force Academy, lists a number of straightforward rules of presentation that should be followed for all papers and essays in the social sciences.

Writing in Business/Business School

http://www.interlog.com/~ohi/www/biz.html

This Web page links to a wide variety of resources for writing in business.

LIBRARY AND LIBRARY-LIKE RESOURCES

http://www.interlog.com/~ohi/www/writesource.html

"Writing Resources," from the WWW Virtual Library, features links to information about different genres of writing and subjects related to writing in the virtual library.

http://www.cs.cmu.edu/Web/books.html

"The On-Line Books Page," maintained by Carnegie Mellon University, is the front page for an index of hundreds of on-line books. It also points to other common repositories of on-line books and other documents.

http://english-www.hss.cmu.edu/reference.html

"English Server-Reference Works" by Carnegie Mellon provides access to an extensive set of phone books, documents, dictionaries, and so on.

http://www.cis.temple.edu/elecbshelf.html

"Electronic Bookshelf-Basic References," from Temple University, includes basic references, as well as links to the White House and Purdue's On-Line Writing Lab.

http://www-cgi.cs.cmu.edu/Web/references.html

"On-Line Reference Works" from CMU is a small collection of on-line reference works such as dictionaries, Internet resources, and geography-oriented references, both at CMU (preferred) and elsewhere.

http://www.ll.mit.edu/ComLinks/deskref.html

"DeskTop References" provides a listing of general reference works and Internet and geographical resources.

ON-LINE BOOKS AND JOURNALS

http://www.4mesa.com/4mesa/weblist/ejournal.html

"The WWW Virtual Library of Electronic Journals" provides a search engine that allows users to link to any E-journal in the Web Information Library Maintenance Agent.

http://www.nosc.mil/planet_earth/news.html

"Planet Earth Home Page News Information" is a list of available on-line newspapers and news information services.

http://www.december.com/cmc/mag/current/toc.html

CMC Magazine, John December's E-zine, focuses on issues dealing with the Internet. CMC Magazine is the place the heavy-duty internauts want to be published.

http://www.missouri.edu/~rhetnet

Rhetnet is an E-journal that publishes articles, discussions, and other genres centering on how computers and writing intertwine. This academic journal often displays a lighter side that is consistent with the spirit of the Internet.

http://english.ttu.edu/kairos/index.html

"A Journal for Teachers of Writing in Webbed Environments," *Kairos* is sponsored by the Alliance for Computers and Writing. Although the journal addresses teachers primarily, it deals with issues of interest to any internaut, and its staff is extraordinarily helpful and hip.

http://stc.org/region2/phi/resources/index.html

"Internet Resources for Technical Communicators," lists E-journals on technical communications, E-mail groups, newsgroups, and E-magazines that deal with written communication on the Internet.

SUBJECT AREA RESOURCES

General

http://www.w3.org/hypertext/DataSources/bySubject/Overview.html

"WWW Virtual Library" provides a very large general subject guide put out by the Web.

http://www.clark.net/pub/journalism/awesome.html

"The Awesome Lists of Subject Guides" gathers, from one Internet trainer's viewpoint, "the glory and grandeur of the Internet, the sine qua non of Cyberspace, the main characters in the evolving drama" (sixty-eight different subject guides).

http://www.yahoo.com/

"Yahoo Net Directory." One of the earliest and largest 'Net directories on the Web, Yahoo! provides both a powerful search engine and a subject index to practically everything on the Web.

http://www.gnn.com/gnn/wic/index.html

"The Whole Internet Catalog," brought to you by Netscape, provides a resource similar to *Yahoo!* plus links to almost all the major search engines. If you are beginning your exploration with no ideas about where to commence, this is a good place to start.

http://www.december.com/cmc/info internet-searching-subjects.html

"INTERNET—Searching—Subjects," maintained by CMC Information Sources, indexes a megalist of subject guides on the Web.

http://www.lib.uwaterloo.ca/society/webpages.html

"Webpages of Scholarly Societies" includes links produced by or for scholarly societies. In addition to the alphabetical list, there is also a subject guide that groups Web pages and Gopher sites by broad subject area.

gopher://gopher.tc.umn.edu:70/11/Other%20Gopher%20and %20Information%20Servers/all

"All the Gopher Servers in the World" provides a list of all the gopher servers in the world.

http://www.lib.lsu.edu/general/scholar.html

"Scholarly Information," compiled by Steven Harris, is an even more extensive page than the prior link to scholarly information.

http://ukanaix.cc.ukans.edu:80/history/

"Full Index of Available Resources," from Kansas University, contains a full list of Web pages organized by subject in the academic fields, so it provides a kind of filter that eliminates most of the commercial sites that broader search engines include. This site also contains extensive information about different Internet tools and resources.

http://www.einet.net/galaxy/Reference-and-Interdisciplinary-Information.html

"Reference and Interdisciplinary Information" provides a list of general references and lists of government publications and 'Net directories from other collegiate institutions.

gopher://dewey.lib.ncsu.edu/11/library/disciplines

"Gopher Menu–Discipline Specific" is a discipline-specfic menu with subjects such as geography, economics, and agriculture. Like the Kansas University archive, this one allows access by academic discipline. It's also Gopher based, so it accesses a different set of documents from the KU service.

http://www.stpt.com/

"Starting Point" aims to provide the single best starting point for WWW exploration, covering topics such as references, the professions, education, and news.

http://www.llnl.gov/llnl/lists/listsl.html

"The LLNL List of Lists" links to topics in government, science, WWW, and comprehensive Internet resource lists.

Electronic Conferences

http://cygnus.csi.cam.ac.uk/AcadInfoRes/Acadlist.html

"Directory of Scholarly Electronic Conferences" is a comprehensive list of electronic conferences, with searchable indexes by subject, keywords, and contact addresses. At this writing, Diane K. Kovacs had listed 1,790 E-conferences, in sixty-two different academic categories.

**gopher://gopher.usask.ca/11/Computing/Internet%20Information/
Directory%20of%20Scholarly%20Electronic%20Conferences**

"Ninth Revision, Directory of Scholarly Electronic Conferences" Those without access to the Web will appreciate this Gopher-based list of electronic conferences in practically every academic field.

Humanities

http://english-www.hss.cmu.edu/

"English Server–Carnegie Mellon" is a cooperative that has published humanities texts to the Internet since 1990. It links to philosophy guides, drama, and other literature-related areas.

http://www.utexas.edu/depts/uwc/.html/citation.html

MLA- and APA-Style citations of electronic sources is a style sheet on how to cite electronic information sources in the format specified by the Modern Language Association and the American Psychological Association.

http://www.lib.lehigh.edu/footnote/chicelec.html

Citation according to *Chicago Manual of Style.*

http://www.umass.edu/english/women.html

"Women Online" compiled by Gary Beason of Purdue University, is a collection women's studies resources on the Web and a site for publishing essays on women's studies.

Social Sciences

http://www.rsl.ox.ac.uk/isca/index.html

"Anthropology Institute of Social and Cultural Anthropology–University of Oxford" provides a list of local Web pages on anthropology at Oxford University and a listing of other anthropology resources on the Web.

http://arachnid.cm.cf.ac.uk/User/Gwyn.Price/history.html

"History Pages," put out by Gwyn Price and Netscape, is a collection of pages on the Web that either relate directly to history or contain information or materials of interest to historians.

Natural Sciences

http://ivory.lm.com:80/~nab/

"Neurosciences on the Internet": The initial sections of this index list sites that are ideal starting points for the exploration of the many neuroscience resources available on the Internet.

The Internet

http://www.mecklerweb.com/home.htm

"Meckler's Web World," by Meckler Multimedia and IBM, positions itself as Internet users' "First Stop on the Internet," where they can find the very latest Internet news, tips, how-to information, product reviews, resources, directories, and expert commentary.

http://www.cis.ufl.edu/help-system/big-dummy/

"Big Dummy's Guide to the Internet" is intended to be a guide to the Internet for folks with little or no experience with network communications.

http://www.eff.org/archives.html

"Electronic Frontier Foundation Online Library" is an extensive archive of articles on EFF issues such as freedom of speech on the Internet, free and open access to the Internet, and so forth.

http://www.december.com/cmc/info/

"Information Sources: The Internet and Computer-Mediated Communication," by John December, provides information on the technical, social, rhetorical, cognitive, and psychological aspects of networked communication and information.

http://galaxy.einet.net/GJ/index.html

"Gopher Jewels" catalogs many of the best Gopher sites by category (subject tree) and takes you to the relevant information buried somewhere in its gopher hole.

http://gopher.it.lut.fi:70/1/gopher

"Frequently Asked Questions in comp.infosystems.gopher" is a FAQ file on Gopher—with answers.

http://www.rit.edu:80/~easi/

"EASI: EQUAL ACCESS TO SOFTWARE AND INFORMATION," an affiliate to the American Association of Higher Learning, is devoted to guaranteeing access to information technology on the part of people with disabilities.

COLLEGES AND UNIVERSITIES

http://www.clas.ufl.edu/CLAS/american-universities.html

"American Universities" As home pages for American Universities granting bachelor or advanced degrees come onto the Web, they are added here, one page per university.

INTERNET RESOURCES

http://www.clearinghouse.net/

"Clearinghouse for Subject-Oriented Internet Resource Guides," from Argus and the University of Michigan, is an ever-growing subject guide to just about any noncommercial resource on the Internet.

http://www.fsu.edu/Links/Internet.html

"Internet Resources (Lists of Lists, Lists of Lists of Lists...)" provides links to selected major sites that may help users locate specific services. Some resources are organized by subject and others by type of access (Usenet, WWW, Gopher, etc.). This site contains information about the State of Florida. You'll have to scroll down to find links to internet resources.

Usenet

http://www.cis.ohio-state.edu/hypertext/faq/bngusenet/news/
groups/top.html
"Usenet FAQ" includes a listing of all active newsgroups organized by the
Usenet hierarchy, and "Internet Newsgroups" a hypertextual listing of all
active newsgroups, organized under each Usenet hierarchy.

http://www.cis.ohio-state.edu/hypertext/faq/usenet/FAQ-List.html
"USENET FAQs" from Ohio State contains a list of all Usenet FAQs found
in news.answers. The document is (more or less) alphabetized by topic.

http://www.ucssc.indiana.edu/FAQ/USAGN/
"The Usenet Site Administrator's Guide to Netiquette" is a FAQ file dealing
with all aspects of Usenet, including netiquette.

news://D9A3Kq.Fpz@deshaw.com
(Posting from Usenet) "A Primer on How to Work with the Usenet Community," by Mark Moraes, is an essay on what users need to know before
participating in a Usenet community. This article is a very good place to
start.

news://D9A3KE.FMn@deshaw.com
(Posting from Usenet) "Copyright Myths FAQ: Ten Big Myths about Copyright Explained," by Brad Templetion, offers netiquette information about
copyright issues on Usenet.

Mail Lists

http://tile.net/lists/
The "Listserv Home Page," this site is the most complete reference to listserv discussion groups. TileNet also provides other useful information in
other areas of its Web Site.

http://www.yahoo.com/Computers_and_Internet/Internet/
Mailing_Lists/
"Computers and Internet:Internet:Mailing Lists," from Yahoo!, is somewhat bewildering (it's easy to get lost here). It provides a gigantic list of E-
mail lists. If you have an interest, you'll find a list for it here.

http://www.neosoft.com/internet/paml/bysubj.html

"Publicly Accessible Mailing Lists" is an extensive listing of electronic mail lists for hundreds of subjects, indexed by name or subject.

http://galaxy.einet.net/GJ/lists.html

"List of Lists Resource" is a list of thousands of listservs (or listprocs, or majordomos) by subject.

Internet Relay Chat (IRC)

http://wwwnt.thegroup.net/harris/isg.htm

The IRC Survival Guide, by Stuart Harris, is a detailed book on every aspect of IRC, with some excerpts published on-line. Anyone who spends much time in IRC needs to look at this Web Site and the book (information on purchasing the book is in the site).

http://gopher.metronet.com:70/1/ircinfo

"The IRC (Internet Relay Chat)." IRC news, an IRC primer, and two very useful FAQs about IRC.

MUDs AND MOOs

http://lydia.bradley.edu/las/soc/syl/391/papers/text_cyb.html

"Textuality in Cyberspace: Muds and Written Experiences," by Jeffrey R. Young, is a paper describing the nature of MUDs, including social construction and interaction.

http://www.nmusd.k12.ca.us/Resources/Roadmap/map26.html

"IRC/MUDs /MOOs, and Other 'Talkers,'" by Patrick Crispen, part of a hypertexual course about the Internet, describes MUDs and MOOs. Crispen also offers a section dedicated to "warnings" to all users of "talker" programs.

http://www.mudconnect.com/frameless.html

"The Mud Connector" is a complete on-line service designed to provide the most up-to-date listings of registered Multiuser on-line games. Every entry lists the site of the game, the base code used, descriptions of the game as submitted by the administrators, links to WWW homepages (when available), and Telnet links to the game.

http://www.daedalus.com/net/manners.html

"Collected MOO Manner Guidelines" are meant to give you an idea of the ways people are expected to behave in MOOs and MUDs.

gopher://mcmuse.mc.maricopa.edu:70/0ftp%3Aftp.media.mit.edu@/pub/asb/papers/deviance-chi94.txt

"Approaches to Managing Deviant Behavior in Virtual Communities" is an essay on how to handle behavior that is deemed unacceptable in the virtual community.

http://www.en.utexas.edu/~daniel/papers/busstopsbeyond.html

"The Bus Stops beyond Language," by Daniel Anderson, is a paper on the parallelism between the everyday reality and the reality found in MUDs.

WORLD WIDE WEB/HTML

General Information about the World Wide Web

http://www.w3.org/hypertext/WWW/WWW/

"About the World Wide Web" offers background information on the WWW including a time line, the people involved in the Web, and manuals.

http://www.vir.com/eegtti/eeg_213.html

"EFF's guide to the Internet-WWW" is a brief introduction to the Web.

http://oneworld.wa.com/htmldev/devpage/dev-page1.html#doc-b

"Information on the World Wide Web (WWW)" is part of large Web page called the "WWW and HTML Jumpstation"; this section has a FAQ file on the Web.

http://www.december.com/cmc/mag/

"Challenges for Web Information Providers," from *WWW Unleashed* by John December, is a chapter from December's book on how the Web will affect the giving and taking of information in the future.

Getting Started with HTML

http://www.ncsa.uiuc.edu/General/Internet/WWW/HTMLPrimer.html

"A Beginner's Guide to HTML" is a primer for producing documents in HTML, the markup language used by the World Wide Web.

http://www.w3.org/hypertext/WWW/MarkUp/html-spec/
html-spec_toc.html

"Hypertext Markup Language" describes everything you want to know about HTML, in an easy-to-understand Web page.

http://www.webcom.com/html/

"The Web Communications Comprehensive Guide to Publishing on the Web" is intended to provide a comprehensive resource for publishing on the World Wide Web: tutorials, hints, reference, public software tools.

http://www.w3.org/pub/WWW/Provider/Style/Etiquette

"Web Etiquette" presents things to check off when making a Web page.

http://fire.clarkson.edu/edu/tc/guidelines.html

"WWW Publishing Guidelines" offers suggestions for avoiding conflicting signals when creating a Web page.

http://www.thegiim.org/

"How to Publish on the Web," by the Global Institute of Interactive Media, is a primer on how to publish on the Web for specific audiences such as teachers, students, and small-business owners.

Complete Information on HTML

http://info.med.yale.edu/caim/StyleManuaLTop.HTML

"World Wide Web Authoring Resoures" (Yale) is a giant compilation of on-line resources for basic guides to HTML, HTML references, and WWW authoring resources and indexes.

http://oneworld.wa.com/htmldev/devpage/dev-page1.html#doc-av

"Writing HTML Documents" is concerned with getting started with HTML, advanced HTML, how to do fancy stuff with HTML, and HTML standards.

HTML Quick Reference

http://werbach.com/barebones

"The Bare Bones Guide to HTML," by Kevin Werbach, is a quick "cheat sheet" on all the HTML tags.

http://krypton.mankato.msus.edu/reference.html

"Useful References to the HTML" contains FAQ and references for HTML use.

http://www.cc.ukans.edu/info/HTML_quick.html
"HTML Quick References" offers some quick tips on basic HTML.

HTML Style

http://www.w3.org/hypertext/WWW/Provider/Style/Overview.html
"Style Guide for Online Hypertext" is designed to help you create a WWW hypertext database that effectively communicates your knowledge.

http://www.cs.cmu.edu/~tilt/cgh/old/
"Composing Good HTML" (stable until 2000) contains the guidelines for using HTML now and in the future.

http://home.mcom.com/hom/services_docs/impact_docs/creating-high-impact-docs.html
"How to Create High-Impact Documents" describes how to create high-impact documents for use with Netscape Navigator and other browsers.

http://www.earth.com/bad-style/
"Bad Style Page" is a collection of don'ts for HTML.

http://bookweb.cwis.uci.edu:8042/Staff/StyleGuide.html
"Elements of HTML Style," by Cohen and Lee, offers eight tips to consider when writing in HTML.

http://www.ziff.com:8023/~zdpress/9504/feature/laron/la_samp.html
"Chapter 3—Writing HTML Documents," by Larry Aronson, from a book called *HTML Manual of Style,* deals with general HTML principles, good HTML style, creating a home page, and converting an existing document to HTML.

A Couple of Good Examples of Hypertext on the Web

http://raven.ubalt.edu/Kaplan/lit/One_Beginning_417.html
"E-Literacies," by Nancy Kaplan, is a hypertexual essay on the future of electronic writing.

http://jefferson.village.virginia.edu/vshadow/vshadow2.html
"The Valley of the Shadow: Living the Civil War in Pennsylvania and Virginia," by Ed Ayers, is a hypertexual history essay on the Civil War.

APPENDIX **B**

GLOSSARY OF KEY TERMS

Although we have provided definitions of key terms here, we also recommend that you fall back on your own resources to explore the meaning and significance of the terms we've used in this book. To that end, here are some Internet-based locations for all the definitions a person could ever want to read:

"The Free On-Line Dictionary of Computing"
http://www.wombat.doc.ic.ac.uk/

"Internet Glossary"(January 1993)
ftp://nic.merit.edu/documents/fyi/fyi18.txt

"Jargon File"
http://www.fwi.uva.nl/cgi-bin/topicsearch.CGI?back=/~mes/jargon/ &dbase=/~mes/jargon&dbdesc=The+Jargon+File+-+version+3.2

"The Epiphany Project Glossary"
http://www.mason2.gmu.edu/~jwillia9/epiphany-FG-glossary.html

Anonymous FTP   A system that allows any Internet member to retrieve and transfer documents, files, programs and other archived data without needing a log-in name and password. Use "anonymous" as your log-in name and your E-mail address as your password to gain access to publicly accessible files on the remote system.

Archie   A system to gather, index and serve information automatically from FTP sites on the Internet.

Article   A message sent to a USENET newsgroup.

ASCII (American Standard Code for Information Interchange)   The standard character encoding used in current computers. Each character is composed of eight bits, or one byte. Thus, a character's ASCII code might look like this: 00110000.

Compressed file   A file that has been reduced or compacted in size to take up less disk space or to quicken transmission time of files. The file must be later decompressed before it is viewable.

Domain name   A host computer's title on the Internet. This title is also included in an E-mail address.

Download   To transfer files, data, or (especially) code from a host system to a smaller client system.

FAQ (frequently asked questions)   A document about a given Usenet newsgroup, mail list, Web Site, and so on, that is intended to answer the most frequent questions from new readers.

Finger   A program that displays information about a particular user or all users logged on the system or a remote system. Typically shows full name, last log-in time, idle time, terminal line, and terminal location (where applicable).

Flame   An electronic mail or Usenet news article sent out with a frank and strong criticisim intended as a personal attack on the author of an E-mail message or a Usenet posting.

FTP (file transfer protocol)   A client-server protocol that allows a user on one computer to transfer files to and from another computer over a TCP/IP network. Also the client program the user executes to transfer files.

Gopher   An Internet service that allows users to search and retrieve information from any accessible Gopher server. A menuing interface is presented to help users navigate through Gopher space.

HTML (hypertext markup language)   The programming language that enables the creation of hypertextual World Wide Web pages.

Hypermedia   A combination of hypertext and multimedia that includes but is not limited to text, graphics, sound, and video.

Hypertext   A system for linking texts, broadly defined, to other texts in an infinite number of pathways. *Nodes* containing text, graphics, sound, or video can be joined by *links* that allow users to proceed directly from one node to any node that is linked to it. Hypertext can only be composed and read on-screen, because its linking function is impossible to render fully on paper.

Internet relay chat (IRC)   A worldwide "party line" network that lets people join together on the Internet and converse with each other in real time, whether in discussions regarding certain topics or in personal conversations.

Jughead   A Gopher searching tool that "tunnels" through Gopherspace to get various Gopher menu information using a keyword provided by the user. Similar to but not as effective as Veronica, Jughead stands for Jonzy's Universal Gopher Hierarchy Excavation and Display.

Knowbot   Comparable to a "robotic librarian," a knowbot is probably the information retrieval resource of the future.

Listserv   An abbreviation for "list server," an automatic mailing list that enables sets of discussion via E-mail. Listserv also refers to the user name that manages the additions and deletions from discussion groups. List members send messages to the list, but commands that determine how they receive mail from the list must go to the listserv.

Log in   v: The process of creating a link between you and your host computer using your name and password; n: also commonly used to refer to the name you use when making a connection with your host computer.

Mirror site   An FTP site that "mirrors" or replicates the information held in another site. Extremely busy sites often establish a mirror site so that users can put and get files more quickly than they could with only one site.

Modem   Required for most Internet access, a modem (a portmanteau term referring to the functions of *mo*dulation and *dem*odulation) is an electronic device that sends and receives data over phone lines by converting digital information into analog signals and vice versa.

Multimedia   Documents that include different types of media such as text, graphics, video, and audio. Like hypertext and hypermedia, multimedia depends on computer technology because it cannot be reproduced on paper.

Netiquette   Standing for "network etiquette," refers to the customs of polite behavior recognized on Usenet, mail lists, and the Internet in general.

Newsgroup   One of Usenet's huge collection of topic groups. Usenet groups can be unmoderated (anyone can post) or moderated (submissions are automatically directed to a moderator, who edits or filters and then posts the results).

PPP (point-to-point protocol)   The standard procedure for delivering Internet protocol packets over serial point-to-point links.

Public domain software   Software that is not copyrighted by anyone. Anyone may duplicate, modify, or share this software legally without any payment.

Server   A computer or program that volunteers services and various resources to other computers or programs called *clients.*

Shareware   Software that is offered on a trial basis. Users are placed on their honor to pay the author if the user continues to use the software after trying it out.

Telnet   An Internet standard protocol that allows users to log in to other computer systems on the Internet.

URL (uniform resource locator)   The address of a Web document on the World Wide Web. A URL contains a term that indicates the type of resource (http for Web documents, ftp for file transfer, etc.), as well as the location of a file and the file name.

Veronica   Stands for Very Easy Rodent-Oriented Net-wide Index to Computerized Archives. Veronica uses a keyword search to sift through Gopher space using gopher menus.

Virus   Damaging programs that can be transferred from computer to computer. Viruses seek out other programs and "infect" them by duplicating a copy of the harmful virus and placing it in the victim programs. The virus is activated when the program is executed. Some viruses are harmless, but many can destroy all the data stored on an infected computer.

WAIS (wide area information server)   A distribution information service that allows users to search databases on the Internet using keyword/index searching for faster retrieval of relevant documents.

World Wide Web (WWW, The Web, W3)   A hypertext-based, information distribution system in which users (governmental, commercial, scholastic, or individuals) may create, edit, or browse "homepages" that have links to other Internet sites around the world.

INDEX